US Imperialism

This book offers a broad and deep examination of the dynamics of US imperialism. Petras analyzes imperialism not only as economic domination, showing that its impact in the world takes many forms, including cultural, political and historical. He points to the disruptive effects it has on other world regional economies and cultures. Capitalism and imperialism take diverse forms but both are intimately tied to the projection of state power in the service of capital—a strategy designed to advance the geopolitical and economic interests of the US economic elite and ruling class—interests that are equated with the 'US national interest'.

James Petras is Professor Emeritus of Sociology at Binghamton University. He is the author of over sixty books on the dynamics of global power and Latin American development. They include *Power and Resistance: US Imperialism in Latin America* and *Imperialism and Capitalism in the 21st Century*.

'James Petras has consistently demonstrated a profoundly detailed understanding of the global economic and political power dynamics of empire and crisis in our times. Staying true to form, Petras' *US Imperialism: The Changing Dynamics of Global Power*, is a brilliant contribution to the literature that chronicles and analyzes the modus operandi of empires or states that project their power through military and economic means over weaker, poorer foreign countries to dominate their economy and politics to buttress the economic interests of the ruling classes in the empire. Academics, media commentators and political leaders who have ignored the subject matter of *US Imperialism*, must take notice of its scholarship and relevance in today's world.'

—*Dennis C. Canterbury, Department of Sociology, Anthropology, Criminology and Social Work, Eastern Connecticut State University, USA*

'James Petras is the undisputed foremost authority on the global and regional dynamics of US imperialism. This collection of his most recent essays on the contemporary dynamics of US imperialism provides a treasure trove of fascinating facts concerning the projection of state power by the United States in the different macro-regions of the world system. The book is also the most comprehensive study of US global economic and political power in the era of the Obama and Trump administration of the US Empire.'

—*Raúl Delgado Wise, Research Professor and Coordinator, Development Studies PhD, Universidad Autónoma de Zacatecas, Mexico*

'This collection of essays shows in very clear language and without academic jargon that the foreign affairs of the United States, and the actual development of countries in Latin America and elsewhere on the periphery of the world system, both currently and in recent years best be understood through the lens of imperialist theory. Petras is one of the world's foremost authorities on the subject, and the book is a must read for both the scholars and students of international relations and world affairs.'

—*Henry Veltmeyer, Professor Emeritus of International Development Studies, Saint Mary's University, Canada*

'While focusing on America's hegemonic project in the post-Cold era, James Petras provides an incisive understanding of the complex relationship between "military imperialism" and "economic imperialism", which constitutes the pillar of empire building. Global and regional perspectives are presented focussing on regime change in Latin America, US–NATO wars in the Middle East, the rise of Neo-fascism in Ukraine, US–NATO threats directed against Russia, China and Washington's Pivot to Asia. Petras also analyses how imperialism triggers "colonialism at home" including the demise of the welfare state, rising poverty and social inequality in America. In all respects Petras' *US Imperialism* is a carefully documented political economy masterpiece.'

—*Michel Chossudovsky, Professor Emeritus*
of Economics, University of Ottawa, USA

US Imperialism

The Changing Dynamics of Global Power

James Petras

Routledge
Taylor & Francis Group

NEW YORK AND LONDON

First published 2020
by Routledge
52 Vanderbilt Avenue, New York, NY 10017

and by Routledge
2 Park Square, Milton Park, Abingdon, Oxon OX14 4RN

Routledge is an imprint of the Taylor & Francis Group, an informa business

© 2020 Taylor & Francis

Library of Congress Cataloging-in-Publication Data
A catalog record for this title has been requested

ISBN: 978-0-367-25275-5 (hbk)
ISBN: 978-0-367-25278-6 (pbk)
ISBN: 978-0-429-28695-7 (ebk)

Typeset in Bembo
by Taylor & Francis Books

Contents

Foreword   x

PART I
Historical Background   I

1 US Global Power in the 21st Century: Military or Economic
   Imperialism?   3

2 Fifty Years of Imperial Wars   14

3 Empire or Vampire?   29

4 A Century of Wars That Were Lost   36

PART II
Structure of Empire   41

5 Foundations of the US Empire: Axes of Evil   43

6 Networks of Empire and Realignments of World Power   50

7 Imperial Power Centers: Divisions, Indecisions and Civil War   59

PART III
Political Economy of Empire   63

8 Democracy and World Power   65

9 Imperial Wars and Domestic Epidemics   75

10 The Pentagon and Big Oil: Militarism and Capital Accumulation   81

11 Soaring Profits and Soaring Social Costs   85

12   Putting an End to the Welfare State: The Last Cut   88

13   Imperial Recovery and Disappearing Workers   96

14   Global Empire and Internal Colonialism   100

15   Immigration: Western Wars and Imperial Exploitation Uproot
     Millions   105

16   Imperialists' Fear and Loathing ... of Being Colonized   109

PART IV
Geopolitics of Empire   113

17   Dis-Accumulation on a World Scale: Pillage, Plunder and
     Wealth   115

18   Washington's Two-Track Policy: Marines to Central America
     and Diplomats to Cuba   122

19   The United States' Grand Strategy Toward China: Mistaken
     Assumptions and Prescriptions   130

20   Re-mapping the Middle East   137

21   The Offensive Against Venezuela   140

22   The Sun Never Sets but a Mote Remains   151

23   The Emperor's Rage   159

PART V
Ideology of Empire   165

24   The Harvard School of Empire Building   167

25   Lies and Deceptions on the Left   175

26   An Empire Built on Fear at Home and Abroad   183

27   Imperial Road to Conquest: Peace and Disarmament
     Agreements   188

28   Mapping Trump's Empire: Assets and Liabilities   194

29   Latin America in the Time of Trump   197

30   Trump's Protectionism: A Great Leap Backward   202

31   Trump Marches Onward and Downward   206

32   Trump Against the World Order: A Teapot in a Tempest?   211

33   A Decalogue of American Empire Building   214

     Bibliography   219
     Index   223

Foreword

Imperialism is defined by Michael Parenti in his illuminating primer *Against Empire*[1] as a system so organized as to permit economically dominant groups and the ruling class of powerful nations to advance their political and economic interests by appropriating or expropriating the land, raw materials, and markets of subjugated nations for their self enrichment. More generally imperialism can be understood as a policy or practice by which the government of a country increases its power by gaining control over other areas of the world, either by direct territorial acquisitions or, more commonly in the post-Second World War era of Pax Americana, by gaining indirect control over the political or economic life of other countries in order to advance the economic interests of the ruling classes in the advanced capitalist countries. In this context it is common practice for the officials of the imperial state, a state that is oriented towards a belief in both the necessity of using and its right to use the instruments of state power available to it to protect and advance what is perceived to be the national interest, here equating the economic interests of the dominant class with the 'national interest'.

So understood, imperialism has been a powerful force in world history over the last four or five centuries, during which powerful states with an imperialist agenda carved up entire continents, looting and pillaging countries on the periphery of the world capitalist system of their wealth and natural resources while oppressing the indigenous people and nations and obliterating entire civilizations in the process.

Yet, despite the momentous importance and devastating impact of capitalism and imperialism over the years, imperialism is seldom accorded any serious attention by academics, media commentators, and political leaders, or it is viewed as a left-wing ideology without any basis in reality or as the political practice of non-western, non-democratic nations governed by authoritarian regimes. But in actual fact imperialism in its diverse forms over the past four or five centuries—and especially over the past decades of the American empire—is intimately connected to capitalism, a means of advancing the interests of capitalists and the ruling class of the capitalist western democracies where the economic and political interests of the capitalist class are equated with the 'national interest'. In these cases, rather than being directly colonized by the imperial power, the weaker countries subordinated to this power have been granted the trappings of sovereignty and freedom (liberal multi-party democracy) while the owners of finance capital retain control of the lion's share of their profitable resources. This relationship has gone under various names: 'informal empire', 'colonialism without colonies' or 'neocolonialism', and 'the new imperialism'.

As for academics, when not ignored outright the subject of imperialism has been sanitized so that empires become 'commonwealths' and colonies become 'territories' or 'dominions'. By the same token, imperialist pillage and military interventions are transformed into matters of 'national security', leadership of the forces of freedom, or maintaining 'stability' in one or another region.

As noted by Parenti, the preponderant thrust of European and North American imperial power over the years—from the 19th to the 21st century— has been directed against Africa, Asia, and Latin America on the periphery of the world capitalist system. By the 19th century, capitalists saw the Third World of Africa, Asia, and Latin America as not only a source of raw materials and slaves, and a source of wealth and cheap labor, but also a market for manufactured goods in the US. By the 20th century, the western industrial nations were exporting not only goods but also capital in the form of machinery, technology, investments, and loans. But to say that the world entered the most advanced stage of capitalism understood (by Lenin) as 'imperialism' (an era dominated by the export of profit-seeking capital and the territorial division of the world by European colonial powers), is not to imply that imperialist exploitation and the plunder of natural resources that characterized the earlier period of European colonialism and mercantilism ceased.

As argued by Petras in this book of essays written over recent years, if anything the exploitation and pillage of the natural and human 'resources' of the weaker, poorer countries on the periphery of the world capitalist system, and the despoliation of the environment, accelerated in the neoliberal era of free market capitalism—that is, over the past three decades of US imperialism.

Imperialism is older than capitalism. The Persian, Macedonian, Roman, and Mongol empires all existed centuries before the British and American empires of the 20th century. Emperors and the conquistadors were interested mostly in plunder and tribute, gold and glory. But the imperialism of the 19th, 20th and 21st centuries—capitalist imperialism—differs from these earlier forms in the way it systematically accumulates capital through the organized exploitation and penetration of overseas markets. Capitalist imperialism invests in other countries, transforming and dominating their economies, cultures, and political life, integrating their financial and productive structures into an international system of capital accumulation.

Sometimes imperial domination is explained as arising from an innate desire for domination and expansion, a 'territorial imperative' or 'lust for power'. But of the various notions about imperialism circulating today in the United States, Canada, and Europe, the dominant view is that it does not exist. Imperialism is not recognized as a legitimate concept, certainly not in relation to the United States or Canada. One may speak or write of 'Soviet imperialism' or '19th-century British imperialism' but not of US imperialism. As Parenti observes, graduate students in political science at most American universities (and the same is true for Canadian universities) would not be granted the opportunity to research US imperialism, with argument being that such an undertaking would not be scholarly. While many people throughout the world charge the United States with being an imperialist power—and Canada has now acquired this status in Latin America thanks to the destructive operations of Canadian mining companies—those who talk or write of US imperialism are usually judged to be 'mouthing ideological blather', as Parenti puts it.

In the liberal tradition of political science, the projection of imperial power and associated dynamics are generally disconnected from capitalism and its economic dynamics, reducing imperialism to a quest for world domination based on a lust for power or purely geopolitical considerations by the guardians of the national interest in the most powerful countries. On the other hand, in the Marxist tradition of political economy, among world system theorists of the new imperialism there can be found the opposite tendency, in which the institutional specificity of the state as an instrument of class power is ignored and imperialism reduced to a purely economic issue, essentially confusing imperialism with capitalism.

One of the major values of this collection of essays on US imperialism is that capitalism and imperialism are shown to take diverse forms but remain intimately connected—that imperialism is essentially the projection of state power in the service of capital, a strategy and policies designed to advance the geopolitical and economic interests of the economically dominant and politically ruling capitalist class.

Almost all theories of contemporary imperialism, in both its (neo)Marxist and (neo)liberal variants, lack any but the crudest sociological analysis of the class and political character of the governing groups that direct the imperial state and its policies. This is another reason for the importance of this collection of essays: they show in very clear language, and without academic jargon, that the foreign affairs and international relations of the United States and Canada can best be understood through the lens of class analysis and the notion of imperialism.

Most scholars of contemporary imperialism resort to economic reductionism in which the political and ideological dimensions of imperial power are downplayed or ignored, and words such as 'investments', 'trade' and 'markets' are decontextualized and presented as historically disembodied

entities that are comparable across space and time. Changes in the configuration of class relations and associated dynamics are then accounted for in
terms of general economic categories such as 'finance', 'manufacturing',
'banking', and 'services' without any analysis of the political economy of
capitalist development and class formation, or the nature and sources of
financial wealth—illegal drug trade, money laundering, real estate speculation, etc. As for the shifts in the political and economic orientation of
governing capitalist politicians who represent the imperial interests of the
dominant class, they are glossed over in favour of abstract accounts of sta-
tistical shifts in economic measures of capital flows.

Unlike so much contemporary theorizing about imperialism, which generally ignores the sociopolitical and ideological power configurations of
imperial state policy as well as the role of international financial institutions
such as the World Bank in shaping the institutional and policy framework of
the current imperial world order, James Petras shows that the dynamics of
imperial power relations are political as well as economic, and engage not
only the interests of capitalists and the ruling class but also the political apparatus of the state, which is controlled by or put at the service of this class.

Henry Veltmeyer

Note

1   Michael Parenti (1995). *Against Empire*. City Lights Books.

Part I

Historical Background

Chapter 1

US Global Power in the 21st Century

Military or Economic Imperialism?

Despite vast amounts of imperial data to the contrary, the great majority of writers on imperialism continue to describe and analyze US imperialism strictly in economic terms—that is, as an expansion of capital accumulation, accumulation on a world scale.

In fact, the major and minor US imperial wars have more to do with capital *dis-accumulation*, in the sense that trillion-dollar flows have gone out from the US, hundreds of billions of dollars in profits from resource sites have been undermined, markets for exports have been severely weakened, and exploitable productive industry has been uprooted. At the same time that the US imperialist state dis-accumulates capital, multinational corporations, especially in the extractive sector, are expanding, accumulating capital throughout Latin America and other areas of the world system.

This new configuration of power, the conflicting and complementary nature of 21st-century US imperialism, requires that we anchor our analysis in the real, existing behaviour of imperial state and extractive capitalist policymakers. The basic premise informing this essay is that there are two increasingly divergent forms of imperialism: military-driven intervention, occupation, and domination; and economic expansion and exploitation of resources and markets by invitation of the host country.

We will proceed by examining, in a historical-comparative framework, the choices of imperial strategy and the alternatives that were selected or rejected. Through an analysis of the practical decisions taken regarding 'imperial expansion' we can obtain insights into the real nature of US imperialism. The study of imperial strategic choices, past and present, state and corporate, requires three levels of analysis: global, national, and sectoral.

Global Strategies: The US Imperial State and Multinational Corporations

The US imperial state invested trillions of dollars in military expenditures, sent hundreds of thousands of military personnel in wars in the Middle East (Iraq, Yemen, and Syria), North and East Africa (Libya, Somalia), South

Asia (Afghanistan), and imposed sanctions on Iran that cost the US hundreds of billions in capital dis-accumulation.

The US corporate elite, driven out of Iraq, Syria, Libya, and other places where US military imperialism was engaged, chose to invest in manufacturing in China and extractive sectors throughout Latin America. In other words, the imperial state strategists either chose to expand in relatively backward areas (Afghanistan, Pakistan, Somalia and Yemen) or imposed under-development by destroying or sanctioning lucrative extractive economies (Iraq, Libya, Iran).

In contrast, multinational corporations (MNCs) chose the most dynamic expanding zones where militarist imperialism was least engaged: China and Latin America. In other words, capital did not 'follow the flag'; it avoided it.

Moreover, the zones where extractive capital was most successful in terms of access, profits, and stability were those where their penetration was based on negotiated contracts between sovereign nations and CEOs—economic imperialism by invitation.

In contrast, in the priority areas of expansion chosen by imperial state strategists, entry and domination was by force, leading to the destruction of the means of production and loss of access to the principal sites of extractive exploitation. US military-driven imperialism undermined energy companies' agreements in Iraq and Libya. Imperial state sanctions in Iran designed to weaken its nuclear and defense capabilities undercut US corporate extractive, public-private contracts with the Iranian state oil corporations. The drop in production and supply of oil in Iraq, Iran, and Libya raised energy prices and had a negative impact on the 'accumulation of capital on a world scale'.

If imperial state decision-makers had followed the direction of economic rather than military driven policymakers they would have pivoted to Asia and Latin America rather than the Middle East, South Asia and North Africa. They would have channelled funds into economic imperialist strategies, including joint ventures, high and medium-tech trade agreements, and expanded exports by the high-end manufacturing sector, instead of financing 700 military bases, destabilization campaigns and costly military exercises.

Twentieth century military imperialism stands in stark contrast to late twentieth century economic imperialism. In the mid 1960s the US announced a vast new economic program in Latin America—the Alliance for Progress that was designed to finance economic opportunities in Latin America via joint ventures, agrarian reform and investments in the extractive sector. The imperial state's military policies and interventionist policies were designed to secure US business control over mines, banks, factories and agro-business. US backing for the coups in Chile, Bolivia, Brazil, Uruguay and Peru led to the privatization of key resource sectors and the imposition of the neoliberal economic model.

US policy in Asia under Nixon was directed first and foremost to opening economic relations with China, expanding trade agreements with Japan, Taiwan and South Korea. The pivot from war to free trade led to a boom in US exports as well as imports, in private investments and lucrative profits. Military expenditures declined even as the US engaged in covert operations in Afghanistan, Angola, Nicaragua and El Salvador.

Imperial intervention combined military and economic expansion, with the latter dictating policy priorities and the allocation of resources.

The reversal set in with the US military backing of the jihadist extremists in Afghanistan and the demise of the USSR. The former set the stage for the rise to power of the Taliban and the emergence of the Al Qaeda terrorist organization. The latter led US imperial strategists to pursue wars of conquest with impunity—for example, Yugoslavia and Iraq during the 1990s.

Easy military conquests and visions of a 'unipolar' world dominated by US military supremacy encouraged and fostered the emergence of a new breed of imperial strategists—neo-conservative militarists with closer ties to Israel and its military priorities than to the US extractive petrol capitalists in the Middle East.

Military Versus Economic Imperialism at the National Level

In the post-Cold War period, the competition between the two variants of imperialism was played out in all the nations subject to US intervention.

During the first Iraq war the balance between militarists and economic imperialists was in play. The US defeated Iraq but did not shred the state or bomb the oil fields. Sanctions were imposed but did not paralyze oil deals. The US did not occupy Iraq; it partitioned the north—so-called 'Kurdish' Iraq—but left the secular state intact. Extractive capital was actively in competition with the militarist neo-conservatives over the future direction of imperial policy.

The launch of the second Iraq war and the invasion of Afghanistan marked a decisive shift toward military imperialism: the US ignored all economic considerations. Iraq's secular state was destroyed; civil society was pulverized; ethno-religious, tribal and clan warfare was encouraged. US colonial officials ruled by military fiat; top policymakers with links to Israel replaced oil-connected officials. The militarist 'war on terror' ideology replaced free market, free trade imperialism. Afghanistan killing fields replaced the China market as the center of US imperial policy. Billions were spent chasing evasive guerrillas in the mountains of a backward economy while US lost competitive advantages in the most dynamic Asian markets.

In Iraq, imperial policymakers chose to align with sectarian warlords over extractive technocrats. In Afghanistan they chose loyal ex-pat puppets over influential Taliban leaders capable of pacifying the country.

Extractive Versus Military Imperialism in Latin America

Latin American neoliberalism went from boom to bust in the 1990s. By the early 2000s crises enveloped the region. By the turn of the century, US-backed rulers were being replaced by popular nationalist leaders. US policymakers stuck by their neoliberal clients in decline and failed to adapt to the new rulers who pursued modified socially inclusive extractivism. The US military imperialists longed for a return of the neoliberal backers of the 'war on terrorism'. In contrast, multinational extractive corporations were realists—and adapted to the new regimes.

On a global scale, at the beginning of the new millennium two divergent tendencies emerged. US military imperialism expanded throughout the Middle East, North Africa, South Asia and the Caucuses, while Latin American regimes turned in the opposite direction—toward moderate nationalism and populism, with a strong emphasis on poverty reduction via economic development in association with imperial extractive capital.

In the face of these divergent and conflicting trends, the major US extractive multinational corporations chose to adapt to the new political realities in Latin America. While Washington, the imperial state, expressed hostility and dismay toward the new regimes' refusal to back the 'war on terror' (military imperialism), the major MNCs' robust embrace of economic imperialism took advantage of the investment opportunities opened by these regimes' adoption of a new extractivist model to pour billions into the mining, energy and agricultural sectors.

The Specificities of Extractive Imperialism in the Post-neoliberal Era

Extractive imperialism in Latin America has several specific characteristics that sharply demarcate it from earlier forms of agro-mineral imperialism.

First, extractive capital is not dominated by a single imperial country as it was by the Spanish in the 18th century, the British in the 19th century or the US in the 20th century. Imperial extractive capital is very diverse: Canadian, US, Chinese, Brazilian, Australian, Spanish, Indian and other MNCs are deeply involved.

Second, the imperial states of the diverse MNC do not engage in 'gun boat diplomacy' (with the exception of the US). The imperial states provide economic financing and diplomatic support but are not actively involved in subverting Latin American regimes.

Third, the relative weight of US MNCs in the new imperial extractivism is much less than it was a half-century earlier. The rise of diverse extractive MNCs and the dynamism of China's commodity market and deep financial pockets have displaced the US, IMF and WB and established new terms of trade with Latin America.

Fourth, probably the most significant aspect of the new imperial extractivism is that its entry and expansion is by invitation. The Latin American regimes and the extractive MNCs negotiate contracts: MNC entry is not unilaterally imposed by an imperial state. Yet the 'contracts' may result in unequal returns; they provide substantial revenues and profits to the MNC; they grant large multi-million-acre tracts of land for mining or agriculture exploitation; they obligate the national state to dispossess local communities and police/repress the displaced. But they have also allowed the post-neoliberal states to expand their social spending, increase their foreign reserves, eschew relations with the IMF, and diversify their markets and trading partners.

In regional terms extractive imperialism in Latin America has accumulated capital by diverging from the military imperialism practiced by the US in other macro-regions of the world system. Over the past decade and a half, extractive capital has been allied with and relied on both post-neoliberal and neoliberal regimes against petty commodity producers, indigenous communities and other anti-extractive resistance movements. Extractive imperialists do not rely on 'their' imperial state to quell resistance; they turn to their national political partners.

Extractive imperialism by invitation also diverges from the military imperial state in its view toward regional organizations. US military imperialism placed all its bets on US-centered economic integration that Washington could leverage to political, military and economic advantage. Extractive capital, in the great diversity of its 'national identity', welcomed Latin American-centered integration that did not privilege US markets and investors.

However, the predominance of economic imperialism, in particular the extractive version, needs to be qualified by several caveats.

US military imperialism has been present in several forms. The US backed the military coup in Honduras overthrowing the post-neoliberal Zelaya government; likewise it supported an 'institutional coup' in Paraguay.

Second, even as Multinational Corporations (MNCs) poured capital into Bolivian mining and energy sectors, the US imperial state fomented destabilization activities to undermine the MAS government. But the US was defeated and the agencies and operatives were expelled from the country. The crucial issue here, as well as in other instances, was the unwillingness of the MNCs to join forces with the military imperialists via boycotts, trade embargoes or disinvestment. Clearly, the stability and profitability of long-term contracts between the Bolivian regime and extractive MNCs counted for more than ties to the US imperial state.

US military imperialism has expanded its military bases and increased joint military exercises with most Latin American armed forces. Indoctrinated military officials could still be formidable potential allies in any future 'coup', if and when the US pivots from the Middle East to Latin America.

US military imperialism in its manifest multiple forms, from bankrolling non-governmental organizations (NGOs) engaged in destabilization and street riots in Venezuela to its political support of financial speculators in Argentina and right-wing parties and personalities in Brazil, has a continuous presence alongside extractive imperialism. The success of the latter and eclipse of the former is based in part on two contingent circumstances. The US's serial wars in the Middle East divert attention from Latin America; and the commodity boom fuels the growth of extractive capital. The economic slowdown in China and the decline of commodity prices may weaken regimes in opposition to US military imperialism.

Paradoxically, the weakening of ties between the post-neoliberal regimes and extractive imperialism resulting from the decline of commodity prices is strengthening the neoliberal sociopolitical forces allied with US military imperialism.

Latin America's Right Turn: The Cohabitation of Extractive and Military Imperialism?

Throughout Latin America the post-neoliberal regimes that have ruled for the better part of a decade and a half face serious challenges—from consequential social opposition at the micro-level and aggressive political-economic elites at the macro-level. It is worthwhile surveying the prospects for a return to power of neoliberal regimes allied with military imperialism in several key countries.

Several factors are working in favour of a return to power of political parties and leaders who seek to reverse the independent and inclusive policies of the post-neoliberal power bloc.

First, the post-neoliberal regimes' development strategy of depending on foreign extractive capital perpetuated and strengthened the economic basis of imperialism: 'colonial style' trade relations, exporting primary commodities and importing finished goods, allowed the agro-mineral elites to occupy key positions in the politico-social structure. With the decline in commodity prices, some post-neoliberal regimes are experiencing fiscal and balance of payments shortfalls. Inflation and cuts in social expenditures adversely affect the capacity of the post-neoliberal regimes to retain popular and middle-class electoral support.

The divergence between post-neoliberals and economic imperialism are accentuated by the return of the neoliberal right. The agro-mineral sectors perceive an opportunity to rid themselves of their power and revenue-sharing agreements with the state and secure even more lucrative arrangements with the advance of the neoliberal right, which promises tax and royalty reductions, deregulation and lower wage and pension payments.

Second, the post-neoliberal regimes' alliances with the building, construction and other bourgeois sectors was accompanied by corruption involving pay-offs, bribes and other illicit financial transactions designed to finance their mass media-based electoral campaigns and patronage system which ensured electoral majorities. The neoliberal right is exploiting these corruption scandals to erode the middle-class electoral base of the post-neoliberal regimes.

Third, the post-neoliberal regimes increased the supply of social services but ignored their quality, provoking widespread discontent with the inadequate public educational, transport and health services.

Fourth, inflation is eroding the decade-long advance of wage, pension and family allowances. The post-neoliberal regimes are caught between pressures to 'adjust'—to devalue the currency and impose fiscal 'austerity' as proposed by the international bankers mass—and pressures to engage in deeper structural changes which require, among other things, changes in the extractive dependence model and greater public ownership. The crises of the post-neoliberal regimes are leading to irresolution and opening up political space for the neoliberal right that is allied to military and economic imperialism.

Military imperialism, which was weakened by the popular uprisings at the turn of 20th century, is never absent. US military imperialism is first and foremost powerfully entrenched in two major countries: Mexico and Colombia. In both countries neoliberal regimes bought into the militarization of their societies, including the comprehensive and deep presence of US military-police officials in the structures of the state.

In both states, US military and economic imperialism operates in alliance with paramilitary death squads, even as officials proclaimed a 'war on drugs'. The ideology of free market imperialism was put into practice with the elimination of trade barriers, widespread privatization of resources and multi-million-acre land grabs by the MNCs.

Through its regional clients, US imperialism has a springboard to extend its influence. Mexican-style 'militarized imperialism' has spread to Central America; Colombia serves as a launchpad to subvert Venezuela and Ecuador.

Where dissident regimes emerged in regions claimed by militarized imperialism—for example, Honduras and Paraguay—military and civilian coups were engineered. However, because of the regional concentration of US military imperialism in the Middle East, it relies heavily on local collaborators—political, military and economic elites—as vehicles for 'regime change'.

Extractive imperialism is under siege from popular movements in many countries in Latin America. In some cases, the political elites have increasingly militarized the contested terrain. Where this is the case, the regimes invite and accept an increased imperial military presence as advisers, and embrace their militarist ideology, thus fostering a 'marriage' between extractive and military imperialism. This was the case in Peru under President Humala and Santos in Colombia.

In Argentina and Brazil, the moderate reformist policies of the Kirchner and Lula/Rousseff regimes placed under siege. Faltering export earnings, rising deficits and inflationary pressures fuelled a neoliberal offensive, which took a new form: populism at the service of neoliberal collaboration with military imperialism. Extractive capital has become divided—some sectors retaining ties with the regime, while, the majority, are allied with the rising power of the Right.

In Brazil, the Right has promoted a former environmentalist (Silva) to front the hard-line neoliberal financial sector—which has received full support from local and imperial mass media. In Argentina, the imperial state and mass media have backed hedge fund speculators and launched a full-scale economic war, claiming default, in order to damage Buenos Aires' access to capital markets and increase its investments in the extractive sector.

In contrast, Bolivia, the paradigmatic case of the extractive model has moved successfully to oust and weaken the military arm of imperialism, ending the presence of US military advisers and Drug Enforcement Administration officials while deepening and strengthening ties with diverse extractive MNCs on the one hand and on the other consolidating support among the trade unions and Indian peasant movements.

In Ecuador the extractive regime established by Rafael Correa diversified the sources of imperial capital from the US to China and consolidated its power via effective patronage machinery and socioeconomic reforms.

The US-Colombian military threat to Venezuela and Ecuador has diminished, peace negotiations with the FARC advanced and the regime now faces trade union and Indian peasant opposition with regard to its extractive strategy and corporatist reforms.

In both Ecuador and Bolivia, imperial militarism appears to lack the vital strategic military-civilian allies capable of engineering regime change.

The case of Venezuela highlights the continuing importance of imperial militarism in shaping US policy in Latin America. A clear military policy was adopted by Washington prior to any basic social reforms or economic nationalist measures. The coup of 2001 and lockout of 2002 were backed by the US in response to President Chávez' forceful rejection of the 'war on terrorism'. Washington jeopardized its economic stake, its petrol investments, to put in place a regime that conformed to its global military strategy.

And for the following decade and a half US imperial strategy totally ignored investment, trade and resource opportunities in this wealthy petrol state; it chose to spend hundreds of millions in financing opposition NGOs, terrorists, electoral parties, mass media and military officials to effect a regime change. The extractive sector in the US simply became a transmission belt for the agencies of the militarized imperial state. In its place, Russia and China, interested especially in the extractive sector, signed multi-billion-dollar contracts with the Venezuelan state: a case of extractive imperialism by invitation for economic and security reasons.

Apart from the ideological conflict over US militarist expansion, Venezuela's promotion of Latin American-centered regional integration weakened US leverage and control in the region. In its struggle against Latin American-centered regional organizations and to regain its dominance, US imperialism has upgraded its economic profile via the Trans-Pacific Alliance, which includes its most loyal neoliberal allies—Chile, Peru, Colombia and Mexico. The global eclipse of economically driven imperial expansion in favour of the military has not totally displaced several key economic advances in strategic countries and sectors in Mexico, Colombia and Peru.

The privatization and denationalization of the biggest and most lucrative public petrol company in Latin America, the Mexican giant PEMEX, opens up enormous profitable opportunities for US MNCs. The rapid appropriation of oil fields by American MNCs will enhance and compliment the militarization of Mexico undertaken by the US military-security apparatus. The Mexican example highlights several features of US imperialism in Latin America.

Imperial militarization does not necessarily preclude economic imperialism if it takes place within an existing stable state structure. Unlike the imperial wars in Iraq and Libya, the military imperialist policies in Mexico advanced via powerful local political clients willing and able to engage in bloody civil wars costing more than 100,000 civilian lives in over a decade. Under the aegis and guidance of US imperial rulers, the US and Mexican military devastated civil society but safeguarded and expanded the huge mining and manufacturing enclaves open to economic imperialist exploitation. Militarization contributed to a weakening of the bargaining rights of workers. Wages have declined in real terms over the last few decades and the minimum wage is the lowest in the hemisphere.

Mexico highlights the crucial role that collaborator elites play in imperialist capital accumulation. Mexico is an excellent example of imperialism by invitation—the political agreements at the top impose 'acquiescence' below. The extraordinary levels of corruption that permeate the entire political class solidify the longstanding links between Mexican political-business elites, the MNC and the security apparatus of the imperial state. Extractive imperialism is the principal beneficiary of this 'triple alliance'.

In the case of Mexico, militarized imperialism laid the groundwork for the expansion of economic imperialism.

A similar process involving 'triple alliances' is operative in Colombia. For the past decade and a half, militarized imperialism poured over $6 billion in military aid (Plan Colombia) to finance the dispossession, assassination, arrest and torture of over four million Colombians, including the killing of thousands of trade union and social movement leaders.

The scorched earth policy, which was backed by a substantial US military mission and operated through the existing state apparatus with the active support of the agro-mineral and banking elite aided by nearly 40,000-strong paramilitary death squads and drug traffickers, laid the groundwork for the large-scale entry of extractive capital—particularly mining capital.

Military imperialism preceded the long-term, large-scale 'invasion' by economic imperialism in the form of a free trade agreement and multi-million-acre land grants and concessions to mining MNCs.

This general pattern was repeated in Peru. The 'war on terror' under Fujimori and the liberalization of the economy under three subsequent presidents culminated in the massive primarization of the economy under President Humala, who deepened and extended the expansion of imperial extractive capital.

The economic downturn in some of the post-neoliberal economies, namely Brazil, Argentina and Venezuela, and the rightward-moving political spectrum have opened a window of opportunity for US economic imperialism to work in tandem with the rising neoliberal political opposition. The military option, a military coup or US military intervention, is not on the horizon at present. The central focus of imperial state decision-makers regarding regime change is a combination of overt electoral and covert 'street intervention': adopting 'populist', moralist and technocratic rhetoric to highlight corruption in high offices and inefficiency in the delivery of social services with claims of bureaucratic interference in the operation of the market. Business disinvestment, financial speculation on the currency and negative mass media propaganda prompted a wave of strikes and protests against shortages and lagging wages relative to price increases.

Despite costly and failed imperial wars in the Middle East, despite a decade of military retreat in Latin America, economic imperialism is advancing via the electoral route; it has already established a formidable array of allies among the political regimes in Mexico, Colombia and Peru and is poised to re-establish neoliberal allies in Brazil, Argentina and Venezuela.

Conclusion

Imperialism as it has evolved over the past quarter of a century cannot be understood as a 'unified whole' in which the two basic components, military and economic, are always complimentary. Divergences have been graphically illustrated by the imperial wars in the Middle East, South Asia and North Africa. Convergences are more obvious in Latin America, especially in Mexico, Colombia and Peru, where militarization facilitated the expansion of extractive capital.

The theoretical point is that the nature of the political leadership of the imperial state has a high degree of autonomy in shaping the predominance of one or another strand of imperial expansion. The capacity for imperial capital to expand is highly contingent on the strength and structure of the collaborators' state: militarized imperialism that invades and destroys states and the fabric of civil society has led to disinvestment. In contrast, economic imperialism by invitation in neoliberal collaborators' states has been at the center of successful imperial expansion.

The ambiguities and contradictions intrinsic to the post-neoliberal extractivist-based development model have constrained the military component of imperialism while expanding opportunities for economic imperial accumulation. Accumulation by invitation and accumulation by dispossession are simply 'different facets of' in a complex process in which political regime changes intervene and establish the locations and timing for refluxes and influxes of capital.

The rise of new economic imperialist powers like China competing with established imperial powers like the US has led to alternative markets and sources of financing, which eroded the effectiveness of political, military and diplomatic instruments of imperial coercion.

Regional variations in political configurations and imperial priorities and choice of instruments of power have deeply influenced the nature and structure of imperialism. And as the world historic record seems to argue, military-driven empire building in the Middle East has been a disaster, while economically driven imperialism shows signs of rapid recovery and success in Latin America.

Chapter 2

Fifty Years of Imperial Wars

Over the past fifty years, US and European powers have engaged in countless imperial wars throughout the world. The drive for world supremacy has been clothed in the rhetoric of 'world leadership', and the consequences have been devastating for the peoples targeted. The biggest, longest and most numerous wars have been carried out by the United States. Presidents from both parties direct and preside over this quest for world power. The ideology that informs imperialism varies from 'anti-communism' in the past to 'anti-terrorism' today.

In its drive for world domination the US has used and combined many forms of warfare, including military invasions and occupations; proxy mercenary armies and military coups; financing political parties, NGOs and street mobs to overthrow duly constituted governments. The driving forces in the imperial state behind the quest for world power vary with the geographic location and social economic composition of the targeted countries.

What is clear from an analysis of US empire-building over the last half century is the relative decline of economic interests and the rise of politico-military considerations. In part this is because of the demise of the collectivist regimes (the USSR and Eastern Europe) and the conversion of China and leftist Asian, African and Latin American regimes to capitalism. The decline of economic forces as the driving force of imperialism is a result of the advent of global neoliberalism. Most US and EU multinationals (MNCs) are not threatened by nationalizations or expropriations that might trigger imperial state political intervention. In fact, MNCs are invited to invest, trade and exploit natural resources even by post-neoliberal regimes. Economic interests come into play in formulating imperial state policies if and when nationalist regimes emerge and challenge US-based MNCs, as was the case in Venezuela under President Chávez.

The key to US empire building over the past half-century is found in the political, military and ideological power configurations that have come to control the levers of the imperial state. The recent history of US imperial wars has demonstrated that strategic military priorities—military bases, budgets and bureaucracy—have expanded far beyond any localized economic interests of global capital in the form of MNCs. Moreover, the vast expenditures and long-term and expensive military interventions of the US imperial state in the Middle East have been at the behest of Israel. The takeover of strategic political positions in the executive branch and Congress by the powerful Zionist power configuration within the US has reinforced the centrality of military over economic interests.

The 'privatization' of imperial wars—the vast growth and use of mercenaries contracted by the Pentagon—has led to a vast pillage of tens of billions of dollars from the US Treasury. Corporations that supply mercenary military combatants have become a very 'influential' force shaping the nature and consequences of US empire building.

Military strategists, defenders of Israeli colonial interests in the Middle East, mercenary military and intelligence corporations are key actors in the imperial state, and it is their decision-making influence which explains why US imperial wars do not result in a politically stable, economically prosperous empire. Instead their policies have resulted in unstable, ravaged economies in perpetual rebellion.

In this essay we proceed by identifying the changing areas and regions of US empire building from the mid-1970s to the present. We then examine the methods, driving forces and outcomes of imperial expansion. We then turn to describe the current geo-political map of empire building and the varied nature of the anti-imperialist resistance. We conclude by examining the why and how of empire building and, more particularly, the consequences and results of a half century of US imperial expansion.

Imperialism in the Post-Vietnam Period: Proxy Wars in Central America, Afghanistan and Southern Africa

The US imperialist defeat in Indo-China marked the end of one phase of empire building and the beginning of another: a shift from territorial invasions to proxy wars. Hostile domestic opinion precluded large-scale ground wars. Beginning during the presidencies of Gerald Ford and James Carter, the US imperialist state increasingly relied on proxy clients. It recruited, financed and armed proxy military forces to destroy a variety of nationalist and social revolutionary regimes and movements in three continents. Washington financed and armed extremist Islamic forces worldwide to invade and destroy the secular, modernizing, Soviet-backed regime in Afghanistan, with logistical support from the Pakistan military and intelligence agencies and financial backing from Saudi Arabia.

The second proxy intervention was in Southern Africa, where the US imperial state financed and armed proxy forces against anti-imperialist regimes in Angola and Mozambique, in alliance with South Africa.

The third proxy intervention took place in Central America, where the US financed, armed and trained murderous death squad regimes in

Nicaragua, El Salvador, Guatemala and Honduras to decimate popular movements and armed insurgencies, resulting in over 300,000 civilian deaths.

The US imperial state's proxy strategy extended to South America: CIA and Pentagon-backed military coups took place in Uruguay (Alvarez), Chile (Pinochet) Argentina (Videla), Bolivia (Banzer) and Peru (Morales). Empire building by proxy was largely at the behest of US MNCs, which were the principal actors in setting priorities in the imperial state throughout this period.

Accompanying proxy wars were direct military invasions: the tiny island of Grenada (1983) and Panama (1989) under Presidents Reagan and Bush, Sr. Easy targets, with few casualties and low-cost military expenditures: dress rehearsals for relaunching major military operations in the near future.

What is striking about the proxy wars is the mixed results. The outcomes in Central America, Afghanistan and Africa did not lead to prosperous neo-colonies or prove lucrative to US multinational corporations. In contrast, the proxy coups in South America led to large-scale privatization and profits for the American MNCs.

The Afghan proxy war led to the rise and consolidation of the Taliban's Islamic regime, which opposed both Soviet influence and US imperial expansion. The rise and consolidation of Islamic nationalism in turn challenged US allies in South Asia and the Gulf region and subsequently led to a US military invasion in 2001 and a prolonged (15-year) war (which has yet to conclude), and most probably to military retreat and defeat. The main economic beneficiaries were Afghan political clients, US mercenary military contractors, military procurement officers and civilian colonial administrators who pillaged hundreds of billions from the US Treasury in illegal and fraudulent transactions.

Pillage of the US Treasury in no way benefited the non-military MNCs. In fact, the war and resistance movement undermined any large-scale, long-term entry of US private capital in Afghanistan and adjoining border regions of Pakistan.

The proxy war in Southern Africa devastated the local economies, especially the domestic agricultural economy, uprooted millions of workers and farmers and curtailed US corporate oil penetration for over two decades. The positive outcome was the de-radicalization of the former revolutionary nationalist elite. However, the political conversion of the Southern African 'revolutionaries' to neoliberalism did not benefit the US MNCs as much as the rulers turned kleptocratic oligarchs who organized patrimonial regimes in association with a diversified collection of MNCs, especially from Asia and Europe.

The proxy wars in Central America had mixed results. In Nicaragua the Sandinista revolution defeated the US/Israeli-backed Somoza regime but immediately confronted a US-financed, armed and trained counter-revolutionary mercenary army (the 'Contras') based in Honduras. The US war destroyed many of the progressive economic projects, undermined the economy and eventually led to an electoral victory by the US-backed political client Violeta Chamorro. Two decades later the US proxies were defeated by a de-radicalized Sandinista-led political coalition.

In El Salvador, Guatemala and Honduras, the US proxy wars led to the consolidation of client regimes presiding over the destruction of the productive economy and the flight of millions of war refugees to the United States. US imperial dominance eroded the bases for a productive market that spawned the growth of murderous drug gangs.

In short, the US proxy wars succeeded in most cases in preventing the rise of nationalist-leftist regimes but also led to the destruction of the economic and political basis of a stable and prosperous empire of new colonies.

US Imperialism in Latin America: Changing Strategies, External and Internal Contingencies, Shifting Priorities and Global Constraints

To understand the operations, agency and performance of US imperialism in Latin America it is necessary to recognize the specific constellation of competing forces that shaped imperial state policies. Unlike in the Middle East where the militarist Zionist faction has established hegemony, in Latin America the MNCs have played a leading role in directing imperial state policy. In Latin America, the militarists played a lesser role, constrained by the power of the MNCs, the shifts in political power in Latin America from the right to the center-left, and the impact of economic crises and the commodity boom.

In contrast to the Middle East, the Zionist power configuration has little influence over imperial state policy, as Israel's interests are focused on the Middle East and, with the possible exception of Argentina, Latin America is not a priority.

For over a century and a half US MNCs and banks dominated and dictated US imperial policy toward Latin America. US armed forces and the CIA were instruments of economic imperialism via direct intervention (invasions), proxy 'military coups' or a combination of the two.

US imperial economic power in Latin America peaked between 1975 and 1999. Vassal states and client rulers were imposed via proxy military coups, direct military invasions (Dominican Republic, Panama and Grenada) and military/civilian-controlled elections. The result was the dismantling of the welfare state and the imposition of neoliberal policies. The MNC-led imperial state and its international financial appendages (IMF, WB, IDB) privatized lucrative strategic economic sectors, dominated trade and projected a regional integration scheme that would codify US imperial dominance.

Imperial economic expansion in Latin America was not simply a result of the internal dynamics and operations of the MNCs but depended on the receptivity of the 'host' country or, more precisely, the internal correlation of class forces in Latin America, which in turn revolved around the performance of the economy—its growth or susceptibility to crisis.

Latin America demonstrates that contingencies such as the demise of client regimes and collaborators' classes can have a profound negative impact on the dynamics of imperialism, undermining the power of the imperial state and reversing the economic advance of the MNC.

The advance of US economic imperialism during the 1975–2000 period was manifest in the adoption of neoliberal policies, the pillage of national resources, the increase of illicit debts and the overseas transfer of billions of dollars. However, the concentration of wealth and property precipitated a deep socio-economic crisis throughout the region which eventually led to the overthrow or ousting of the imperial collaborators in Ecuador, Bolivia, Venezuela, Argentina, Brazil, Uruguay, Paraguay and Nicaragua. Especially in the countryside, powerful anti-imperialist social movements emerged in Brazil and the Andean countries. Urban unemployed workers' movements and unions of public employees in Argentina and Uruguay spearheaded electoral changes, bringing to power center-left regimes which 're-negotiated' relations with the US imperial state.

The influence of US-based MNCs in Latin America waned as they could not count on the full battery of military resources of the imperial state to intervene and re-impose neoliberal clients because of its military priorities elsewhere in the Middle East, South Asia and North Africa.

Unlike the past, US-MNCs in Latin America lacked two essential props of power: the full backing of the US armed forces and powerful civilian-military clients in Latin America.

The strategy of US-centered integration was rejected by the center-left regimes. The imperial state turned to bilateral free trade agreements with Mexico, Chile, Colombia, Panama and Peru. As a result of the economic crises and collapse of most Latin American economies, neoliberalism, the dominant ideology of imperialism, was discredited. And the advocates of neoliberalism were marginalized.

Changes in the world economy had a profound impact on US–Latin American trade and investment relations. The dynamic growth of China and the subsequent boom in demand and the rising prices of commodities led to a sharp decline in US dominance in Latin American markets.

Latin American states diversified trade and sought and gained new overseas markets, especially in China. The increase in export revenues created greater capacity for self-financing. The IMF, WB and IDB, economic instruments for leveraging US financial impositions ('conditionality'), were sidelined.

The US imperial state faced Latin American regimes that embraced diverse economic options, markets and sources of finance. With powerful domestic popular support and unified civilian-military command, Latin America moved tentatively out of the US sphere of imperialist domination.

The imperial state and its MNCs, deeply influenced by their 'success' in the 1990s, responded to the decline of influence by proceeding by trial and error in the face of the negative constraints of the 21st century. The MNC-backed policymakers in the imperial state continued to back the collapsing neoliberal regimes, losing all credibility in Latin America. The imperial state failed to accommodate changes—deepening popular and center-left regime opposition to 'free markets' and the deregulation of banks. No large-scale economic aid programs, like President Kennedy's effort to counter the revolutionary appeal of the Cuban revolution by promoting social reforms via the 'Alliance for Progress', were fashioned to win over the center-left, probably because of budget constraints resulting from costly wars elsewhere.

The demise of neoliberal regimes, the glue that held the different factions of the imperial state together, led to competing proposals of how to regain dominance. The militarist faction resorted to and revived the military coup formula for restoration: coups were organized in Venezuela, Ecuador, Bolivia, Honduras and Paraguay, but all were defeated except for the last two. The defeat of US proxies led to the consolidation of the independent, anti-imperialist center-left regimes. Even the 'success' of the US coup in Honduras resulted in a major diplomatic defeat as every Latin American government condemned it and the US role, further isolating Washington in the region.

The defeat of the militarist strategy strengthened the political and diplomatic factions of the imperial state. With positive overtures toward ostensibly 'center-left regimes', this faction gained diplomatic leverage, retained military ties and deepened the expansion of MNCs in Uruguay, Brazil, Chile and Peru. With the last two countries the economic imperialist faction of the imperial state secured bilateral free trade agreements.

A third MNC-military faction, overlapping with the previous two, combined diplomatic-political accommodations toward Cuba, with an aggressive political destabilization strategy aimed at regime change (via a coup d'état) in Venezuela.

The heterogeneity of imperial state factions and their competing orientations reflects the complexity of interests engaged in empire building in Latin America and results in seemingly contradictory policies, a phenomenon less evident in the Middle East where the militarist-Zionist power configuration dominates imperial policymaking. For example, the promotion of military bases and counter-insurgency operations in Colombia (a priority of the militarist faction) is accompanied by bilateral free market agreements and peace negotiations between the Santos regime and the FARC-armed insurgency (a priority of the MNC faction).

Regaining imperial dominance in Argentina involves (i) promoting the electoral fortunes of the neoliberal governor of Buenos Aires, Mauricio Macri, (ii) backing the pro-imperial media conglomerate Clarin, which faces legislation breaking up its monopoly, (iii) exploiting the death of prosecutor and CIA-Mossad collaborator Alberto Nisman to discredit the Kirchner-Fernandez regime, and (iv) backing a New York speculators' (vulture) investment fund attempting to extract exorbitant interest payments and, with the aid of a dubious judicial ruling, block Argentina's access to financial markets.

Both the militarist and MNC factions of the imperial state converge in backing a multi-pronged electoral and coup approach that seeks to restore US-controlled neoliberal regimes to power.

The contingencies that forestalled the recovery of imperial power over the past decade are now acting in reverse. The drop in commodity prices has weakened post-neoliberal regimes in Venezuela, Argentina and Ecuador. The ebbing of anti-imperialist movements resulting from center-left co-optation tactics has strengthened imperial state-backed right-wing movements and street demonstrators. The decline in Chinese growth has weakened the Latin American market diversification strategies. The internal balance of class forces has shifted to the right in the direction of US-backed political clients in Brazil, Argentina, Peru and Paraguay.

Theoretical Reflections On Empire Building in Latin America

US empire building in Latin America is a cyclical process, reflecting the structural shifts in political power and the restructuring of the world economy—forces and factors which 'override' the imperial state and capital's drive to accumulate. Capital accumulation and expansion does not depend merely on the impersonal forces of 'the market' because the social relations under which the 'market' functions operate under the constraints of the class struggle.

The centerpiece of imperial state activities—namely the prolonged territorial wars in the Middle East—are absent in Latin America. The driving force of US imperial state policy is the pursuit of resources (agro-mining), power (low-paid autoworkers), markets (size and purchasing power of 600 million consumers). The economic interests of the MNCs are the motives for imperial expansion.

From a geo-strategic vantage point, the Caribbean, Central America as well as South America are most proximate to the US, but economic not military objectives predominate. However, the militarist-Zionist faction in the imperial state ignores these traditional economic motives and deliberately chooses to act on other priorities: control over oil-producing regions, destruction of Islamic nations or movements or simply anti-imperialist adversaries. The militarist-Zionist faction considered the 'benefits' to Israel, its Middle East military supremacy, as more important than the US securing economic supremacy in Latin America. This is clearly the case if we measure imperial priorities by state resources expended in pursuit of political goals.

Even if we take the goal of national security, interpreted in the broadest sense of securing the safety of the territorial homeland of the empire, the US military assault of Islamic countries driven by accompanying Islamophobic ideology and the resulting mass killings and uprooting of millions of Islamic people, has led to blowback: reciprocal terrorism. US 'total war' against civilians has provoked Islamic assaults against the citizens of the West.

Latin America countries targeted by economic imperialism are less belligerent than Middle Eastern countries targeted by US militarists. A cost/benefit analysis would demonstrate the totally 'irrational' nature of militarist strategy. However, if we take account of the specific composition and interests that motivate particularly imperial state policymakers, there is a kind of perverse 'rationality'. The militarists defend the rationality of costly and unending wars by citing the advantages of seizing the 'gateways to oil', and the Zionists cite their success in enhancing Israel's regional power.

For over a century Latin America was a priority region of imperial economic conquest, but by the 21st century it had lost primacy to the Middle East.

The Demise of the USSR and China's Turn Toward Capitalism

The greatest impetus to successful US imperial expansion did not take place via proxy wars or military invasions. Rather, the US empire achieved its greatest growth and conquest with the aid of client political leaders, organizations and vassal states throughout the USSR, Eastern Europe, the Baltic States, the Balkans and the Caucuses. Long-term and large-scale US and EU political penetration and funding succeeded in overthrowing the hegemonic collectivist regimes in Russia and the USSR and installing vassal states. They would soon serve NATO and be incorporated in the European Union. Bonn annexed East Germany and dominated the markets of Poland, the Czech Republic and other Central European states. American and London bankers collaborated with Russian-Israeli gangster-oligarchs in joint ventures plundering resources, industries, real estate and pension funds. The European Union exploited tens of millions of highly trained scientists, technicians and workers by importing them or stripping them of their welfare benefits and rights and utilizing them as cheap reserves in their own country.

'Imperialism by invitation' hosted by the vassal Yeltsin regime easily appropriated Russian wealth. The ex-Warsaw Pact military forces were incorporated into a foreign legion for US imperial wars in Afghanistan, Iraq and Syria. Their military installations were converted into military bases and missile sites encircling Russia.

US imperial conquest of the East created a unipolar world in which Washington decision-makers and strategists believed that, as the world's supreme power, they could intervene in every region with impunity.

The scope and depth of the US world empire was enhanced by China's embrace of capitalism and its ruler's invitation to US and EU MNCs to enter and exploit cheap Chinese labor. The global expansion of the US empire led to a sense of unlimited power, encouraging its rulers to exercise power against any adversary or competitor.

In the 1990s the US extended its military bases to the borders of Russia. US MNCs moved into China and Indo-China. US-backed client regimes throughout Latin America dismantled national economies, privatizing and denationalizing over five thousand lucrative strategic firms. Every sector was affected: natural resources, transport, telecommunications and finance.

Throughout the 1990s the US continued to increase its presence via political penetration and military force. George H. W. Bush launched a war against Iraq. Clinton bombed Yugoslavia and Germany and the EU joined the US in dividing Yugoslavia into 'mini-states'.

2000, a Pivotal Year: The Pinnacle and Decline of Empire

The very rapid and extensive imperial expansion 1989–1999 and the easy conquests and accompanying plunder created the conditions for the decline of the US empire.

The pillage and impoverishment of Russia led to the rise of a new leadership under President Putin intent on reconstructing the state and economy and ending vassalage.

The Chinese leadership harnessed its dependence on the West for capital investments and technology into instruments for creating a powerful export economy and growing a dynamic national public–private manufacturing complex. The imperial centers of finance that flourished under lax regulation crashed. The domestic foundations of empire were severely strained. The imperial war machine competed with the financial sector for federal budgetary expenditures and subsidies.

The easy growth of empire led to its over-extension. Multiple areas of conflict reflected worldwide resentment and hostility at the destruction wrought by bombings and invasions. Collaborative imperial client rulers were weakened. The worldwide empire exceeded the capacity of the US to successfully police its new vassal states. The colonial outposts demanded new infusions of troops, arms and funds at a time when countervailing domestic pressures were demanding retrenchment and retreat.

All the recent conquests—outside of Europe—were costly. The sense of invincibility and impunity led imperial planners to overestimate their capacity to expand, retain, control and contain inevitable anti-imperialist resistance.

The crisis and collapse of the neoliberal vassal states in Latin America accelerated. Anti-imperialist uprisings spread from Venezuela (1999), to Argentina (2001), Ecuador (2000–2005) and Bolivia (2003–2005). Center-left regimes emerged in Brazil, Uruguay and Honduras. Mass movements in rural regions and indigenous and mining communities gained momentum. Imperial plans formulated to secure US-centered integration were rejected. Instead, multiple regional pacts that excluded the US proliferated: ALBA, UNASUR, CELAC. Latin America's domestic rebellion coincided with the economic rise of China. A prolonged commodity boom severely weakened US imperial supremacy. The US had few local allies in Latin America and over-ambitious commitments to control the Middle East, South Asia and North Africa.

Washington lost its automatic majority in Latin America: its backing of coups in Honduras and Paraguay and intervention in Venezuela (2002) and blockade of Cuba was repudiated by every regime, even conservative allies.

Having easily established a global empire, Washington found it less easy to defend. Imperial strategists in Washington viewed the Middle East wars through the prism of Israeli military priorities, ignoring the global economic interests of the MNC.

Imperial military strategists overestimated the military capacity of vassals and clients, ill-prepared by Washington to rule in countries with growing armed national resistance movements. Wars, invasions and military occupations were launched in multiple sites. Yemen, Somalia, Libya, Syria, Pakistan were added to Afghanistan and Iraq. US imperial state expenditures far exceeded any transfer of wealth from the occupied countries.

A vast civilian-military-mercenary bureaucracy pillaged hundreds of billions of dollars from the US Treasury.

The centrality of wars of conquest destroyed the economic foundations and institutional infrastructure necessary for MNC entry and profit.

Once entrenched in strategic military conceptions of empire, the military-political leadership of the imperial state fashioned a global ideology to justify and motivate a policy of permanent and multiple warfare. The doctrine of the 'war on terror' justified war everywhere and nowhere. The doctrine was 'elastic'—adapted to every region of conflict and inviting new military engagements: Afghanistan, Libya, Iran and Lebanon were all designated as war zones.

The terror doctrine, global in scope, provided a justification for multiple wars and the massive destruction (not exploitation) of societies and economic resources. Above all, the war on terrorism justified torture (Abu Ghraib), concentration camps (Guantanamo) and, anywhere, civilian targets (via drones). Troops were withdrawn and returned to Afghanistan and Iraq as the nationalist resistance advanced. Thousands of Special Forces in scores of countries were active, purveying death and mayhem. Moreover, the violent uprooting, degradation and stigmatization of an entire civilization led to the spread of violence in the imperial centers of Paris, New York, London, Madrid and Copenhagen. The globalization of imperial state terror led to personal terror.

Imperial terror evoked domestic terror, the former on a massive, sustained scale encompassing entire civilizations and conducted and justified by elected political officials and military authorities, the latter by a cross-section of 'internationalists' who directly identified with the victims of imperial state terror.[1]

Contemporary Imperialism: Current and Future Perspectives

To understand the future of US imperialism it is important to sum up and evaluate the experience and policies of the past quarter of a century. If we compare US empire building between 1990 and 2015 it is clearly in decline economically, politically and even militarily in most regions of the world—though the process of decline is not linear and probably not irreversible.

Despite talk in Washington of reconfiguring imperial priorities to take account of MNC economic interests, little has been accomplished. Obama's so-called 'pivot to Asia' has resulted in new military base agreements with Japan, Australia and the Philippines that surround China and reflect an inability to fashion free trade agreements that exclude China. Meantime, the US has militarily restarted the war in Iraq and Afghanistan in addition to launching new wars in Syria and the Ukraine. It is clear that the primacy of the militarist faction is still the determining factor in shaping imperial state policies.

The imperial military drive is most evident in the US intervention in support of the coup in the Ukraine and its subsequent financing and arming of the Kiev junta. The imperial takeover of the Ukraine and plans to incorporate it into the EU and NATO represents military aggression in its most blatant form: the expansion of US military bases and installations and military manoeuvres on Russia's borders and the US-initiated economic sanctions have severely damaged EU trade and investment with Russia. US empire building continues to prioritize military expansion even at the cost of Western imperial economic interests in Europe.

The US-EU bombing of Libya destroyed the burgeoning trade and investment agreements between imperial oil and gas MNCs and the Gaddafi regime. NATO air assaults destroyed the economy, society and political order, converting Libya into a territory overrun by warring clans, gangs, terrorists and armed thuggery.

Over the past half century, the political leadership and strategies of the imperial state have changed dramatically. During the period 1975–1990, the MNCs played a central role in defining the direction of imperial state policy: leveraging markets in Asia; negotiating market openings with China; promoting and backing neoliberal military and civilian regimes in Latin America; installing and financing pro-capitalist regimes in Russia, Eastern Europe, the Baltic and Balkan states. Even in cases where the imperial state resorted to military intervention, Yugoslavia and Iraq, the bombings led to favourable economic opportunities for the US-based MNCs. The Bush, Sr. regime promoted US oil interests via an oil-for-food exchange agreement with Saddam Hussein in Iraq. Clinton promoted free market regimes in the mini-states resulting from the break-up of socialist Yugoslavia.

However, the imperial state's leadership and policies shifted dramatically during the late 1990s onward. President Clinton's imperial state was composed of long-standing MNC representatives, Wall Street bankers and newly ascending militarist Zionist officials. The result was a hybrid policy in which the imperial state actively promoted MNC opportunities under neoliberal regimes in the ex-communist countries of Europe and Latin America and expanded MNC ties with China and Vietnam while launching destructive military interventions in Somalia, Yugoslavia and Iraq.

The correlation and balance of force within the imperialist state shifted dramatically in favour the militarist-Zionist faction with 9/11: the terrorist attack of dubious origins and false flag demolitions in New York and Washington served to entrench the militarists in control of a vastly expanded imperial state apparatus. As a consequence of 9/11, the militarist-Zionist faction of the imperial state subordinated the interests of the MNC to its strategy of total war. This in turn led to the invasion, occupation and destruction of civilian infrastructure in Iraq and Afghanistan (instead of harnessing it to MNC expansion). The US colonial regime dismantled the Iraqi state (instead of re-ordering it to serve the MNC). The assassination and forced out-migration of millions of skilled professionals, administrators, police and military officials (rather than their incorporation as servants of the colonial state and MNCs) crippled any economic recovery.

The militarist-Zionist ascendancy in the imperial state introduced major changes in the policy, orientation, priorities and modus operandi of US imperialism. The ideology of the 'global war on terror' replaced the MNC doctrine of 'economic globalization'.

Perpetual wars vs. 'terrorists', not confined to place and time, replaced limited wars or interventions directed at opening markets or changing regimes that would implement neoliberal policies benefiting US MNCs.

The locus of imperial state activity shifted from exploiting economic opportunities in Asia, Latin America and the ex-communist countries of Eastern Europe to wars in the Middle East, South Asia and North Africa— targeting Muslim countries that opposed Israel's colonial expansion in Palestine, Syria, Lebanon and elsewhere.

The new militarist power configuration's conception of empire building required vast—trillion-dollar—expenditures, without thought of returns to private capital. In contrast, under the hegemony of the MNC, the imperial state intervened to secure concessions of oil, gas and minerals in Latin America and the Middle East. The costs of military conquest were more than compensated for by the returns to MNCs. The militarist imperial state configuration pillaged the US Treasury to finance its occupations, financing a vast army of corrupt colonial collaborators, private mercenary 'military contractors' and soon-to-be millionaire US military procurement (sic) officials.

Previously, MNC-directed overseas exploitation led to healthy returns to the US Treasury both in terms of direct tax payments and via the revenues generated from trade and the processing of raw materials.

Over the past decade and a half, the biggest and most stable returns to MNCs occur in regions and countries where the militarized imperial state is least involved—China, Latin America and Europe. US MNCs have profited least and lost most in areas of greatest imperial state involvement.

The 'war zones' that extend from Libya, Somalia, Lebanon, Syria and Iraq to Ukraine, Iran, Afghanistan and Pakistan are the regions where imperial MNCs have suffered the biggest decline and exodus.

The main 'beneficiaries' of the current imperial state policies are the war contractors and the security-military-industrial complex in the US. Overseas the state beneficiaries include Israel and Saudi Arabia. In addition, Jordanian, Egyptian, Iraqi, Afghani and Pakistani client rulers have squirreled away tens of billions in off-shore private bank accounts.

The non-state beneficiaries include mercenary, proxy armies. In Syria, Iraq, Libya, Somalia and the Ukraine, tens of thousands of collaborators in self-styled 'nongovernmental' organizations—civil society—have also profited.

Empire Building Under the Aegis of the Militarist-Zionist Imperial State

Sufficient time has passed over the past decade and a half of militarist-Zionist dominance of the imperial state to evaluate their performance.

The US and its Western European allies, especially Germany, successfully expanded their empire in Eastern Europe, the Balkans and the Baltic regions without firing a shot. These countries were converted into EU vassal states, their markets dominated and industries denationalized. Their armed forces were recruited as NATO mercenaries. West Germany annexed the East, allowing it to access a reserve of cheap, highly qualified and educated immigrant labor, and increasing profits for both EU and US-based MNCs. Russia was temporarily reduced to a vassal state between 1991 and 2001. Living standards plunged and welfare programs were reduced. Mortality rates increased. Class inequalities widened. Millionaires and billionaires seized public resources and joined with the imperial MNC in plundering the economy. Socialist and communist leaders and parties were repressed or co-opted. In contrast, imperial military expansion in the 21st century was a costly failure. The war in Afghanistan was costly in lives and expenditure and ended in ignominious retreat. What remained was a fragile puppet regime and an unreliable mercenary military. The US-Afghanistan war was the longest war in US history and one of the biggest failures. The nationalist-Islamist resistance movements—the so-called Taliban and allied ethno-religious and nationalist anti-imperialist resistance groups—now dominate the countryside, repeatedly penetrate and attack urban centers and prepare to take power.

The Iraq war and the imperial state's invasion and decade-long occupation decimated the economy. The occupation fomented ethno-religious warfare. The secular Ba'thist officers and military professionals joined with Islamist-nationalists and subsequently formed a powerful resistance movement (ISIS) that defeated the imperial-backed Shia mercenary army during the second decade of the war. The imperial state was condemned to re-enter and engage directly in a prolonged war. The cost of war spiralled to over a trillion dollars. Oil exploitation was hampered, and the US Treasury poured in tens of billions to sustain a 'war without end'.

The US imperial state and the EU, along with Saudi Arabia and Turkey, financed armed Islamic mercenary militias to invade Syria and overthrow the secular, nationalist, anti-Zionist Bashar Assad regime. The imperial war opened the door for the expansion of the Islamic Ba'thist forces—ISIS—into Syria. The Kurds and other armed groups seized territory, fragmenting the country. After nearly five years of warfare and rising military costs, US and EU MNCs have been cut off from the Syrian market.

US support for Israeli aggression against Lebanon has led to the growth in power of the anti-imperialist Hezbollah armed resistance. Lebanon, Syria and Iran now represent a serious alternative to the US, EU, Saudi Arabia, Israeli axis.

The US sanctions policy toward Iran has failed to undermine the nationalist regime and totally undercut the economic opportunities of all the major US and EU oil and gas MNCs as well as US manufacturing exporters. Chinese companies have replaced them.

The US-EU invasion of Libya led to the destruction of the economy, the flight of billions in MNC investments and the disruption of exports.

The US imperial state seizure of power via a proxy coup in Kiev provoked a powerful anti-imperialist rebellion led by armed militia in the east (Donetsk and Luhansk) and the decimation of the Ukraine economy.

To summarize, the military-Zionist takeover of the imperial state has led to prolonged, unwinnable and costly wars that have undermined markets and investment sites for US MNCs. Imperial militarism has undermined the imperial economic presence and provoked long-term, growing anti-imperialist resistance movements, as well as chaotic, unstable and unviable countries out of imperial control.

Economic imperialism has continued to profit in parts of Europe, Asia, Latin America and Africa despite the imperial wars and economic sanctions pursued by the highly militarized imperial state elsewhere.

However, the US militarist seizure of power in the Ukraine and its sanctions against Russia have eroded the EU's profitable trade and investments in Russia. The Ukraine under IMF–EU–US tutelage has become a heavily indebted and broken economy run by kleptocrats who are totally dependent on foreign loans and military intervention.

Because the militarized imperial state prioritizes conflict and sanctions with Russia, Iran and Syria it has failed to deepen and expand its economic ties with Asia, Latin America and Africa. The political and economic conquest of East Europe and parts of the USSR has lost significance. The perpetual lost wars in the Middle East, North Africa and the Caucasus have weakened the imperial state's capacity for empire building in Asia and Latin America.

The outflow of wealth and the domestic cost of perpetual wars have eroded the electoral foundations of empire building. Only a fundamental change in the composition of the imperial state and a re-orientation of priorities toward economic expansion can alter the current decline of empire. The danger is that as the militarist–Zionist imperialist state pursues losing wars it may escalate and raise the ante and move toward a major nuclear confrontation: an empire amidst nuclear ashes!

Note

1 It has been estimated that the US imperialist state's offensive against Islam and 'anti-terrorist' war has cost two million lives in just three countries (Resumen Latinoamericano, 27/3/2015).

Chapter 3

Empire or Vampire?

To the growing army of critics of US military intervention who reject the mendacious claims by American officials and their apologists of 'world leadership', Washington is engaged in a project of empire building. But the notion that the US is building an empire by engaging in wars to exploit and plunder markets and resources defies the realities of the past two decades. US wars, including invasions, bombings, occupations, sanctions, coups and clandestine operations, have not resulted in the expansion of markets, greater control and exploitation of resources or the ability to exploit cheap labor. Instead, US wars have destroyed enterprises, reduced access to raw materials, killed, wounded or displaced productive workers around the world, and limited access to lucrative investment sites and markets via sanctions.

In other words, US global military interventions and wars have done the exact opposite of what all previous empires have pursued: Washington has exploited (and depleted) the domestic economy to expand militarily abroad instead of enriching it.

Why and how the US global wars differ from those of previous empires requires us to examine the forces that are driving overseas expansion; the political conceptions accompanying the conquest, the displacement of incumbent rulers and the seizure of power, and the reorganization of the conquered states and the accompanying economic and social structures to sustain neo-colonial relations over the long term.

Empire Building in the Past

Europe built durable, profitable and extensive empires that enriched the 'mother country', stimulated local industry, reduced unemployment and trickled down wealth in the form of better wages to privileged sectors of the working class. Imperial military expeditions were preceded by the entry of major trade enterprises (British East India Company) and followed by large-scale manufacturing, banking and commercial firms. Military invasions and political takeovers were driven by competition with economic rivals in Europe, and later, by the US and Japan.

The goal of military interventions was to monopolize control over the most lucrative economic resources and markets in the colonized regions. Imperial repression was directed at creating a docile low-wage workforce and buttressing subordinate local collaborators or client-rulers who facilitated the flow of profits, debt payments, taxes and export revenues back to the empire.

Imperial wars were the beginning, not the end, of empire building. What followed these wars of conquest was the incorporation of pre-existing elites into subordinate positions in the administration of the empire. The 'sharing of revenues' between the imperial economic enterprises and pre-existing elites was a crucial part of empire building. The imperial powers sought to instrumentalize existing religious, political and economic elites and harness them to the new imperial-centered division of power. Pre-existing economic activity, including local manufacturers and agricultural producers, which competed with imperial industrial exporters were destroyed and replaced by malleable local traders and importers (compradors). In short, the military dimensions of empire building were informed by the economic interests of the mother country. The occupation was pre-eminently concerned with preserving local collaborative powers and, above all, restoring and expanding the intensive and extensive exploitation of local resources, as well as the capture and saturation of local markets with goods from the imperial center.

Empire Building Today

The results of contemporary US military interventions and invasions stand in stark contrast with those of past imperial powers. The targets of military aggression are selected on the basis of ideological and political criteria. Military action does not follow the lead of 'pioneer' economic entrepreneurs like the British East India Company. Military action is not accompanied by the large-scale expansion of capitalist enterprise. Multinational construction companies of the empire, which build great military bases, are a drain on the imperial treasury.

Contemporary US intervention does not seek to secure and take over the existing military and civilian state apparatus; instead, the invaders fragment the conquered state and decimate its cadres, professionals and experts at all levels, thus providing an entry for the most retrograde ethno-religious regional, tribal and clan leaders to engage in intra-ethnic, sectarian wars against each other: in a word, chaos. Even the Nazis, in their expansion phase, chose to rule through local elites and maintained established administrative structures at all levels.

With US invasions, entire existing socio-economic structures are undermined, not taken over: all productive activity is subject to the military priorities of leaders bent on permanently crippling the conquered state and its advanced economic, administrative, educational, cultural and social sectors. While this is militarily successful in the short run, the medium and long-term results are a non-functioning state, not a sustained inflow of plunder and an expanding market for an empire. What is gained is a chain of US military bases surrounded by a sea of hostile, largely unemployed populations and warring ethno-religious groups in decimated economies.

The US claims to 'world leadership' are based exclusively on failed-state empire building. Nevertheless, the dynamic for continuing to expand into new regions, to militarily and politically intervene and establish new client entities, continues. And, most importantly, this expansionist dynamic further undermines domestic economic interests, which, theoretically and historically, form the basis for empire. We therefore have *imperialism without empire*, a *vampire state* preying on the vulnerable and devouring its own in the process.

Empire or Vampire? The Results of US Global Warfare

Empires, throughout history, have violently seized political power and exploited the riches and resources (both material and human) of the targeted regions. Over time, they would consolidate a working relationship, ensuring the ever-increasing flow of wealth into the mother country and the expanding presence of imperial enterprises in the colony. Every recent major military conquest and occupation by the US has had the opposite effect.

Iraq: Vampires Pillage

Under Saddam Hussein, the Republic of Iraq was a major oil producer and profitable partner for major US oil companies, as well as a lucrative market for US exports. It was a stable, unified secular state. The first Gulf War in the 1990s led to the first phase of its fragmentation with the de facto establishment of a Kurdish mini-state in the north under US protection. The US withdrew its military forces but imposed brutal economic sanctions limiting economic reconstruction from the devastation of the first Gulf War. The second US-led invasion and full-scale occupation in 2003 devastated the economy and dismantled the state, dismissing tens of thousands of experienced civil servants, teachers and police. This led to utter social collapse and fomented ethno-religious warfare that led to the killing, wounding or displacement of millions of Iraqis. The result of G. W. Bush's conquest of Baghdad was a 'failed state'. US oil and energy companies lost billions of dollars in trade and investment and the US economy was pushed into recession.

Afghanistan: Endless Wars, Endless Losses

The US war against Afghanistan began with the arming, financing and political support of Islamist jihadi-fundamentalists in 1979. They succeeded in destroying and dismantling a secular, national government. With the decision to invade Afghanistan in October 2001 the US became an occupier in Southwest Asia. For the next thirteen years the US-puppet regime of Hamid Karzai and the 'NATO coalition' occupation forces proved incapable of defeating the Taliban guerrilla army. Billions of dollars were spent devastating the economy and impoverishing the vast majority of Afghans. Only the opium trade flourished. The effort to create an army loyal to the puppet regime failed. The forced retreat of US armed forces beginning in 2014 signalled the bitter demise of US 'empire building' in Southwest Asia.

Libya: From Lucrative Trading Partner to Failed State

Libya under President Gaddafi was evolving into a major US and European trading partner and influential power in Africa. The regime signed large-scale, long-term contracts with major international oil companies that were backed by a stable secular government. The relationship with the US and EU was profitable. The US opted to impose a 'regime change' through massive US-EU missile and bombing strikes and the arming of a motley collection of Islamist terrorists, ex-pat neoliberals and tribal militias. While these attacks succeeded in killing President Gaddafi and most of his family (including many of his grandchildren) and dismantling the secular Libyan government and administrative infrastructure, the country was ripped apart by tribal warlord conflicts, political disintegration and the utter destruction of the economy. Oil investors fled. Over one million Libyans and immigrant workers were displaced. The US and EU 'partners in regime change' have even fled their own embassies in Tripoli, while the Libyan 'parliament' operates offshore from a casino boat. None of this devastation would have been possible under President Gaddafi. The US vampire bled its new prize, Libya, but certainly could not incorporate it into a profitable empire. Not only were its oil resources denied to the empire, even oil exports disappeared. Not even one imperial military base has been secured in North Africa.

Syria: Wars On Behalf of Terrorists, Not Empire

Washington and its EU allies backed an armed uprising in Syria hoping to install a puppet regime and bring Damascus into their 'empire'. The mercenary assaults have caused the deaths of nearly 200,000 Syrians, the displacement of over 30 percent of the population and the seizure of the Syrian oil fields by the Sunni extremist army, ISIS. ISIS has decimated the pro-US mercenary army, recruiting and arming thousands of terrorists from around the world. It invaded neighbouring Iraq, conquering the northern third of that country. This was the ultimate result of the deliberate US dismantling of the Iraqi state in 2003.

The US strategy, once again, was to arm Islamist extremists to overthrow the secular Bashar al-Assad regime in Damascus and then to discard them for a more pliable client. The strategy 'boomeranged' on Washington. ISIS devastated the ineffective Iraqi armed forces of the Maliki regime in Baghdad and America's much over-rated Peshmerga proxy 'fighters' in Iraqi 'Kurdistan'. Washington's mercenary war in Syria didn't expand the 'empire'. Indeed, it undermined existing imperial outposts.

The Ukrainian Power Grab, Russian Sanctions and Empire Building

In the aftermath of the collapse of the USSR, the US and EU incorporated the Baltic, Eastern European and Balkan ex-communist countries into their orbit. This clearly violated major agreements with Russia by incorporating most of the neoliberal regimes into NATO and bringing NATO forces to the very border of Russia. During the corrupt regime of Boris Yeltsin, the 'West' absolutely looted the Russian economy in co-operation with local gangster-oligarchs, who took up EU or Israeli citizenship to recycle their pillaged wealth. The demise of the vassal Yeltsin regime and the ascent and recovery of Russia under Vladimir Putin led the US and EU to formulate a strategy to deepen and extend their empire by seizing power in the Caucasus and Ukraine. A power and land grab by the puppet regime in Georgia attacking Russian forces in Ossetia in 2012 was decisively beaten back. This was a mere dress rehearsal for the coup in Kiev. In late 2013/early 2014, the US financed a violent right-wing putsch ousting the elected government and imposing a hand-picked pro-NATO client to assume power in Kiev.

The new pro-US regime moved quickly to purge all independent, democratic, federalist, bilingual and anti-NATO voices, especially among the bilingual citizens concentrated in south-eastern Ukraine. The coup and subsequent purge provoked a major armed uprising in the southeast, which successfully resisted the invading NATO-backed neo-fascist armed forces and private armies of the oligarchs. The failure of the Kiev regime to subdue the resistance fighters of the Donbass region resulted in a multi-pronged US-EU intervention designed to isolate, weaken and undermine the resistance. First and foremost they attempted to pressure Russia to close its borders on the eastern front, where hundreds of thousands of Ukrainian civilians eventually fled the bombardment. Second, the US and EU applied economic sanctions on Russia to abandon its political support for the southeast region's democratic and federalist demands. Third, it sought to use the Ukraine conflict as a pretext for a major military build-up on Russia's borders, expanding NATO missile sites and organizing an elite rapid interventionist military force capable of bolstering a faltering puppet regime or backing a future NATO-sponsored putsch against any adversary.

The Kiev regime is economically bankrupt. Its war against its own civilians in the southeast has devastated Ukraine's economy. Hundreds of thousands of skilled professionals, workers and their families have fled to Russia. Kiev's embrace of the EU has resulted in the breakdown of vital gas and oil agreements with Russia, undermining the Ukraine's principal source of energy and heating with winter only months away. Kiev cannot pay its debts and faces default. The rivalries between neo-fascists and neoliberals in Kiev will further erode the regime. In short, the US-EU power grab in the Ukraine has not led to any sort of 'expansion of empire'; rather it has ushered in the total destruction of an emerging economy and precipitated a sharp reversal of financial, trade and investment relations with Russia and Ukraine. The economic sanctions against Russia exacerbate the EU's current economic crisis. The belligerent posture of military confrontation toward Russia will result in an increase in military spending among the EU states and further divert scarce economic resources form job creation and social programs. The loss by significant sectors of the EU of agricultural export markets, as well as the loss of several billion-dollar military-industrial contracts with Russia, weakens, rather than expands, the Empire as an economic force

Iran: 100-Billion-Dollar Punitive Sanctions Do Not Build Empires

The US-EU sanctions on Iran carry a very high political, economic and political price tag. They do not strengthen empire, if we understand 'empire' to mean the expansion of multinational corporations and increasing access to oil and gas resources to ensure stable, cheap energy for strategic economic sectors within the imperial center.

The economic war on Iran has been at the behest of US allies, including the Gulf monarchies and especially Israel. These are dubious 'allies' for US 'empire' ... widely reviled potentates and a racist regime that manage to exact tribute from the imperial center!

In Afghanistan, Iraq and elsewhere, Iran has demonstrated its willingness to co-operate in power-sharing agreements with US global interest. However, Iran is a regional power, which will not submit to becoming a vassal state of the US. The sanctions policy has not provoked an uprising among the Iranian masses nor has it led to regime change. Sanctions have not weakened Iran to the extent of making it an easy military target. While sanctions have weakened Iran's economy, they have also worked against any kind of long-range empire-building strategy because Iran has strengthened its economic and diplomatic ties with the US's rivals, Russia and China.

Conclusion

As this brief survey indicates, US-EU wars have not been instruments of empire building in the conventional or historical sense. At most they have destroyed some adversaries of empire. But these have been pyrrhic victories. Along with the overthrow of a target regime, the systematic break-up of the state has unleashed powerful chaotic forces that have doomed any possibility of creating stable neo-colonial regimes capable of controlling their societies and securing opportunities for imperialist enrichment via economic exploitation.

At most, the US overseas wars have secured military outposts, foreign islands in seas of desperate and hostile populations. Imperial wars have provoked continuous underground resistance movements, ethnic civil wars and violent terrorist organizations that threaten blowback on the imperial center.

The US and EU's easy annexations of the ex-communist countries, usually via the stage-managed ballot-box or 'color revolutions', led to the takeover of the enormous reservoir of wealth accumulated over decades of communist rule. However, Euro-American empires bloody campaigns to invade and conquer the Middle East, South Asia, North Africa and the Caucasus have created nightmarish 'failed states'—continuously draining imperial coffers and leading to a state of permanent occupation and warfare.

The bloodless takeover of the Eastern European satellites with their accommodating, corrupt elites has ended. The 21st-century reliance on militarist strategies contrasts sharply with the successful multi-pronged colonial expansions of the 19th–20th centuries, where economic penetration and large-scale economic development accompanied military intervention and political change. Today's imperial wars cause economic decay and misery within the domestic economy, as well as perpetual wars abroad, an unsustainable drain.

The current US/EU military expansion into Ukraine, the encirclement of Russia, NATO missiles aimed at the very heart of a major nuclear power and the economic sanctions may lead to a global nuclear war, which may indeed put an end to militarist empire-building ... and the rest of humanity.

Chapter 4

A Century of Wars That Were Lost

Despite having the biggest military budget in the world, five times larger than the next six countries, the largest number of military bases—over 180—in the world and the most expensive military industrial complex, the US has failed to win a single war in the 21st century. In this chapter we will enumerate the wars and proceed to analyze why, despite the powerful material basis for war, it has led to failures.

Imperialism in Decline: The Lost Wars

The US has been engaged in multiple wars and coups since the beginning of the 21st century. These include Afghanistan, Iraq, Libya, Syria, Somalia, Palestine, Venezuela and the Ukraine. In addition, Washington's secret intelligence agencies have financed five surrogate terrorist groups in Pakistan, China, Russia, Serbia and Nicaragua.

The US has invaded countries, declared victories and subsequently faced resistance and prolonged warfare that required a large US military presence to merely protect garrison outposts.

The US has suffered hundreds of thousands of casualties—dead, maimed and deranged soldiers. The more the Pentagon spends, the greater the losses and subsequent retreats.

The more numerous the vassal regimes, the greater the corruption and flourishing of incompetence.

Every regime subject to US tutelage has failed to accomplish the objectives designed by its US military advisers.

The more that is spent on recruiting mercenary armies, the greater the rate of defection and the transfer of arms to US adversaries.

Success in Starting Imperial Wars and Failures in Finishing Them

The US invaded Afghanistan, captured the capital (Kabul) and defeated the standing army ... and then spent the next two decades engaged in losing irregular warfare. The initial victories laid the groundwork for future defeats. Bombing drove millions of peasants and farmers, shopkeepers and artisans into the local militia. The invaders were defeated by the forces of nationalism and religion linked to families and communities. The indigenous insurgents overcame arms and dollars in many of the villages, towns and provinces.

Similar outcomes were repeated in Iraq and Libya. The US invaded, defeated the standing armies, occupied the capital and imposed its clients—which set the terrain for long-term, large-scale warfare by local insurgent armies.

The more frequent the Western bombings, the greater the opposition forcing the retreat of the proxy army.

Somalia has been bombed frequently. Special Forces have recruited, trained and armed the local puppet soldiers, sustained by mercenary African armies, but they have remained holed up in the capital city, Mogadishu, surrounded and attacked by poorly armed but highly motivated and disciplined Islamic insurgents.

Syria is targeted by a US-financed and armed mercenary army. In the beginning they advanced, uprooted millions, destroyed cities and homes and seized territory. All of which impressed their US-EU warlords. Once the Syrian army united the populace, with their Russian, Lebanese (Hezbollah) and Iranian allies, Damascus routed the mercenaries.

After the better part of a decade the separatist Kurds, alongside the Islamic terrorists and other Western surrogates, retreated and made a last stand along the northern borders—the remaining bastion of Western surrogates.

The Ukrainian coup of 2014 was financed and directed by the US and EU. They seized the capital (Kiev) but failed to conquer eastern Ukraine and the Crimea. Corruption among the US-supported ruling kleptocrats devastated the country—over three million fled abroad to Poland, Russia and elsewhere in search of a livelihood. The war continues, and the corrupt US clients are discredited and will suffer electoral defeat unless they rig the vote.

Surrogate uprisings in Venezuela and Nicaragua were bankrolled by the US National Endowment for Democracy (NED). They ruined economies but lost the street wars.

Conclusion

Wars are not won by arms alone. In fact, heavy bombing and extended military occupations ensure prolonged popular resistance, ultimate retreats and defeats.

The major and minor wars of the US in the 21st century have failed to incorporate targeted countries into the empire.

Imperial occupations are not military victories. They merely change the nature of the war, the protagonists of resistance, the scope and depth of the national struggle.

The US has been successful in defeating standing armies, as it did in Libya, Iraq, Afghanistan, Somalia and the Ukraine. However, the conquest was limited in time and space. New armed resistance movements led by former officers, religious activists and grassroots activists took charge... .

The imperial wars slaughtered millions, savaged traditional family, workplace and neighborhood relations and set in motion a new constellation of anti-imperialist leaders and militia fighters. The imperial forces beheaded established leaders and decimated their followers. They raided and pillaged ancient treasures. The resistance followed by recruiting thousands of uprooted volunteers who served as human bombs, challenging missiles and drones.

The US's imperial forces lack ties to the occupied lands and peoples. They are 'aliens' serving time; they seek to survive, secure promotions and exit with a bonus and an honorable discharge. In contrast, the resistance fighters are there for the duration. As they advance, they target and demolish the imperial surrogates and mercenaries. They expose the corrupt client rulers who deny subject people the elementary conditions of existence—employment, potable water, electricity, etc.

The imperial vassals are not present at weddings, sacred holidays or funerals, unlike the resistance fighters. The presence of the latter signals a pledge of loyalty unto death. Resistance forces circulate freely in cities, towns and villages with the protection of local people; and by night they rule enemy terrain, under cover of their own people, who share intelligence and logistics.

Inspiration, solidarity and light arms are more than a match for the drones, missiles and helicopter gunships.

Even the mercenary soldiers trained by the Special Forces defect from and betray their imperial masters. Temporary imperial advances serve only to allow resistance forces to regroup and counter-attack. They view surrender as a betrayal of their traditional way of life, submission to the boot of Western occupation forces and their corrupt officials.

Afghanistan is a prime example of an imperial 'lost war'. After two decades of warfare, a trillion dollars in military spending and tens of thousands of casualties, the Taliban controls most of the countryside and towns; enters and takes over provincial capitals and bombs Kabul. They will take full control the day after the US departs.

US military defeats are the product of a fatal flaw: imperial planners cannot successfully replace indigenous people with colonial rulers and their local look-alikes.

Wars are not won by high-tech weapons directed by absentee officials divorced from the people: they do not share their sense of peace and justice.

Exploited people informed by a spirit of communal resistance and self-sacrifice have demonstrated greater cohesion than rotating soldiers eager to return home and mercenary soldiers with dollar signs in their eyes.

The lessons of lost wars have not been learned by those who preach the power of the military-industrial complex—which makes, sells and profits from weapons but lacks the mass of humanity with lesser arms but great conviction who have demonstrated their capacity to defeat imperial armies.

The Stars and Stripes fly in Washington but remain folded in embassy offices in Kabul, Tripoli, Damascus and other lost battlegrounds.

Part II

Structure of Empire

Chapter 5

Foundations of the US Empire
Axes of Evil

Empires are not easy to sustain given the multiple enemies that they provoke: at the international level (imperial rivals and emerging new powers), at the national level (national resistance movements, unreliable clients and untrustworthy 'Sepoy' armies) and at the local level (boycotts, sabotage and strikes). Imperial difficulties are multiplied when an empire is in economic decline (loss of market shares with growing debt), facing domestic unrest as the economic costs to the taxpayers exceed the returns by a substantial margin; and when the political elite is internally divided between militarists and free market advocates.

The US empire today is in the midst of long-term decline, during which it has suffered a series of costly defeats. In addition, Washington has assumed long-term burdensome commitments to allies who have imposed their own ambitions of seeking 'mini empires' (Israel, Turkey, and Saudi Arabia).

The US White House has increasingly adopted a military definition of 'imperial leadership' at the expense of reconfiguring imperial relations to accommodate potential new political and economic partners.

As the empire slides, the political elite, operating with a highly militarized mind set, has expanded its intrusive global intelligence networks to spy on allies, adversaries and its own citizens. Washington has risked deepening hostilities among key allies (Germany and Brazil) and exacerbating conflicts with conciliatory competitors (Russia) by refusing to curtail its massive espionage. Spying is a clear hostile act and part of the policy of military-driven empire building.

Empires Depend on Alliances

The entire edifice of the US empire, like the earlier British empire, is sustained through a series of complex alliances. US military forces are injected into a country to ensure that local military and police forces efficiently control their population and become available as mercenaries to fight overseas wars for the US empire.

In the past two centuries, European colonial empires, especially the French and English, invaded and subjugated nations using colonial soldiers of color under the command of European imperial officers.

Today the US empire builders are making a transition back to the 19th-century colonial model. The Pentagon has been moving from reliance on US ground troops to recruiting colonial troops under US military command. To that end, Washington's empire has turned toward creating alliances with regional powers to sustain imperial pre-eminence. These 'alliances' are in place in Africa, Latin America, Asia and, in particular, in the Middle East. The empire's Middle East alliances have been operative for decades, but in recent years they have absorbed the greatest resources, with devastating consequences to the empire, as we shall see.

The empire today operates and can only be sustained by these alliances or 'axes of regional power', which are therefore worth analyzing in greater detail.

The Middle East as an Axis of Imperial Power

US empire builders have constructed three regional axes of power in the Middle East. In order of importance, they are: the US-Israel axis of power, the US-Saudi axis and the US-Turkey axis of power.

The US-Israel axis of power is based on a longstanding agreement. The US militarily and financially supports Israel's colonial expansion into Palestine and Syria, while Israel backs US projections of military and political power throughout the region. Thanks to US military and financial aid, Israel has become the dominant military power in the Middle East and the only nuclear power in the region. The US has used Israel's wars and invasions of its neighbors to secure several Arab collaborator client states (notably Jordan and Egypt). More recently the US-Israeli power axis has been expanded to include the client regime in Kurdistan (northern Iraq). In addition, the US-Israeli axis has been deeply involved in financing and promoting collaborators' opposition forces in Lebanon (currently the Hariri political formation), sectors of the armed mercenaries in Syria, Kurdish Peshmerga militias in Iraq and the so-called 'Mujahedeen al Khalq' terrorists in Iran. The US CIA and Israel's Mossad engage in clandestine violent operations, directly intervening to destabilize secular and Islamic nationalist regimes like Iran by—for example—disrupting their communications and assassinating their scientists and leaders. Israel has secured political and intelligence agreements with Egypt and Jordan to isolate and dispossess the Palestinians. The US has secured military bases and operational platforms in Egypt and Jordan to attack Hezbollah in Lebanon, President Bashar al Assad in Syria and the Iranian government.

However, while in the past each country benefited from the US-Israel axis of power, recently it has turned into a costly, asymmetrical relation, a zero-sum game, where Israel's regional power increases as the US empire deteriorates.

This turn of events is easily understood if one examines the way in which Middle East policy is formulated in the US. Over the past three decades Israel has constructed the most formidable organized power configuration in the United States that has ever penetrated an imperial state. Linked by tribal loyalties and blind obedience, over a half-million Jewish Zionists have embraced Israel's interests and pursued them with a zeal and single-mindedness that is unmatched by any other foreign-based lobby. Prominent Zionists have permeated key state institutions, from the US Treasury, Department of Commerce and Pentagon to the White House and National Security Council. They dominate the US Congress and the two-party system, especially the nomination and electoral process, ensuring that only candidates who swear allegiance to Israel are allowed to run and be elected. That way no political debate regarding Israel's subversive influence is permitted. They dominate the mass media, ensuring that all news and commentary is favorable to Israel and all criticism of the Jewish state is excluded.

Here we have the paradox of an imperial ally: Israel colonizing an imperial power and extracting tribute, with foreign aid to Tel Aviv exceeding $3.6 billion. More importantly, the Zionist power configuration plays a key role in waging wars against Israel's designated enemies and providing diplomatic cover for the Jewish state's ethnic slaughter of the people of Palestine.

The Israel-US alliance has been set up wholly on Israel's terms. Even as Israel rains thousands of tons of bombs on the captive people of Gaza, to the horror of world public opinion, the White House applauds and the US Congress unanimously approves resolutions supporting Israel's war crimes at the behest of the powerful Zionists ensconced in Washington.

Whatever the US empire has gained from Israel in the way of intimidating and humiliating Arab leaders in the region it has lost in economic terms. Major oil companies have lost hundreds of billions of dollars in trade and investment from the wars in Iraq, Syria and Libya and from sanctions against Iran. The US domestic economy has lost hundreds of billions of dollars in income and investment as a result of the high cost of oil imports resulting from the wars.

Strategically, the asymmetrical US-Israeli alliance has turned the US into an empire dominated by militarists, and one exclusively focused on the Middle East. This transformation into a military-driven empire has resulted in neglect, decline and displacement of the imperial influence in the most dynamic growth sectors of the world economy: Asia, Latin America and Russia.

It is a paradox that the lopsided strength of the US-Israeli axis in the Middle East has profoundly undermined the US global economic and domestic foundations of empire. Moreover, the brutal colonial-style wars in the Middle East promoted by US Zionist strategists in Iraq, Libya and Afghanistan have destroyed any possibility of re-constructing viable client states and markets out of these conquered nations. Israeli military strategists have long wanted these regimes destroyed, their state institutions dismantled and their societies embroiled in sectarian, tribal strife. As a result, the US wars have not produced a single functioning client state: the US military invaded, occupied and destroyed Iraq and Afghanistan while losing the wars in political terms. This came at no cost to Israel, the unchallenged regional hegemon, while the US Treasury will struggle with a trillion-dollar price tag and the US public will experience economic decline for generations.

The US-Saudi Axis of Power

The second most important axis of power in the Middle East is the US–Saudi Arabia alliance. From the perspective of the US empire, the Saudi connection has many advantages, as well as costs. Saudi financing, in collaboration with the US, was instrumental in recruiting, arming and financing the Islamist guerrillas, which overthrew the secular pro-Soviet government in Afghanistan. Saudi links to the Pakistani intelligence services and military has ensured Pakistan will remain a client state of the US empire. Saudi intervention in Yemen and Bahrain propped up the pro-empire, anti-democratic puppet regimes while ensuring US access to its strategic military bases.

Saudi Arabia is the principal backer of US sanctions and confrontation with Iran. It provides air bases, military intelligence operations and funding of anti-Iranian terrorists such as 'Mujahedeen al Khalq'. Saudi Arabia is the biggest market for US military exports. Saudi increased its oil output to compensate for a decline of oil in world markets due to the US embargo against and the destruction of oil production following US attacks on and devastation of Iraq and Libya. In exchange, Saudi Arabia's absolutist monarchy obtains US protection, security and assistance in repressing its domestic unrest. Saudi billionaires, no matter how brutal and corrupt, have full access to lucrative financial markets in the US. The Saudi theocratic-monarchic dictatorship has clearly benefited from the US destruction of secular nationalist Arab regimes in the region. Indeed, secular nationalism has been the Saudi's primary target since the monarchy was set up by the British.

Nevertheless, the Saudi–US axis is fraught with tensions. The Saudi regime actively promotes Sunni extremist jihadi movements in Iraq, Syria and Lebanon, undermining Washington-backed neoliberal clients. The Saudi-backed terrorists in Libya have destabilized the US proxies. The Saudis promoted and financed the bloody military coup in Egypt of General Sisi. The Saudi royals support the brutal military overthrow of the elected president Morsi and the suppression of the Egyptian Muslim Brotherhood because of Morsi's rapprochement with Iran. This ruined Obama's more moderate goal of setting up a Muslim Brotherhood-Egyptian military power-sharing arrangement in Cairo.

In other words, the US and Saudi Arabia converge in opposition to secular-nationalist regimes but diverge on the alternatives. The Saudis tend to choose the most retrograde Islamic extremist groups, excluding and antagonizing all other tendencies, from conservative-secular neoliberals to democratic, nationalist and socialist parties and movements. They end up with political polarizations unfavorable to US long-term imperial interests. The Saudi choice of political alternatives tends to be minorities incapable of sustaining or overtly hostile to the US imperial order. Moreover, Saudi Arabia opposes Israel on religious grounds, the principal US political partner in the region, even as it works with the Jewish state against the secular or nationalist governments of Syria, Iran and Lebanon.

Like its alliance with Israel, the connection to Saudi Arabia axis comes at a very high cost. Saudi financing of the Taliban and other Islamic groups has cost the US empire builders hundreds of billions of dollars, thousands of military casualties and a humiliating retreat after a thirteen-year war.

Saudi funding for Sunni terrorists in Syria has decimated US-backed neoliberal armed groups. Equally damaging, the same Saudi-backed jihadi groups have severely destabilized the US-imposed Maliki regime in Iraq. Saudi attacks on the US-Iranian nuclear negotiations have strengthened the Zionist-led opposition in the US Congress.

In other words, the US-Saudi axis has buttressed the US empire in the short run but become a strategic liability. Saudi Arabia's overseas projection of its most reactionary internal politics undermines US efforts to create stable imperial clients. Not to be overlooked is the Saudi role in financing Al Queda and its operatives in the attack on the US on September 11.

The US-Turkey Axis

Turkey has been a major US-NATO asset, especially during the Cold War. The secular-military regimes in Ankara mobilized the largest number of combat troops on the USSR border and provided the US with numerous air bases and intelligence centers. In recent times, under an Islamist regime, Turkey has become the axis for the US and EU-backed mercenary invasion of Syria, providing military sanctuaries, training, arms and financing to overthrow the secular Baathist regime in Damascus.

The Erdogan regime has sought to regain a pivotal role within NATO by backing the empire's effort to topple nationalist leaders and movements in the region.

Turkey has worked closely with the US and Israel in building up the political, economic and military capacities of the Iraqi Kurds. They are seen as a counter-force to Saudi-backed jihadis, the failed Shia regime in Baghdad and Iraqi petrol-nationalists.

While pursuing neoliberal policies congruent with US imperial design and collaborating with Washington's clients in Kurdistan, Turkey has its own regional ambitions. President Erdogan supported the Muslim Brotherhood regime in Egypt and opposed the military coup of General Sisi, fearing, perhaps, a similar coup by the Turkish military. Up until quite recently Turkey had its own 'mini-imperial' agenda via trade and investment in Syria, Iraq, Kurdistan and Afghanistan. The recent imperial conflicts and regional instability have undermined Erdogan's dreams of a neo-Ottoman revival. Ninety-five percent of Turks according to public opinion polls support the rights of the Palestinian people; this has forced Erdogan to pull away from the Israeli-US axis, at least temporarily. Likewise the Turkish regime, while not in opposition to the Saudi dictatorship, has refrained from overt collaboration apart from trade and Gulf investments.

With the US-EU in the process of isolating and demonizing Russia, it remains to be seen whether Turkey will once again become the military axis for NATO. Russia is an important energy supplier and market for Turkish goods. If Turkey decides to join the new US axis confronting Russia, it will lose out economically and will have to find alternative markets and energy sources in an increasingly unstable region. A weakened Turkey may be more submissive to empire but it will be more vulnerable to internal opposition.

Conclusion

The US empire, like earlier empires, depends on a host of alliances and axes of power to sustain it and compensate for military, political and economic limitations in resources and personnel. With regard to the main region of direct US involvement, the Middle East, Washington has embraced three sets of alliances with partners who have played a paradoxical role in both sustaining and eroding the US empire.

Israel, the primary ally of the US, is largely a political and military construct of US policymakers over the past years. It was originally designed to serve and police the region for the US. Instead, over the years the relationship has been totally reversed: US imperial power has been subordinated to serve Israel's ambitions to impose unchallenged regional superiority over the Middle East. For the first time in the history of empires, a satrap of empire has systematically penetrated the principal imperial institutions. Decision-makers and elites loyal to Israeli interests have expended vast amounts of US military resources and American soldiers to wage wars with the goal of decimating Israel's enemies. Five hundred thousand well-organized and well-financed American Jewish-Zionist activists have directed the global empire into focusing on one region: the Middle East. The mass media, US Congress and the principal advisory bodies (dubbed 'thinktanks') in Washington are engaged in formulating US policies in line with Israel's colonial interests, with disastrous consequences for the American people. In effect, the US state and society are 'colonized' by unconditional supporters of Israel. The Zionist power configuration's influence found its most macabre expression so far in Congress's unanimous endorsement of the Israeli slaughter of hundreds of trapped Palestinian civilians and children during the July 2014 terror bombing of Gaza. This repugnant act is the culmination of the forced servility of an ostensibly global imperial power subject to the dictates of its lawless, genocidal ally.

The Israeli-US axis has led the empire into a blind ally: a totally one-sided relation has inflated the military dimensions of empire in Israel's interests. Economically, this has become the most perverse of all imperial partnerships, where the satrap extracts billions of dollars a year in political tribute and advanced weaponry in return for nothing! Strategically, the global decline of the US empire, its loss of market shares and political influence in the most dynamic regions of Asia, Latin America and Africa, can be wholly attributed to its sustained focus on the Middle East.

The disastrous 'exclusive Middle East focus' can be attributed to the leadership, organization and policies of the empire.

The US political leadership, beholden to unconditional supporters of Israel, has committed the most damaging policies in US history. First and foremost, these elite-educated policymakers have degraded the entire economic dimensions of empire by pursuing a relentless military agenda—destroying oil producers, raising world prices, sowing instability and bleeding the US Treasury of trillions of dollars—with few returns.

These self-proclaimed 'best and brightest', with advanced degrees from the most prestigious universities, includes policymakers who have committed the US to endless wars which only benefit Israel. Most of these key policymakers, including Wolfowitz, Emmanuel, Feith, Libby, Abrams, Greenspan, Levy, Cohen, Frohman, Lew, Fischer, Bernanke and Yellen, have deliberately pillaged the US Treasury in order to sustain Middle Eastern wars for Israel and Wall Street bankers. The 'leading lights' among the Zionist policymakers, occupying influential positions in the imperial power structures, are responsible for an unmitigated disaster: they have initiated failed wars, dismantled whole societies, fomented financial crises and promoted a one-way 'partnership' with a genocidal state. If only they had pursued respectable and successful careers as dentists, doctors, investors, bankers or ivory tower academics, millions of precious lives would not have been destroyed.

However, it is not only the empire's alliance with Israel that is driving it to crisis. The Saudi-US axis has given immense power to the most retrograde armed insurgents running amok in Libya, Syria, Iraq, Afghanistan and Pakistan. An empire associated with the most parasitic rentiers who send their own fanatical offspring to self-immolate for a head-beheading new world order has little resonance in the modern world.

An empire organized around axes of evil and directed by political leaders loyal to satraps has no material or moral foundations to justify its existence.

Chapter 6

Networks of Empire and Realignments of World Power

Imperial states build networks that link economic, military and political activities into a coherent, mutually reinforcing system. This task is largely performed by the various institutions of the imperial state. Thus, imperial action is not always directly economic, as military action in one country or region is necessary to open or protect economic zones. Nor are all military actions decided by economic interests if the leading sector of the imperial state is decidedly militarist.

Moreover, the sequence of imperial actions may vary according to the particular conditions necessary for empire building. Thus, state aid may buy collaborators; military intervention may secure client regimes, followed later by private investors. In other circumstances, the entry of private corporations may precede state intervention.

In either private or state economic and/or military led penetration, in furtherance of empire building, the strategic purpose is to exploit the special economic and geopolitical features of the targeted country to create empire-centered networks. In the post-Eurocentric colonial world, the privileged position of the US vis-à-vis its empire-centered policies, treaties, trade and military agreements is disguised and justified by an ideological gloss, which varies with time and circumstances. In the war to break up Yugoslavia and establish client regimes, imperial ideology utilized humanitarian rhetoric, as in Kosovo. In the genocidal wars in the Middle East, anti-terrorism and anti-Islamic ideology is central. Against China, democratic and human rights rhetoric predominates. In Latin America, receding imperial power relied on democratic and anti-authoritarian rhetoric aimed at the democratically elected Chávez government.

The effectiveness of imperial ideology is in direct relation to the capacity of empire to promote viable and dynamic development alternatives to their targeted countries. By that criterion, imperial ideology has had little persuasive power among target populations. Islamophobic and anti-terrorist rhetoric has had no impact on the people of the Middle East but alienated the Islamic world. The rejection by all Latin American governments of the history of US intervention, and the associated anti-imperialist sentiment across the region mobilized by the Bolivarian Revolution, as well as Latin America's lucrative trade relations with the Chavist regime in Venezuela, has undermined Washington's ideological campaign to isolate Venezuela. Even the US's staunchest ally, Colombia, rejected Obama's move against Venezuela in the form of declaring it to be a national security threat. The US human rights campaign against China has been totally ignored throughout the EU, Africa, Latin America and Oceania and by the 500 biggest US MNCs (and even by the US Treasury busy selling treasury bonds to China to finance the ballooning US budget deficit).

The weakening influence of imperial propaganda and the declining economic leverage of Washington means that the US imperial networks built over the past half-century are being eroded or at least subject to centrifugal forces. Former fully integrated networks in Asia are now merely military bases as the economies secure greater autonomy and orient toward China and beyond. In other words, the imperial networks are now being transformed into outposts of limited operations, not centers for imperial economic plunder.

Imperial Networks: The Central Role of Collaborators

Empire building is essentially a process of penetrating a country or region, establishing a privileged position and retaining control in order to secure (i) lucrative resources, markets and cheap labor, (ii) a military platform to enable expansion into adjoining countries and regions, (iii) military bases to establish a chokehold over strategic road networks or waterways to deny or limit access by competitors or adversaries, and (iv) intelligence and clandestine operations against adversaries and competitors.

History has demonstrated that the lowest cost in sustaining long-term, long-scale imperial domination is by developing local collaborators in the form of political, economic and/or military leaders operating from client regimes. Overt imperial rule results in costly wars and disruption, especially among a broad array of classes adversely affected by the imperial presence.

The formation of collaborator rulers and classes results from diverse short and long-term imperial policies ranging from direct military, electoral and extra-parliamentary activities to middle to long-term recruitment, training and orientation of promising young leaders via propaganda and educational programs, cultural-financial inducements, promises of political and economic backing on assuming political office and substantial clandestine financial backing.

The most basic offer by imperial policymakers to the 'new ruling class' in emerging client states is the opportunity to participate in an economic system tied to the imperial center—that is, for local elites to share economic wealth with their imperial benefactors. To secure mass support, the collaborator classes obfuscate the new forms of imperial subservience and economic exploitation by emphasizing political independence, personal freedom, economic opportunity and private consumerism.

The mechanisms for the transfer of power to an emerging client state combine imperial propaganda, financing of mass organizations and electoral parties, as well as violent coups or 'popular uprisings'. Authoritarian, bureaucratically ossified regimes relying on police controls to limit or oppose imperial expansion are 'soft targets'. Selective human rights campaigns become the most effective organizational weapon to recruit activists and promote leaders for the imperial-centered new political order. Once the power transfer takes place, the former members of the political, economic and cultural elite are banned, repressed, arrested and jailed. A new homogenous political culture of competing parties embracing the imperial-centered world order emerges. The first order of business beyond the political purge is the privatization and handover of the commanding heights of the economy to imperial enterprises.

The client regimes proceed to provide soldiers to engage in imperial wars as paid mercenaries and to transfer military bases to imperial forces as platforms of intervention. The entire 'independence charade' is accompanied by the massive dismantling of public social welfare programs (pensions, free health and education), codes and full-employment policies. Promotion of a highly polarized class structure is the ultimate consequence of client rule. The empire-centered economies of client regimes—a replica of any commonplace satrap state—are justified (or legitimated) in the name of an electoral system dubbed democratic; in fact a political system dominated by new capitalist elites and their heavily funded mass media.

Empire-centered regimes run by collaborating elites spanning the Baltic states, Central and Eastern Europe and the Balkans is the most striking example of imperial expansion in the 20th century. The break-up and takeover of the Soviet Union and Eastern bloc and its incorporation into the US-led NATO alliance and the European Union resulted in imperial hubris. Washington made premature declarations of a unipolar world, while Western Europe proceeded to plunder public resources, ranging from factories to real estate, and exploiting a formidable reserve of cheap labor overseas via immigration, to undermine living standards of unionized labor at home.

The unity of purpose of European and US imperial regimes allowed for the peaceful joint takeover of the wealth of the new regions by private monopolies. The imperial states initially subsidized the new client regimes with large-scale transfers and loans on the condition that imperial firms were allowed to seize resources, real estate, land, factories, service sectors, media outlets, etc. Heavily indebted states went from a sharp crisis in the initial period to 'spectacular' growth to profound and chronic social crises involving double-digit unemployment in the twenty-year period of client building. Worker protests emerged as wages deteriorated, unemployment soared and welfare provisions were cut, and destitution spread. However, the 'new middle class', embedded in the political and media apparatus and in joint economic ventures, was sufficiently funded by imperial financial institutions for their dominance to be protected.

However, the dynamic of imperial expansion in Eastern, Central and Southern Europe did not provide the impetus for strategic advance because of the ascendancy of highly volatile financial capital and a powerful militarist caste in the Euro-American political centers. In important respects, military and political expansion was no longer harnessed to economic conquest. The reverse was true: economic plunder and political dominance served as instruments for projecting military power.

Imperial Sequences: From War for Exploitation to Exploitation for War

The relations between imperial military policies and economic interests are complex and change over time and according to historical context. In some circumstances an imperial regime will invest heavily in military personnel and augment monetary expenditures to overthrow an anti-imperialist ruler and establish a client regime far beyond any state or private economic return. For example, US wars in Iraq and Afghanistan and proxy wars in Somalia and Yemen have not resulted in greater profits for US multinational corporations; nor have they enhanced private exploitation of raw materials or markets. At best, imperial wars have provided profits for mercenary contractors, construction companies and related 'war industries' profiting through transfers from the US Treasury and the exploitation of US taxpayers, mostly wage and salary earners.

After the Second World War, the emerging US imperial state directed a multi-billion-dollar loan and aid program at Western Europe. The Marshall Plan forestalled anti-capitalist social upheavals and restored capitalist political dominance. This allowed the emergence of NATO (a military alliance led and dominated by the US). Subsequently, US multinational corporations invested in and traded with Western Europe, reaping lucrative profits once the imperial state created favourable political and economic conditions. In other words, imperial state politico-military intervention preceded the rise and expansion of US multinational capital. A myopic, short-term analysis of the initial post-war activity would downplay the importance of private US economic interests as the driving force of US policy. Extending the time period to the following two decades, the interplay between initial high-cost state military and economic expenditures and later private high-return gains provides a perfect example of how the process of imperial power operates.

The role of the imperial state as an instrument for opening, protecting and expanding private markets and resource exploitation corresponds to a time in which both the state and the dominant classes were primarily motivated by industrial empire building.

US-directed military intervention and coups in Iran (1953), Guatemala (1954), Chile (1973) and the Dominican Republic (1965) were linked to specific imperial economic interests and corporations. For example, US and English oil corporations sought to reverse the nationalization of oil in Iran. The US United Fruit Company opposed the agrarian reform policies in Guatemala. Major US copper and telecommunication companies supported and called for the US-backed coup in Chile.

In contrast, current US military interventions and wars in the Middle East, South Asia and the Horn of Africa are not promoted by US multinationals. The imperial policies are promoted by militarists and Zionists embedded in the state, mass media and powerful 'civil society' organizations. The same imperial methods (coups and wars) serve different imperial rulers and interests.

Clients, Allies and Puppet Regimes

Imperial networks involve securing a variety of complementary economic, military and political 'resource bases' which are part of the imperial system but retain varying degrees of political and economic autonomy.

In the dynamic earlier stages of US empire building, roughly from the 1950s to the 1970s, US multinational corporations and the economy as a whole dominated the world economy. Its allies in Europe and Asia were highly dependent on US markets, financing and development. US military hegemony was reflected in a series of regional military pacts that secured almost instant support for US regional wars, military coups and the construction of military bases and naval ports on their territory. Countries were divided into 'specializations' that served the particular interests of the US empire. Western Europe was a military outpost, industrial partner and ideological collaborator. Asia, primarily Japan and South Korea, served as 'frontline military outposts' as well as industrial partners. Indonesia, Malaysia, the Philippines were essentially client regimes that provided raw materials as well as military bases. Singapore and Hong Kong were financial and commercial entrepôts. Pakistan was a client military regime serving as a frontline pressure on China.

Saudi Arabia, Iran and the Gulf mini-states, ruled by client authoritarian regimes, provided oil and military bases. Egypt and Jordan and Israel anchored imperial interests in the Middle East. Beirut served as the financial center for US, European and Middle Eastern bankers. Africa and Latin America, including client and nationalist-populist regimes, were a source of raw materials as well as markets for finished goods and cheap labor.

The prolonged Vietnam War and Washington's eventual defeat eroded the power of the empire. Western Europe, Japan and South Korea's industrial expansion challenged US industrial primacy. Latin America's pursuit of nationalist, import-substitution policies forced US investment toward overseas manufacturing. In the Middle East, nationalist movements toppled US clients in Iran and Iraq and undermined military outposts. Revolutions in Angola, Namibia, Mozambique, Algeria, Nicaragua and elsewhere curtailed Euro-American 'open-ended' access to raw materials, at least temporarily.

The decline of the US empire was temporarily arrested by the collapse of communism in the Soviet Union and Eastern Europe and the establishment of client regimes throughout the region. Likewise, the upsurge of imperially centered client regimes in Latin America between the mid-1970s and the end of the 1990s gave the appearance of an imperialist recovery. However, the 1990s were not the beginning of a repeat of the imperial take-off of the early 1950s: it was a 'last hurrah' before long-term irreversible decline. The entire imperial political apparatus, so successful in its clandestine operations in subverting the Soviet and Eastern European regimes, played a marginal role when it came to capitalizing on the economic opportunities that ensued. Germany and other EU countries led the way in the takeover of lucrative privatized enterprises. Russian-Israeli oligarchs (seven of the top eight) seized and pillaged privatized strategic industries, banks and natural resources. The principal US beneficiaries were the banks and Wall Street firms that laundered billions of illicit earnings and collected lucrative fees from mergers, acquisitions, stock listings and other less than transparent activities. In other words, the collapse of Soviet collectivism strengthened the parasitical financial sector of the US empire. Worse still, the assumption of a 'unipolar world', fostered by US ideologues, played into the hands of the militarists, who now assumed that former constraints on US military assaults on nationalists and Soviet allies had disappeared. As a result, military intervention became the principal driving force in US empire building, leading to the first Iraq war, the Yugoslav and Somali invasions and the expansion of US military bases throughout the former Soviet bloc and Eastern Europe.

At the very pinnacle of US global-political and military power during the 1990s, with all the major Latin American regimes enveloped in the empire-centered neoliberal warp, the seeds of decay and decline set in.

The economic crises of the late 1990s led to major uprisings and electoral defeats of practically all US clients in Latin America, spelling the decline of US imperial domination. China's extraordinary dynamic and cumulative growth displaced US manufacturing capital and weakened US leverage over rulers in Asia, Africa and Latin America. The vast transfer of US state resources to overseas imperial adventures, military bases and the shoring up of clients and allies led to domestic decline.

The US empire, passively facing economic competitors displacing the US in vital markets and engaged in prolonged and unending wars which drained the treasury, attracted a cohort of mediocre policymakers who lacked a coherent strategy for rectifying policies and reconstructing the state to serve productive activity capable of 'retaking' markets. Instead, the policies of open-ended and unsustainable wars played into the hands of a special sub-group (sui generis) of militarists, American Zionists. They capitalized on their infiltration of strategic positions in the state, enhanced their influence in the mass media and across a vast network of organized 'pressure groups' to reinforce US subordination to Israel's drive for Middle East supremacy.

The result was the total unbalancing of the US imperial apparatus: military action was unhinged from economic empire building. A highly influential upper caste of Zionist-militarists harnessed US military power to an economically marginal state (Israel) in perpetual hostility toward the 1.5 billion Muslim world. Equally damaging, American Zionist ideologues and policymakers promoted repressive institutions and legislation and Islamophobic ideological propaganda designed to terrorize the US population. Equally important, Islamophobic ideology served to justify permanent war in South Asia and the Middle East and the exorbitant military budgets, at a time of sharply deteriorating domestic socio-economic conditions. Hundreds of billions of dollars were spent unproductively on 'Homeland Security' that strived in every way to recruit, train, frame and arrest Afro-American Muslim men as 'terrorists'. Thousands of secret agencies with hundreds of thousands of national, state and local officials spied on US citizens who at some point may have sought to speak or act to rectify or reform the militarist-financial Zionist-centered imperialist policies.

By the end of the first decade of the 21st century, the US empire could only destroy adversaries (Iraq, Pakistan, Afghanistan), provoke military tension (Korean peninsula, China Sea) and undermine relations with potentially lucrative trading partners (Iran, Venezuela). Galloping authoritarianism fused with fifth column Zionist militarism to foment Islamophobic ideology. The convergence of authoritarian mediocrities, upwardly mobile knaves and fifth column tribal loyalists in the Obama regime precluded any foreseeable reversal of imperial decay.

China's growing global economic network and dynamic advance in cutting-edge applied technology in everything from alternative energy to high-speed trains stands in contrast to the Zionist, militarist-infested empire of the US.

The US demands on client Pakistan rulers to empty their treasury in support of US Islamic wars in Afghanistan and Pakistan stands in contrast to the thirty-billion-dollar Chinese investments in infrastructure, energy and electrical power and multi-billion-dollar increases in trade.

The States' three-billion-dollar military subsidies to Israel stand in contrast to China's multi-billion-dollar investments in Iranian oil and trade agreements. US funding of wars against Islamic countries in Central and South Asia stands in contrast to Turkey's expanding economic trade and investment agreements in the same region. China has replaced the US as the key trading partner in leading South American countries, while the US unequal 'free trade' agreement (NAFTA) impoverishes Mexico. Trade between the European Union and China exceeds that with the US.

In Africa, the US subsidizes wars in Somalia and the Horn of Africa, while China signs up to multi-billion-dollar investment and trade agreements, building up African infrastructure in exchange for access to raw materials. There is no question that the economic future of Africa is increasingly linked to China.

The US empire, in contrast, is in a deadly embrace with an insignificant colonial militarist state (Israel), failed states in Yemen and Somalia, corrupt stagnant client regimes in Jordan and Egypt and the decadent, rent-collecting, absolutist petrol-states of Saudi Arabia and the Gulf. All form part of an unproductive atavistic coalition bent on retaining power via military supremacy. Yet empires of the 21st century are built on the bases of productive economies with global networks linked to dynamic trading partners.

Recognizing the economic primacy and market opportunities linked to becoming part of the Chinese global network, former or existing US clients and even puppet rulers have begun to edge away from submission to US mandates. Fundamental shifts in economic relations and political alignments have occurred throughout Latin America. Brazil, Venezuela, Bolivia and other countries support Iran's non-military nuclear program in defiance of Zionist-led Washington aggression. Several countries have defied Israel-US policymakers by recognizing Palestine as a state. Trade with China surpasses trade with the US in the biggest countries in the region.

Puppet regimes in Iraq, Afghanistan and Pakistan have signed major economic agreements with China, Iran and Turkey even while the US pours in billions to bolster its military position. Turkey, an erstwhile military client of the US–NATO command, broadens its own quest for capitalist hegemony by expanding economic ties with Iran, Central Asia and the Arab Muslim world, challenging US-Israeli military hegemony.

The US empire still retains major clients and nearly a thousand military bases around the world. As client and puppet regimes decline, Washington increases the role and scope of extra-territorial death squad operations from fifty to eighty countries. The growing independence of regimes in the developing world is fuelled in particular by an economic calculus: China offers greater economic returns and less political-military interference than the US.

Washington's imperial network is increasingly based on military ties with allies: Australia, Japan, South Korea, Taiwan in the Far East and Oceana; the European Union in the West; and a smattering of Central and South American states in the south. Even here, the military allies are no longer economic dependencies: Australia and New Zealand's principal export markets are in Asia (China). EU-China trade is growing exponentially.

Japan, South Korea and Taiwan are increasingly tied by trade and investment with China ... as is Pakistan and India.

Equally important, new regional networks that exclude the US are growing in Latin America and Asia, creating the potential for new economic blocs.

In other words, the US imperial economic network constructed after World War II and amplified by the collapse of the USSR is in the process of decay, even as the military bases and treaties remain a formidable 'platform' for new military interventions.

What is clear is that the military, political and ideological gains in network building by the US around the world with the collapse of the USSR and the post-Soviet wars are not sustainable. On the contrary, the over-development of the ideological military-security apparatus raised economic expectations and depleted economic resources, resulting in the incapacity to exploit economic opportunities or consolidate economic networks. US-funded 'popular uprisings' in the Ukraine led to client regimes incapable of promoting growth. In the case of Georgia, the regime engaged in an adventurous war with Russia resulting in trade and territorial losses. It is only a matter of time before existing client regimes in Egypt, Jordan, Saudi Arabia, the Philippines and Mexico face major upheavals due to precarious bases of rule by corrupt, stagnant and repressive rulers.

The process of decay of the US empire is both cause and consequence of the challenge by rising economic powers establishing alternative centers of growth and development. Changes within countries at the periphery of the empire and growing indebtedness and trade deficits at its center are eroding it. The US governing class, in both its financial and militarist variants, show neither will nor interest in confronting the causes of decay. Instead, each mutually supports the other: the financial sector lowers taxes, deepening public debt, and plunders the treasury. The military caste drains the treasury in pursuit of wars and military outposts and increases the trade deficit by undermining commercial and investment undertakings.

Chapter 7

Imperial Power Centers
Divisions, Indecisions and Civil War

Some of the most important outcomes of the Trump presidency are the revelations describing the complex competing forces and relations engaged in retaining and expanding US global power (the empire). The commonplace reference to 'the empire' fails to specify the interface and conflict among institutions engaged in projecting different aspects of US political power.

In this essay we will outline the current divisions of power, interests and direction of the competing configurations of influence.

The Making of Empire: Countervailing Forces

'The empire' is a highly misleading concept insofar as it presumes to discuss a homogeneous, coherent and cohesive set of institutions pursuing similar interests. It is a simplistic general phrase that covers a vast field contested by institutions, personalities and centers of power, some allied, others in growing opposition.

While 'the empire' may describe the general notion that all pursue a common general goal of dominating and exploiting targeted countries, regions, markets and resources, the dynamics (the timing and focus of action) are determined by countervailing forces.

In the present conjuncture, the countervailing forces have taken a radical turn: one configuration is attempting to usurp power and overthrow another. Up to this point, the usurping power configuration has resorted to judicial, media and procedural–legislative mechanism to modify policies. However, below the surface, the goal is to oust an incumbent enemy and impose a rival power.

Who Rules the Empire?

In recent times, *executive officials rule empires*. They may be prime ministers, presidents, autocrats, dictators, generals or a combination of them. Imperial rulers largely 'legislate' and 'execute' strategic and tactical policies. In a crisis executive officials may be subject to review by competing legislators or judges, leading to impeachment (soft coup d'état).

Normally, the executive centralizes and concentrates power, even as they may consult, evade or deceive key legislators and judicial officials. At no point in time or place do the voters play any significant role. The executive power is exercised via specialized departments or secretariats—Treasury, Foreign Affairs (Secretary of State), Interior, and the various security services. In most instances there is greater or lesser inter-agency competition over budgets, policy and access to the chief executive and leading decision-makers.

In times of crises, when the ruling executive leadership is called into question, this vertical hierarchy crumbles. The question then arises of who will rule and dictate imperial policy.

With the ascent of Donald Trump to the US presidency, imperial ruler-ship has become openly contested terrain, fought over amid unyielding aspirants seeking to overthrow the democratically elected regime.

While presidents rule, today the entire state structure is riven by rival power centers, with power seekers at war to impose their rule over the empire. In the first place, the strategically placed security apparatus is no longer under presidential control: it operates in coordination with insurgent Congressional power centers, mass media and extra-governmental power configurations among the oligarchs (business, merchants, arms manu-facturers, Zionists and special interest lobbies).

Sectors of the state apparatus and bureaucracy investigate the executive, freely leaking damaging reports to the media, distorting, fabricating and/or magnifying incidents. They publicly pursue the goal of regime change.

The FBI, Homeland Security, the CIA and other power configurations are acting as crucial allies of the coup-makers, seeking to undermine presidential control over the empire. No doubt many factions within the regional offices look on nervously, waiting to see if the president will be defeated by these opposing power configurations or survive and purge their current directors.

The Pentagon contains both elements, pro as well as anti-presidential power: some active generals are aligned with the prime movers pushing for regime change, while others oppose this movement. Both contending forces influence and dictate imperial military policies.

The most visible and aggressive advocates of regime change are found in the militarist wing of the Democratic Party. They are embedded in Con-gress and allied with police state militarists in and out of Washington.

From their institutional vantage points, the coup-makers have initiated a series of 'investigations' to generate propaganda fodder for the mass media and prepare mass public opinion to favor or at least accept extraordinary regime change.

The Democratic Party congressional-mass media complex draws on the circulation of selective security agency revelations of dubious national security value, including smutty gossip, which is highly relevant for over-throwing the current regime.

Presidential imperial authority has split into fragments of influence among the legislative, Pentagon and security apparatus. Presidential power depends on the Cabinet and its apparatus in a ruthless fight over imperial power, polarizing the entire political system.

The President Counter-Attacks

The Trump regime has many strategic enemies and few powerful supporters. His advisers are under attack: some have been ousted, others are under investigation and face subpoenas for hysterical McCarthyite hearings; still others may be loyal but are incompetent and outclassed. His Cabinet appointees have attempted to follow the president's stated agenda, including the repeal of Obama's disastrous Affordable Care Act and the rollback of federal regulatory systems, with little success, despite the fact that this agenda has strong backing from Wall Street bankers and 'Big Pharma'.

The president's Napoleonic pretensions have been systematically undermined by continuous disparagement from the mass media and the absence of plebeian support after the election.

The president lacks a mass media base of support and has to resort to the internet and personal messages to the public, which are immediately savaged by the mass media.

The principal allies supporting the president should be found among the Republican Party, which forms the majority in both Congress and Senate. These legislators do not act as a uniform bloc—with ultra-militarists joining the Democrats in seeking his ouster.

From a strategic perspective, all the signs point to the weakening of presidential authority, even as his bulldog tenacity allows him to retain formal control over foreign policy. But his foreign policy pronouncements are filtered through a uniformly hostile media that has succeeded in defining allies and adversaries, as well as the failures of some of his ongoing decisions.

The September 2018 Showdown

The big test of power was focused on the raising of the public debt ceiling and the continued funding of the entire federal government. Without an agreement (achieved in January 2019) there would have been a massive governmental shutdown—a kind of 'general strike' paralyzing essential domestic and foreign programs—including the funding of Medicare, the payment of Social Security pensions and the salaries of millions of government and Armed Forces employees.

The pro-regime-change forces (coup-makers) have decided to go for broke in order to secure the programmatic capitulation of the Trump regime or its ouster.

The presidential power elite may choose the option of ruling by decree based on the ensuing economic crisis. They may capitalize on the hue and cry from a Wall Street collapse and claim an imminent threat to national security along national borders and on overseas bases, declaring a military emergency. Without support from the intelligence services, success is doubtful.

Both sides will blame each other for the mounting breakdown. Temporary Treasury expedients will not save the situation. The mass media will go into hysterical mode, from political criticism to openly demanding regime change. The presidential regime may assume dictatorial powers in order 'to save the country'.

Congressional moderates will demand a temporary solution: a week-to-week trickle of federal spending. However, the coup-makers and the Bonapartists will block any rotten compromise. The military will be mobilized, along with the entire security and judicial apparatus, to dictate the outcome.

Civil society organization will appeal to the emerging power configurations to defend their special interests. Discharged public and private employees will march as pensioners and schoolteachers go without funding. Lobbyists, ranging from oil and gas interests to defenders of Israel, will each demand their priority treatment.

The power configuration will flex their muscles, while the foundations of congressional, judicial and presidential institutions will shake and shutter.

On the positive side, internal chaos and institutional divisions will relieve the mounting threat of more overseas wars for the moment. The world will breathe a sigh of relief. Not so the world of stock markets: the dollar and speculators will plunge.

The dispute and indecision over who rules the empire will allow for regional powers to lay claim to contested regions. The EU, Japan, Saudi Arabia and Israel will face off Russia, Iran and China. No one will wait for the US to decide which power center will rule.

Part III

Political Economy of Empire

Chapter 8

Democracy and World Power

The principal reason why Washington engages in military wars, sanctions and clandestine operations to secure power abroad is because its chosen clients cannot and do not win free and open elections.

A brief survey of recent election outcomes testifies to the electoral unattractiveness of Washington-backed clients. The majority of democratic electorates reject candidates and parties which back the US global agenda: neoliberal economic policies; a highly militarized foreign policy; Israeli colonization and annexation of Palestine; the concentration of wealth in the financial sector; the military escalation against China and Russia. While the US policy attempts to re-impose the pillage and dominance of the 1990s via recycled client regimes the democratic electorates want to move on toward less bellicose, more inclusive governments that restore labor and welfare rights.

The US seeks to impose the unipolar world of the Bush, Sr. and Clinton era, failing to recognize the vast changes in the world economy, including the rise of China and Russia as world powers, the emergence of the BRIC and other regional organizations and above all the growth of popular democratic consciousness.

Failing to convince electorates by reason or manipulation, Washington has opted to intervene by force and to finance organizations to subvert the democratic electoral process. The frequent resort to bullets and economic coercion when ballots fail to produce the appropriate outcome is testimony to the profoundly reactionary nature of US foreign policy—reactionary in the double sense of ends and means. Programmatically, the imperial socioeconomic policies deepen inequalities and depress living standards. The means to achieve power, the instruments of policy, include war, intervention and covert operations and are more akin to those of extremist, quasi-fascist, far-right regimes.

Free Elections and the Rejection of US Clients

US-backed electoral parties and candidates have suffered defeat throughout most of the world, despite generous financial backing and international mass media propaganda campaigns. What is striking about the negative voting outcomes is the fact that the vast majority of adversaries are neither anti-capitalist nor socialist. Equally striking is that all of the US clients are rightist or far-rightist parties and leaders. In other words, the polarization is usually between center-left and rightist parties; the choice is between reform or reaction, between an independent or a satellite foreign policy.

Washington and Latin America: Masters of Defeats

Over the past decade Washington has backed losing neoliberal candidates throughout Latin America and then sought to subvert the democratic outcome.

Bolivia

Since 2005, Evo Morales, the center-left leader favoring social reform and an independent foreign policy, has won three presidential elections against Washington-backed rightist parties, each time by a greater margin. In 2008 he ousted the US ambassador for intervening and expelled the Drug Enforcement Agency (DEA); he expelled USAID in 2013 and the Military Mission after foiling an aborted coup in Santa Cruz.

Venezuela

The United Socialist Party of Venezuela (PSUV) and its predecessor have won every presidential and congressional election (over a dozen) except one over the past fifteen years despite US multi-million-dollar funding of neo-liberal opposition parties. Unable to defeat the Chávez-led radical reform government, Washington backed a violent coup (2002), a boss's lockout (2002/3) and decades-long paramilitary attacks of pro-democracy leaders and activists.

Ecuador

The US has opposed the center-left government of President Correa for ousting it from the military base in Manta, renegotiating and repudiating some of its foreign debt and backing regional pacts that exclude the US. As a result Washington backed an abortive police-led coup in 2010 that was quickly defeated.

Honduras

During democratically elected President Manual Zelaya's tenure in office as a center-left leader, Honduras sought to pursue closer relations with

Venezuela in order to receive greater economic aid and shed its reputation as a US-dominated 'banana republic'. Washington, unable to defeat him at the ballot box, responded by supporting a military coup (2009) which ousted Zelaya and returned Honduras to the US fold. Since the coup Honduras has experienced more killings of popular leaders (200) than any other country in Latin America.

Brazil

The center-left Workers Party won four straight elections against US-backed neoliberal candidates, beginning in 2002 and continuing through the 2014 elections. The US propaganda machine—which included the National Security Agency spying on President Rousseff and the strategic state petrol company, Petrobras—and the international financial press went all out to discredit the reformist government. To no avail! The voters preferred an 'inclusive' social liberal regime pursuing an independent foreign policy to an opposition embedded in the discredited, socially regressive neoliberal politics of the Cardoso regime (1994–2002). In the run-up to the 2014 elections, Brazilian and US financial speculators attempted to strike fear into the electorate by betting against the currency (real) and driving the stock market into a precipitous fall. To no avail. Rousseff won with 52 percent of the vote.

Argentina

In Argentina a massive popular revolt overthrew the US-backed neoliberal regime of De la Rua in 2001. In 2003, voters elected the center-left Kirchner government over the rightist, US-backed Menem candidacy. Kirchner pursued a reformist agenda, imposing a moratorium on the debt and combining high economic growth with large-scale social expenditures and an independent foreign policy. US opposition escalated with the election of his wife Cristina Fernandez. Financial elites, Wall Street, the US judiciary and US Treasury intervened to destabilize the government after failing to defeat Fernandez's re-election. Extra-parliamentary financial pressures were matched by political and economic support for rightist politicians in preparation for the 2015 elections.

Earlier, in 1976, the US backed a military coup and political terror that led to the murder of 30,000 activists and militants. In 2014 the US backed a 'financial coup', with a federal judge siding with vulture funds and financial terror sown in international markets to undermine a democratically elected government.

Paraguay

President Fernando Lugo was a moderate former bishop who pursued a watered-down center-left agenda. Nevertheless, he raised issues that conflicted with Washington's extremist agenda, including Paraguay's membership in regional organizations that excluded the US (MERCOSUR). He appealed to landless rural workers and retained ties to other Latin American center-left regimes. He was deposed by Congress in 2012 in a highly dubious 'institutional coup', quickly supported by the White House, and replaced by Federico Franco, a straight-line neoliberal with tight links to Washington and hostile to Venezuela.

Globalizing US Threats to Democracy

US subversion of democracy when center-left political formations compete for power is not confined to Latin America: it has 'gone global'.

The Ukraine

The most egregious example is the Ukraine, where the US spent more than six billion dollars in over a decade and a half. Washington financed, organized and promoted pro-NATO shock troops to seize power against an elected regime (headed by President Yevtushenko) that tried to balance ties between the West and Russia. In February 2014, an armed uprising and mob action led to the overthrow of the elected government and the imposition of a puppet regime totally beholden to the US. The violent putschists met resistance from a large swathe of pro-democracy activists in the eastern region. The Kiev junta led by oligarch Petro Poroshenko dispatched air and ground troops to repress the popular resistance with the unanimous backing of the US and EU. When the rightist regime in Kiev moved to impose its rule over the Crimea and break its military base treaty with Russia, Crimean citizens voted, by a large margin (85 percent), to separate and merge with Russia.

In both the Ukraine and Crimea, US policy involved the use of force to subordinate democracy to NATO's drive to encircle Russia and undermine its democratically elected government.

Russia

Following the election of Vladimir Putin to the presidency, the US organized and financed a large number of opposition 'thinktanks' and NGOs to destabilize the government. Large-scale demonstrations by well-funded NGOs were given wide play by all the Western mass media.

Failing to secure an electoral majority and after suffering defeats in the executive and legislative elections, Washington and the EU, using the pretext of Russian 'intervention' in the Ukraine, launched a full-scale economic war on Russia. Economic sanctions were enforced in the hopes of provoking economic collapse and a popular upheaval. Nothing of the sort occurred. Putin gained greater popularity and stature in Russia and consolidated ties with China and the other BRIC countries.

In short, facing independently elected governments in the Ukraine, Crimea and Russia, Washington resorted to a mob uprising, military encirclement and an escalation of economic sanctions.

Iran

Iran has periodic elections in which pro and anti-Western parties compete. Iran has drawn the wrath of Washington because of its support for Palestinian liberation from the Israeli yoke; its opposition to the Gulf absolutist states; and its ties to Syria, Lebanon (Hezbollah) and post-Saddam Hussein Iraq. As a result, the US has imposed economic sanctions to cripple its economy and finances and funded pro-Western neoliberal opposition NGOs and political factions. Unable to defeat the Islamist power elite electorally, it chooses to destabilize via sanctions (to disrupt its economy), cyber warfare and the assassination of scientists.

Egypt

Washington backed the Hosni Mubarak dictatorship for over three decades. Following the popular uprising in 2011, which overthrew the regime, Washington retained and strengthened its ties to the Mubarak police, military and intelligence apparatus. While promoting an alliance between the military and the newly elected President Mohammed Morsi, Washington funded NGOs that acted to subvert the government through mass demonstrations. The military, under the leadership of US client General Abdel Fattah el-Sisi, seized power, outlawed the Muslim Brotherhood and abolished democratic freedoms.

Washington quickly renewed military and economic aid to the el-Sisi dictatorship and strengthened its ties with the authoritarian regime. In line with US and Israeli policy, General el-Sisi tightened the blockade of Gaza, allied with Saudi Arabia and the Gulf despots, strengthened its ties with the IMF and implemented a regressive neoliberal program by eliminating fuel and food subsidies and lowering taxes on big business. The US-backed coup and restoration of dictatorship was the only way Washington could secure a loyal client relationship in North Africa.

Libya

The US and NATO and Gulf allies launched a war (2011) against the independent, nationalist Libyan government as the only way to oust the popular, welfare-oriented government of Colonel Gaddafi. Unable to defeat him via internal subversion or to destabilize the economy, Washington and its NATO partners launched hundreds of bombing missions accompanied by arms transfers to local Islamic satraps and tribal, clan and other violent authoritarian groups. The subsequent 'electoral process', lacking the most basic political guarantees and fraught by corruption, violence and chaos, led to several competing power centers. Washington's decision to undermine democratic procedures led to a violent Hobbesian world, replacing a popular welfare regime with chaos and terrorism.

Palestine

Washington has pursued a policy of backing Israeli seizures and colonization of Palestinian territory, the savage bombings and mass destruction of Gaza. Israel's determination to destroy the democratically elected Hamas government has received unconditional US backing. The Israeli colonial regime has imposed racist, armed colonies throughout the West Bank, financed by the US government, private investors and US Zionist donors. Faced with the choice between a democratically elected nationalist regime (Hamas) and a brutal militarist regime (Israel), US policymakers have never failed to back Israel in its quest to destroy the Palestinian mini-state.

Lebanon

The US, along with Saudi Arabia and Israel, has opposed the freely elected Hezbollah-led coalition government formed in 2011. The US backed the Israeli invasion in 2006, which was defeated by the Hezbollah militias. Washington backed the right-wing Hariri-led coalition (2008–2011) that was marginalized in 2011. It sought to destabilize society by backing Sunni extremists, especially in northern Lebanon. Lacking popular electoral support to convert Lebanon into a US client state, Washington relies on Israeli military incursions and Syria-based terrorists to destabilize Lebanon's democratically elected government.

Syria

Syria's Bashar Assad regime has been the target of US, EU, Saudi and Israeli enmity because of its support for Palestine and its ties with Iraq, Iran, Russia and Hezbollah. Its opposition to Gulf despotism and its refusal to become a US client state (like Jordan and Egypt) has been another source of NATO hostility. Under pressure from its internal democratic opposition and external allies, Russia and Iran, the Bashar Assad regime convoked a conference of non-violent opposition parties, leaders and groups to find an electoral solution to the ongoing conflict. Washington and its NATO allies rejected a democratic electoral road to reconciliation. They and their Turkish and Gulf allies financed and armed thousands of Islamic extremists who invaded the country. Over a million refugees and 200,000 dead Syrians were a direct result of Washington's decision to pursue regime change via armed conflict.

China

China has become the world's largest economy. It has become a leading global investment and trading country. It has replaced the US and the EU in Asian, African and Latin American markets. Faced with peaceful economic competition and offers of mutually beneficial free trade agreements, Washington has chosen to pursue a policy of military encirclement, internal destabilization and Pan Pacific integration agreements that exclude China. The US has expanded military deployments and bases in Japan, Australia and the Philippines. It has heightened naval and air force surveillance just beyond China's limits. It has fanned the rival maritime claims of China's neighbours, encroaching on vital Chinese waterways.

The US has supported violent Uighur separatists, Tibetan terrorists and protests in Hong Kong in order to fragment and discredit China's rule over its sovereign territory. Fomenting separation via violent means results in harsh repression, which in turn can alienate a domestic constituency and provide grist for the Western media mills. The key to the US countering China's economic ascent is political: fomenting domestic divisions and weakening central authority. The democratization which Chinese citizens favour has little resonance with US-financed 'democracy' charades in Hong Kong or separatist violence in the provinces.

Washington's effort to exclude China from major trade and investment agreements in Asia and elsewhere has been a laughable failure. The principal US 'partners', Japan and Australia, are heavily dependent on the Chinese market. Washington's (free trade) allies in Latin America, namely Colombia, Peru, Chile and Mexico, are eager to increase trade with China. India and Russia are signing off on multi-billion-dollar trade and investment deals with China. Washington's policy of economic exclusion miscarried in the first month.

In short, Washington's decision to pursue confrontation over conciliation and partnership, military encirclement over cooperation, exclusion over inclusion is counter to a democratic foreign policy designed to promote democracy in China and elsewhere. An authoritarian choice in pursuit of unachievable Asian supremacy is not a virtue; it is a sign of weakness and decay.

Conclusion

In our global survey of US policy relating to democracy, center-left governments and free elections we find overwhelming evidence of systematic hostility and opposition. The political essence of the 'war on terrorism' is Washington's worldwide, long-term pernicious assault on independent governments, especially center-left democratic regimes engaged in serious efforts to reduce poverty and inequality.

Washington's methods of choice range from financing rightist political parties via USAID and NGOs to supporting violent military coups; from backing street mobs engaged in destabilization campaigns to air and ground invasions. Washington's animus against democratic processes is not confined to any particular region or religious, ethnic or racial group. The US has bombed black Africans in Libya; organized coups in Latin America against Indians and Christians in Bolivia; supported wars against Muslims in Iraq, Palestine and Syria; financed neo-fascist 'battalions' and armed assaults against Orthodox Christians in eastern Ukraine; denounced atheists in China and Russia.

Washington subsidizes and backs elections only when neoliberal client regimes win. It consistently destabilizes center-left governments that oppose US imperial policies.

None of the targets of US aggression are, strictly speaking, anti-capitalist. Bolivia, Ecuador, Brazil, Argentina are capitalist regimes that attempt to regulate, tax and reduce disparities of wealth via moderate welfare reforms.

Throughout the world, Washington routinely supports extremist political groups engaged in violent and unconstitutional activities that victimize democratic leaders and supporters. The coup regime in Honduras has murdered hundreds of rank and file democratic activists, farm workers and poor peasants.

The US-armed Islamic jihadist and ex-pat allies in Libya have fallen out with their NATO mentors and are at war among themselves, engaging in mutual bloodletting.

Throughout the Middle East, South Asia, North Africa, Central America and the Caucasus, wherever US intervention has taken place extreme right-wing groups have served, at least for a time, as Washington's and Brussels' principal allies.

Pro EU-NATO allies in the Ukraine include a strong contingent of neo-Nazis, paramilitary thugs and 'mainstream' military forces given to bombing civilian neighbourhoods with cluster bombs.

In Venezuela, Washington bankrolls terrorist paramilitary forces and political extremists who have murdered a socialist congressional leader and dozens of leftists.

In Mexico, the US has advised, financed and backed rightist regimes whose military, paramilitary and narco-terrorist forces recently murdered and burned alive forty-three teachers' college students and are deeply implicated in the killing of 100,000 'other' Mexicans in less than a decade.

Over the past eleven years the US has pumped over $6 billion dollars in military aid to Colombia, funding its seven military bases and several thousand special operations forces and doubling the size of the Colombian military. As a result, thousands of civil society and human rights activists, journalists, trade union leaders and peasants have been murdered. Over three million small landholders have been dispossessed.

The mass media cover up the US support for right-wing extremism by describing ruling mass murderers as 'center-right regimes' or 'moderates': linguistic perversions and grotesque euphemisms are as bizarre as the barbarous activities perpetrated by the White House.

In the drive for world power, no crime is left undone; no democracy that opposes it is tolerated. Countries as small and marginal as Honduras or Somalia and as great and powerful as Russia and China are subject to the wrath and covert destabilization efforts of the White House.

The quest for world domination is driven by a subjective belief in the 'triumph of the will'. Global supremacy depends entirely on force and violence: ravaging country after country, from the carpet bombing of Yugoslavia, Iraq, Afghanistan and Libya to proxy wars in Somalia, Yemen and Ukraine to mass killings in Colombia, Mexico and Syria.

Yet there are limits to the spread of the 'killing fields'. Democratic processes are defended by robust citizen movements in Venezuela, Ecuador and Bolivia. The spread of imperial-backed terrorist seizures of power are stymied by the emergence of global powers: China in the Far East and Russia in Crimea and eastern Ukraine have taken bold steps to limit US imperial expansion.

In the United Nations, the president of the United States and his delegate Samantha Powers rant and rave, in fits of pure insanity, against Russia as 'the greatest world terrorist state' for resisting military encirclement and the violent annexation of the Ukraine.

Extremism, authoritarianism and political insanity know no frontiers. The massive growth of the secret political police, the National Security Agency, the shredding of constitutional guarantees, the conversion of electoral processes into elite-controlled multi-billion-dollar charades, the growing impunity of police involved in civilian murders speaks to an emerging totalitarian police state inside the US as a counterpart to the violent pursuit of world power.

Citizen movements, consequential center-left parties and governments and organized workers in Latin America, Asia and Europe have demonstrated that authoritarian extremist proxies of Washington can be defeated. That disastrous neoliberal policies can be reverted. That welfare states, reductions in poverty, unemployment and inequalities can be legislated despite imperial efforts to the contrary.

The vast majority of Americans, here and now, are strongly opposed to Wall Street, big business and the financial sector. The presidency and Congress are despised by three-quarters of the American public. Overseas wars are rejected. The US public, for its own reasons and interests, shares with the pro-democracy movement worldwide a common enmity toward Washington's quest for world power. Here and now in the United States of

America we must learn from this and build our own powerful democratic political instruments.

Through force of reason we must contain and defeat the 'reason of force': the political insanity that informs Washington's 'will to power'. We must degrade the empire to rebuild the republic. We must turn from intervening against democracy abroad to building a democratic welfare republic at home.

Chapter 9

Imperial Wars and Domestic Epidemics

Washington has escalated its military interventions abroad, launching simultaneous air and ground attacks in Syria, Iraq and Afghanistan; multiplying drone attacks in Pakistan, Yemen and Somalia; training, arming and financing proxy mercenaries in Jordan, the Gulf States and Iraq; and dispatching National Guard battalions to West Africa, ostensibly to combat the Ebola epidemic, though they lack the most elementary public health capabilities. All in all over the past six years the US spent $3.5 trillion for military invasions and the cost of these military adventures and imperial wars are rising.

At the same time, US domestic public health services have deteriorated. At both state and local levels and at the national level, officials and major institutions demonstrate an inability to effectively detect and manage cases of Ebola infection among the general population in a timely manner.

An infected Liberian immigrant was not diagnosed correctly when he presented at a major Dallas hospital emergency room. Instead he received irrelevant and unnecessary 'imaging studies' and was sent home with oral antibiotics. This confirmed the widespread belief that emergency room physicians and nurses are under pressure from their administration to order costly CT scans and MRIs of patients as a way of making money for the hospital and to cover up their incompetence in basic patient history and physical examination. Despite the patient's informing hospital workers of his recent arrival from Liberia, an Ebola outbreak hot spot, personnel failed to put on basic protective gowns, gloves, hoods and masks and allowed the febrile, vomiting, desperately sick man to contaminate large areas of the emergency department, waiting room and MRI suite. Quarantine was not even considered.

The director of the Dallas hospital attempted to cover up his organization's incompetence by a series of blaming assertions aimed at the patient, the computer system, the nurses ... . National health guidelines may have been inadequate at the time, but Ebola was clearly on the national radar and the CDC had provided basic guidelines and measures. All hospitals have infectious control committees, disaster preparedness committees and receive state and national alerts.

As the crisis and public panic deepened, President Obama engaged in vigorous political fund-raising. Meanwhile, Vice President Biden was pre-occupied by his 40+- year-old son's expulsion from the Navy Reserve for cocaine use. The defense secretary was busy picking targets to bomb in Syria and Iraq ... .

The Cabinet met over 'National Security' issues like ISIS, expanding military interventions around the world, while US medical personnel, international travellers and their family members, as well as average American citizens, felt more threatened by the apparent breakdown of the public health system, at both local and national levels, in the face of a deadly viral infection.

The inadequacy, indeed breakdown, of the US public health system as it confronted the first cases of Ebola in the country and the simultaneous escalation of military intervention in Syria and Iraq typifies, in microcosm, the demise of the US republic accompanying the rise of the US military empire.

The Dallas hospital that had initially turned the desperately sick Liberian immigrant away was run as a for-profit enterprise, directed by business managers eager for high returns and dismissive of basic health procedures and even more of the advice of competent, experienced health workers: they had made their biggest investments in high technology and multi-million-dollar equipment irrelevant to the diagnosis and treatment of tropical and infectious diseases. The pressure to use the most expensive technology inappropriately and recoup the corporate investment resulted in a deadly delay in diagnosis and contaminated at least a dozen healthcare workers. The corporate hospital director eventually apologized for their 'mistakes'. But the fault goes far beyond bad decisions.

Procedures and protocols built into the 'for profit' model emphasize the need show a healthy return on multi-million-dollar advanced technological investments. There is a stark contrast between the high tech advances in imaging and surgery in a modern American hospital and the regressive, socially backward ignorance of the socio-medico context in which critically ill, infectious patients are embedded. It is as if such patients are not supposed to enter the techno-medical world where only the most highly remunerative procedures and protocols are available ... to those who can pay.

At a deeper level, the entire national public health system is increasingly dependent on the formulation of rules and flows of information, corrupted and distorted by 'market demands' and political priorities heavily weighted towards expanding the police state at home and militarism abroad. These political priorities, in turn, were influenced by the massive shift in resources to support the permanent war policies of the Obama regime and the US Congress.

The proliferation and escalation of military interventions dominated the Obama administration's real agenda. According to Assistant Secretary of State for Eastern European Affairs Victoria Nuland, six billion dollars of public money was spent on subverting the elected government of the Ukraine—six billion dollars shifted from US domestic sectors like healthcare and real disaster preparedness. Meanwhile, hundreds of hospitals have been closed in major American cities and rural clinics abandoned for lack of personnel. The entire healthcare system in the US, in its current 'for profit' corporate form, is devoid of competent, effective leadership. At the same time, the US military is seen as the solution to the world's (and increasingly its domestic) problems, while the social roots of conflict and disaster are contemptuously ignored.

The militarization of the minds of our political leaders has led to the most grotesque decisions: in the face of the Ebola epidemic in West Africa, the Obama regime sent 2,000 National Guard combatants to Africa. These are soldiers who lack the most elementary knowledge, skill, capability and training to deal with the complexities of a major public health crisis in a devastated, war-torn part of the world. One must recall how Washington pressured the United Nations to send 'peacekeepers' to Haiti after the earthquake—UN soldiers from Nepal, who brought not peace but an epidemic of cholera killing additional tens of thousands of Haitian civilians. The immediate question regarding US National Guard troops in West Africa was not whether they could build rural clinics or maintain camps of quarantined Africans, the real concern was whether these heavily armed 'health aides' could avoid being infected and bringing Ebola home. This concern led the Pentagon to impose mandatory quarantine on its own soldiers returning from West Africa—a knee-jerk reaction motivated more by fearmongering than science.

In contrast, Cuba sent hundreds of highly skilled health workers with a proven track record in forming teams to confront public health crises in the tropics and elsewhere. Cuban teams typically include skilled epidemiologists who develop effective local programs, based on real-time, on-the-ground fact-finding and assessment of available resources. The enormous differences between the Cuban and US responses to the Ebola crisis reflects the profound contrast in their social and health systems: Cuba has a free national health system and strong public health and civil defence structures that use rigorous procedures and effective guidelines to set up clinics and camps appropriate to the objective conditions. They emphasize the social context of disease and are not invested in expensive high tech medical equipment and tests irrelevant to the challenges at hand. Their budget is not skewed toward promoting imperial wars: for the Cubans, health and welfare is an integral political priority.

In contrast, healthcare in the US has become big business, while military metaphysics dominate the minds and policies of the political and business elite. The deterioration of basic healthcare delivery in general and the public health sector in particular is not only a consequence of a failure of political leadership, it also reflects the recurring and deepening economic crises. Under the 'war on terrorism', fearmongering over bio-weapons—namely, threatened Anthrax attack—led to tens of billions of public money being diverted from public health at both national and state level, and the corrupted, crippled system has never recovered.

The economic crisis gripping the US, the European Union and beyond is clearly manifested in the stagnation of the US economy. The private corporate elite who form the ruling class are unable to sustain growth without massive US Treasury subsidies—$4.5 trillion dollars according to the *Financial Times* (10/14/14). The US has experienced extreme volatility in its stock market, together with the impoverishment of its working class and diminution of its middle class. Heightened social inequalities are everywhere, especially in relation to access to decent, effective healthcare. In the EU, Germany's economy is plunging from zero to negative growth, while France, Italy and Holland are in deep recession. Greece, Spain and Portugal are in a prolonged depression, burdened by unpayable debts and unable to escape the downward social and economic spiral because of austerity programs imposed by Brussels.

Washington's war policies, the concentration of state resources on financing military invasions and subsidizing the grossly inflated financial sector, account for the fatal deterioration of health and welfare services in the US. Growing majorities feel the pain, and many more are alienated from the presidential and Congressional elite—as well as from their own corrupt and incompetent local elected officials.

To safeguard the power of the military-financial elite, the political rulers have resorted to a series of 'Horror Shows'—orchestrating vast propaganda spectacles designed to strike fear and loathing of 'external enemies' into the American public and secure their submission and obedience to police state policies.

In 2014 there was the lurid media shock of Muslim terrorists in 'ISIS' beheading two American captives. The public 'horror' was manipulated to justify the large-scale US military re-entry in Iraq and the air war against Syria—policies largely opposed by the war-weary US citizenry.

Close on the heels of the 'beheading' atrocities came the spectacle of a fearsome African Ebola epidemic, spreading to the US and threatening Americans with brutally painful deaths ... . This was used to justify Obama's sending thousands of US National Guard to West Africa to act as 'health workers'.

The total collapse of the public health systems throughout Africa follows decades of civil wars fomented by US and EU military policies aimed at plundering Africa's economies and rich natural resources—while marketing western arms and mercenaries. Militarizing the problems of Africa and creating millions of refugees has naturally led to plagues: Ebola today, malaria yesterday and other infectious diseases and miseries tomorrow.

The immensely complex and catastrophic health crisis in West Africa is the stark backdrop to years of Western propaganda hailing the massive growth of foreign investment in Africa's extractive sectors—notably, energy and mining. The business press (*Financial Times, The Economist, Wall Street Journal* ...) featured images of 'Africa: The Sleeping Giant Awakes', describing the emergence of wealthy mineral enclaves powered by large-scale foreign investments that create vast private foreign and local fortunes while ignoring the massive sea of poverty, broken public health clinics, non-existent schools and devastating living conditions, as well as the war-lord-ravaged masses of refugees fleeing fights over mineral-rich lands. This created the 'perfect storm' for the emergence and spread of epidemics such as Ebola.

In Africa, under IMF and Western corporate dictates, entire budgets and foreign aid programs were channelled to finance infrastructure (roads, transport, ports, etc.) for extractive imperialism—while virtually nothing, in terms of public policy, was or is allocated to basic public health and preventative medicine. The 'poverty focused' programs of the 'Gates Foundation' and others serve to divert African health workers and resources to NGO, rather than national, priorities and encourage the flight of African doctors and nurses to the West.

The recent cases of Ebola in the US highlight the deterioration of national and local public health systems—the result of deregulation, privatization and corporatization of medicine. The 'profit ethos' permeates medical care in the US. Cutbacks in preventive medicine, the divorce of medical care from the social context of illness and the lack of accountability and transparency in the face of erroneous diagnoses and inappropriate or incompetent care are the consequences of larger failures in public policy. This ethos also explains the emergence and rampant spread of multi-drug-resistant bacterial infections within hospitals and out in the community. The preference for expensive, profitable techno-medicine (marketed as 'personalized' healthcare) over competent 'hands-on', science-based medicine rooted in an understanding of objective social conditions has fuelled the crisis and spread mass confusion among the public.

When the government engages in long-term, large-scale wars abroad, when the US Treasury allocates trillions of public dollars to Wall Street for the better part of a decade, when the government secures submission ('consent') via horrific scenarios that replace public accountability with fear and loathing, the US public ends up paying a steep price in terms of funding programs of public health, education and welfare.

The recent 'police state' response to the American nurse, Kaci Hickox, highlights the corrupt arrogance of US politicians and opinion leaders long accustomed to control via fearmongering and criminalizing dissent. The fact that Nurse 'Kaci' arrived at Newark Liberty International Airport in perfect health from her months of heroic work in West Africa, where she set up clinics and hospitals to help stem the Ebola crisis at its source, did not dissuade the thuggish governor of New Jersey from confining her, like an animal, in a clear plastic cage in the parking lot of a Newark hospital. Her successful fight for freedom against this arbitrary confinement exposed Governor Christie and his sidekick, New York Governor Cuomo, as ignorant bellowing thugs intent on making her 'an example'. Nurse Kaci Hickox' victory of science and civil rights over brutal scaremongering may be temporary, as the tendency has long been to militarize crises and erode citizen rights.

The American public is beginning to understand the relationship between this policy of scaremongering, the bail-out of billionaires and rampant militarism with the daily erosion of their standard of living, health and security and civil rights. It will take more than a Nurse 'Kaci' to reverse the tide, but one tough competent nurse has set a glorious example.

Chapter 10

The Pentagon and Big Oil
Militarism and Capital Accumulation

There is no question that in the immediate aftermath of and for several years following US military conquests, wars, occupations and sanctions, US multinational corporations lost out on profitable sites for investments. The biggest losses were in the exploitation of natural resources—in particular, gas and oil—in the Middle East, the Persian Gulf and South Asia.

As a result some observers speculated that there were deep fissures and contradictory interests within the US ruling class. They argued that, on the one hand, political elites linked to pro-Israel lobbies and the military industrial power configuration promoted a highly militarized foreign policy agenda and, on the other hand, some of the biggest and wealthiest multinational corporations sought diplomatic solutions.

Yet this seeming 'elite division' did not materialize. There is no evidence, for example, that multinational oil companies sought to oppose the Iraq, Libyan, Afghan, Syrian wars. Nor did the powerful ten largest oil companies with a net value of over 1.1 trillion dollars mobilize their lobbyists and influentials in the mass media to support the cause of peaceful capital penetration and domination of the oil fields via neoliberal political clients.

In the run-up to the Iraq war, the three major US oil companies, Exxon Mobil, Chevron, Conoco Phillips, eager to exploit the third largest oil reserves in the world, did not engage in Congressional lobbying or exert pressure on the Bush or later the Obama administration for a peaceful resolution of the conflict. At no point did the Big Ten challenge the pro-war Israel lobby and its phony argument that Iraq possessed weapons of mass destruction by coming up with an alternative policy.

Similar political passivity was evidenced in the run-up to the Libyan war. 'Big Oil' was actually signing off on lucrative oil deals when the militarists in Washington struck again—destroying the Libyan state and tearing asunder the entire fabric of the Libyan economy.

Big Oil may have bemoaned the loss of oil and profits but there was no concerted effort, before or after the Libyan debacle, to critically examine or evaluate the loss of a major oil-producing region. In the case of economic sanctions against Iran, which possessed the second largest oil reserves in the world, MNCs were again notable by their absence from the halls of Congress and the Department of the Treasury where the sanctions policy was decided. Prominent Zionist policymakers, Stuart Levey and David Cohen, designed and implemented sanctions that prevented US (and EU) oil companies from investing in or trading with Teheran.

In fact, despite the seeming divergence of interest between a highly militarized foreign policy and the drive of MNCs to pursue the global accumulation of capital, no political conflicts erupted. The basic question that this paper seeks to address is: why did the major MNCs submit to an imperial foreign policy that resulted in lost economic opportunities?

Why MNCs Fail to Oppose Imperial Militarism

There are several possible hypotheses accounting for the MNC accommodation of a highly militarized version of imperial expansion.

In the first instance, the CEOs of the MNCs may have believed that the wars, especially the Iraq war, would be short term and would lead to a period of stability under a client regime willing and able to privatize the oil and gas sector. In other words, the petrol elites bought into the arguments of Rumsfeld, Chaney, Wolfowitz and Feith that the invasion and conquest would 'pay for itself'.

Second, even after the prolonged decade-long destructive war and the deepening sectarian conflict, many CEOs believed that a lost decade would be compensated by long-term gain. They believed that profits would flow once the country was stabilized. However, the entry of the oil majors after 2010 was immediately threatened by the ISIS offensive. The time frame of the MNC strategic planners was understated if not totally wrong-headed.

Third, most CEOs believed that the US-NATO invasion of Libya would lead to monopoly ownership and greater profits than they had received from a public-private partnership with the Gaddafi regime. The oil majors believed that they would secure total or majority control. In other words, the war would allow the oil MNCs to secure monopoly profits for an extended period. Instead, the end of a stable partnership led to a Hobbesian world in which anarchy and chaos inhibited any large-scale, long-term entry of MNCs.

Fourth, the MNCs, including the big oil corporations, have invested in hundreds of sites in dozens of countries. They are not tied to a single location. They depend on the militarized imperial state to defend their global interests. Hence they are probably not willing to contest or challenge the militarists in, say, Iraq for fear that it might endanger US imperial intervention in other sites.

Fifth, many MNCs interlock across economic sectors: they invest in oil fields and refineries; banking, financing and insurance as well as extractive sectors. To the degree that multinational capital is diversified they are less dependent on a single region, sector or source for profit. Hence, destructive wars, in one or several countries, may not have as great a prejudicial effect as in the past when 'Big Oil' was just 'oil'.

Sixth, the agencies of the US imperial state are heavily weighted in favour of military rather than economic activity. The international bureaucracy of the US is overwhelmingly made up of military, intelligence and counter-insurgency officials. In contrast, China, Japan, Germany and other emerging states (Brazil, Russia and India) have a large economic component in their overseas bureaucracy. The difference is significant. US MNCs do not have access to economic officials and resources in the same way as China's MNCs. The Chinese overseas expansion and its MNCs are built around powerful economic support systems and agencies. US MNCs have to deal with Special Forces, spooks and highly militarized 'aid officials'. In other words, the CEOs who look for state support perforce have mostly military counterparts who view the MNCs as *instruments* rather than *subjects* of policy.

Seven, the recent decade has witnessed the rise of the financial sector as the dominant recipient of state support. As a result, big banks exercise major influence on public policy. To the extent that this is true, much of what is 'oil money' has gone over to finance and profits accrue by pillaging the US Treasury. As a result, oil interests merge with the financial sector and their 'profits' are as much dependent on the state as on exploiting overseas sites.

Eight, while Big Oil has vast reserves of capital, its diverse locations, multiple activities and dependence on state protection (military) weaken its opposition to US wars in lucrative oil countries. As a result, other powerful pro-war lobbies that have no such constraints have a free hand. For example, the pro-Israel power configuration has far less 'capital' than any of the top ten oil companies. But it has a far greater number of lobbyists with much more influence over Congress people. Moreover, it has far more effective propaganda—media leverage—than Big Oil. Critics of US foreign policy, including its military and sanctions policies, are much more willing to criticize Big Oil than Zionist lobbies.

Finally, the rise of domestic oil production resulting from fracking opens new sites for Big Oil to profit outside of the Middle East, even though the costs may be higher and the duration shorter. The oil industry has replaced losses in Middle East sites (due to war) with domestic investments.

Nevertheless, there is tension and conflict between oil capital and militarism. A recent case involved ExxonMobil's plans to invest $38 billion in a joint venture in the Russian Arctic with the Russian oil giant Rosneft. Obama's sanctions against Russia shut down the deal, much to the dismay of the senior executives of ExxonMobil, which had already invested $3.2 billion in an area the size of Texas.

Conclusion

The latent conflicts and overt difference between military and economic expansion may eventually find greater articulation in Washington. However, up to now, because of the global structures and orientation of the oil industry, because of their dependence on the military for 'security', the oil industry in particular and MNCs in general have sacrificed short- and medium-term profits for 'future gains' in the hope that the wars will end and lucrative profits will return.

Chapter 11

Soaring Profits and Soaring Social Costs

There are two major beneficiaries of the two major wars launched by the US government: one domestic and one foreign. The three major domestic arms manufacturers, Lockheed Martin (LMT), Northrop Grumman (NOG) and Raytheon (RTN), have delivered record-shattering returns to their investors, CEOs and investment banks during the past decade and a half. The Israeli regime is the overwhelming foreign beneficiary of the war, expanding its territory through its dispossession of Palestinians and positioning itself as the regional hegemon. Israel benefited from the US invasion that destroyed Iraq, a major ally of the Palestinians; the invasion provided cover for Israel's massive settler expansion in the Occupied Palestinian territories. In the course of its invasion and occupation Washington systematically destroyed Iraq's armed forces and civil infrastructure, shredding its complex modern society and state. By doing so, the US occupation removed one of Israel's major regional rivals.

Apart from the enormous costs to the Iraqis, Americans have paid a huge price for this military adventure. In terms of the cost to the US, hundreds of thousands of soldiers who served in the war zones have sustained severe physical and mental injuries, while thousands have died directly or indirectly through an epidemic of soldier suicides. The invasion and occupation of Iraq has cost the US trillions of dollars and counting. Despite the immense costs to the American people, the military-industrial complex and the pro-Israel power configuration continue to keep the US government on a wartime economy—undermining the domestic social safety net and standard of living of many millions.

No peaceful economic activity can match the immense profits enjoyed by the military-industrial complex in war. This powerful lobby continues to press for new wars to sustain the Pentagon's huge budget. As for the pro-Israel power configuration, any substantive diplomatic peace negotiations in the Middle East would end their naked land grabs, reduce or curtail new weapons transfers and undermine pretexts to sanction or attack countries, like Iran, that stand in the way of Tel Aviv's vision of 'Greater Israel', unrivalled in the region.

The cost of almost fifteen years of warfare weighs heavily on the US Treasury and electorate. The wars have been dismal failures if not outright defeats. New sectarian conflicts have emerged in Syria, Iraq and, now, Ukraine—opportunities for the US arms industry and pro-Israel lobbies to make even greater profits and gain more power.

The horrendous ongoing costs of past and continuing wars make the launch of new military interventions more difficult for US and Israeli militarists. The US public has expressed widespread discontent over the burden of recent wars and shows even less stomach for new wars that profit the military-industrial complex and further strengthen Israel.

War Profits

The power and influence of the military-industrial complex in promoting serial wars has resulted in extraordinary rates of profit. According to a recent study by Morgan Stanley (cited in *Barron's*, 6/9/14, p. 19), shares in the major US arms manufacturers have risen 27,699 percent over the past fifty years, in contrast to 6,777 percent for the broader market. In the past three years alone Raytheon has returned 124 percent, Northrup Grumman 114 percent and Lockheed Martin 149 percent to their investors and masters.

The Obama regime made a grand public show of reducing the military budget via the annual appropriation bill, and then turned around and announced emergency supplemental funds to cover the costs of these wars … thereby actually increasing military spending, all the while waving the banner of 'cost cutting'. Obama's theatrics fattened the profits for the US military-industrial complex.

War profits have soared with the series of military interventions in the Middle East, Africa and South Asia. Arms industry lobbyists pressure Congressional and Pentagon decision-makers to link up with the pro-Israel lobby as it promotes even deeper direct US military involvement in Syria, Iraq and Iran. The growing ties between Israeli and US military industries reinforce their political leverage in Washington by working with liberal interventionists and neo-conservatives. They attacked Obama for not bombing Syria and for his withdrawal of troops from Iraq and Afghanistan. They then clamoured to send US troops back to Iraq and called for intervention in Ukraine. Obama argued that proxy wars without direct US troop involvement do not require the heavy Pentagon expenditures demanded by the arms industry. The Obama regime presented the withdrawal from Iraq and Afghanistan as a necessary step to reduce US financial and military losses. This was in response to Wall Street's pressure to cut the budget deficit. Obama's attempt to meet the demands of the US financial sector came at the price of cutting potential profit for the military industrial complex as well as infuriating Israel and its fanatical supporters in Congress.

The Fight Over the Military Budget: Veterans Versus the IMC Complex Lobby

In the face of rising domestic pressure to reduce the budget deficit and cut military spending, the US military-industrial complex and its Zionist accomplices are fighting to retain their share by eliminating programs designed to serve the health needs of active and retired soldiers. Soaring disability costs related to the recent wars will continue for decades. Veteran healthcare costs are expected to double to 15 percent of the defense budget in the next five years. The huge public cost of caring for soldiers and veterans means 'bad news for defense stocks', according to financial analysts (*Barron's*, 6/9/14, p. 19).

This is why the arms industries promote the closure of scores of Veterans Health Administration hospitals and a reduction in retiree benefits, using the pretexts of fighting fraud and incompetence and poor-quality service compared with the private sector. The same corporate warlords and lobbyists who clamour to send US troops back to Iraq and to new wars in Syria and Ukraine, where young lives, limbs and sanity are at great risk, are also in the forefront of a fight to slash funding for the veterans' medical care. Economists have long noted that the more dollars spent on veterans' and military retirees' healthcare, the less is allocated for war materials, ships and aircraft. Today it is estimated that over $900 billion dollars will have been spent on long-term VHA medical and disability services for veterans of the wars in Afghanistan and Iraq. That number is clearly set to rise with each new intervention.

The corporate warlords are urging Congress to increase co-pays, enrollment fees and deductibles for veterans, retirees and active duty personnel enrolled in military health insurance plans such as Tricare, as well as limiting access to VHA services.

The fight over Pentagon expenditures is a struggle over war or social justice: health services for troops and veterans versus weapons programs that fatten corporate profits for the arms industry.

Chapter 12

Putting an End to the Welfare State

The Last Cut

The American welfare state was created in 1935 and continued to develop through 1973. Since then, over a prolonged period the capitalist class has been steadily dismantling the entire welfare state. Between the mid-1970s and the present (2017), laws, welfare rights and benefits and the construction of and subsidies for affordable housing have been gutted. 'Workfare' (under President 'Bill' Clinton) ended welfare for the poor and displaced workers. Meanwhile the shift to regressive taxation and steadily declining real wages have increased corporate profits to an astronomical degree.

What started as incremental reversals during the 1990s under Clinton has snowballed over the last two decades, decimating welfare legislation and institutions. The earlier welfare 'reforms' and the current anti-welfare legislation and austerity practices have been accompanied by a series of endless imperial wars, especially in the Middle East.

In the 1940s through the 1960s, world and regional wars (Korea and Indo-China) were combined with significant welfare programs—a form of 'social imperialism', which 'buys off' the working class while expanding the empire. However, recent decades are characterized by multiple regional wars and the reduction or elimination of welfare programs—and a massive growth in poverty, domestic insecurity and poor health.

New Deals and Big Wars

The 1930s witnessed the advent of social legislation and action, which laid the foundations of what is called the 'modern welfare state'.

Unions were organized as working-class strikes and progressive legislation facilitated trade union organization, elections, collective bargaining rights and a steady increase in union membership. Improved work conditions, rising wages, pension plans and benefits, employer or union-provided health care and protective legislation improved the standard of living for the working class and provided for two generations of upward mobility.

Social security legislation was approved along with workers' compensation and the forty-hour workweek. Jobs were created through federal programs (WPA, CCC, etc.). Protectionist legislation facilitated the growth of domestic markets for US manufacturers. Workplace shop steward councils organized 'on the spot' job action to protect safe working conditions.

World War II led to full employment and increases in union membership, as well as legislation restricting workers' collective bargaining rights and enforcing wage freezes. Hundreds of thousands of Americans found jobs in the war economy, but a huge number were also killed or wounded in the war.

The post-war period witnessed a contradictory process: wages and salaries increased while legislation curtailed union rights via the Taft Hartley Act and the McCarthyist purge of left-wing trade union activists. So-called 'right to work' laws effectively outlawed unionization, particularly in southern states, which drove industries to relocate to the anti-union states.

Welfare reforms, in the form of the GI bill, provided educational opportunities for working-class and rural veterans, while federal-subsidized low-interest mortgages encourage home ownership, especially for veterans.

The New Deal created concrete improvements but did not consolidate influence at any level. Capitalists and management still retained control over capital, the workplace and the location of production plants. Trade union officials signed pacts with capital: higher pay for the workers and greater control of the workplace for the bosses. Trade union officials joined management in repressing rank and file movements seeking to control technological changes by reducing hours ("thirty hours work for forty hours pay"). Dissident local unions were seized and gutted by the trade union bosses— sometimes through violence.

Trade union activists, community organizers for rent control and other grassroots movements lost both the capacity and the will to advance toward large-scale structural changes of US capitalism. Living standards improved for a few decades but the capitalist class consolidated strategic control over its relations with labor and civil society. While unionized workers' incomes increased, inequalities, especially in the non-union sectors, began to grow. With the end of the GI bill, veterans' access to high-quality subsidized education diminished.

While a new wave of social welfare legislation and programs began in the 1960s and early 1970s, it was no longer the product of a mass trade union or workers' class struggle. Moreover, trade union collaboration with capitalist regional war policies led to the killing and maiming of hundreds of thousands of workers in two wars—the Korean and Vietnamese wars.

Much of the social legislation resulted from the civil and welfare rights movements. While specific programs were helpful, none of them addressed structural racism and poverty.

The Last Wave of Social Welfarism

The 1960s witnessed the greatest racial war in modern US history: mass movements in the south and north rocked state and federal governments while advancing the cause of civil, social and political rights. Millions of black citizens, joined by white activists and, in many cases, led by African American Vietnam War veterans, confronted the state. At the same time, millions of students and young workers, threatened with military conscription, challenged the military and social order.

Energized by mass movements, a new wave of social welfare legislation was launched by the federal government to pacify mass opposition among blacks, students, community organizers and middle-class Americans. Despite this mass popular movement, the union bosses at the AFL-CIO openly supported the war, police repression and the military or, at best, were passive impotent spectators of the drama unfolding in the nation's streets. Dissident union members and activists were the exception, as many had multiple identities to represent: African American, Hispanic, draft resisters, etc.

Under presidents Lyndon Johnson and Richard Nixon, Medicare, Medicaid, OSHA, the EPA and multiple poverty programs were implemented. A national health program, extending Medicare to all Americans, was introduced by President Nixon and sabotaged by the Kennedy Democrats and the AFL-CIO. Overall, social and economic inequalities diminished during this period.

The Vietnam War ended in defeat for the American militarist empire. This coincided with the beginning of the end of social welfare as we knew it, as the bill for militarism placed even greater demands on the public treasury.

With the election of President Carter, social welfare in the US began its long decline. The next series of regional wars were accompanied by even greater attacks on welfare via the 'Volker Plan'—freezing workers' wages as a means of combating inflation.

'Guns without butter' became the legislative policy of the Carter and Reagan administrations. The welfare programs were based on politically fragile foundations.

The Debacle of Welfarism

Private-sector trade union membership declined from a post-World War peak of 30 percent to 12 percent in the 1990s. Today it has sunk to 7 percent. Capitalists embarked on a massive program of closing thousands of factories in the unionized north, which were then relocated to the non-unionized low-wage southern states and then overseas to Mexico and Asia. Millions of stable jobs disappeared.

Following the election of 'Jimmy' Carter, neither Democratic nor Republican presidents felt any need to support organizations. On the contrary, they facilitated contracts dictated by management, which reduced wages, job security, benefits and social welfare.

The anti-offensive from the Oval Office intensified under President Reagan, whose direct intervention led to the firing of tens of thousands of striking air controllers and the arrest of union leaders. Under presidents Carter, Reagan, George H. W. Bush and William Clinton, cost of living adjustments failed to keep up with the price of vital goods and services. Healthcare inflation was astronomical. Financial deregulation led to the subordination of American industry to the financial sector and the Wall Street banks. De-industrialization, capital flight and massive tax evasion reduced domestic capital's share of national income.

The capitalist class followed a trajectory of decline, recovery and ascendance. Moreover, during the earlier world depression, at the height of mobilization and organization, the capitalist class never faced any significant political threat to its control of the commanding heights of the economy.

The New Deal was, at best, a de facto 'historical compromise' between the capitalist class and the unions, mediated by the Democratic Party elite. It was a temporary pact in which the unions secured legal recognition while the capitalists retained their executive prerogatives.

The Second World War secured the economic recovery for capital and subordinated through a federally mandated 'no strike' production agreement. There were a few notable exceptions: the coal miners' union organized strikes in strategic sectors and some leftist leaders and organizers encouraged slow-downs, work to rule and other in-plant actions when employers ran roughshod over the workers with particular brutality. The recovery of capital was the prelude to a post-war offensive against independently based political organizations. The quality of organization declined even as the quantity of trade union membership increased.

Union officials consolidated internal control in collaboration with the capitalist elite. Capitalist-class official collaboration was extended overseas, with strategic consequences.

The post-war corporate alliance between the state and capital led to a global offensive—the replacement of European-Japanese colonial control and exploitation by US business and bankers. Imperialism was later re-branded as 'globalization'. It pried open markets, secured cheap, docile labor and pillaged resources for US manufacturers and importers.

US unions played a major role by sabotaging militant unions abroad in cooperation with the US security apparatus: they worked to co-opt and bribe nationalist and leftist leaders and supported police-state regime repression and the assassination of recalcitrant militants.

'Hand in bloody glove' with the US empire, the American trade unions planted the seeds of their own destruction at home. The local capitalists in newly emerging independent nations established industries and supply chains in cooperation with US manufacturers. Attracted to these sources of low-wage, violently repressed workers, US capitalists relocated their factories overseas and turned their backs on those at home.

Union officials had laid the groundwork for the demise of stable jobs and social benefits for American workers. Their collaboration increased the rate of capitalist profit and overall power in the political system. Their complicity in the brutal purges of militants, activists and leftist union members and leaders at home and abroad put an end to the government's capacity to sustain and expand the welfare state.

Trade unions in the US did not use their collaboration with empire in its bloody regional wars to win social benefits for rank and file workers. The time of social-imperialism, when workers within the empire benefited from imperialism's pillage, was over. Gains in social welfare henceforth could only result from mass struggles led by the urban poor, especially Afro-Americans, the community-based working poor and militant youth organizers.

The last significant social welfare reforms were implemented in the early 1970s—coinciding with the end of the Vietnam War (and victory for the Vietnamese people)—and ended with the absorption of the urban and anti-war movements into the Democratic Party. Henceforward, the US corporate state advanced through the overseas expansion of multi-national corporations and via large-scale, non-unionized production at home.

The technological changes of this period did not benefit the US population. The belief, common in the 1950s, that science and technology would increase leisure, decrease work and improve living standards for the working class was shattered. Instead, technological changes displaced well-paid industrial jobs while increasing the number of mind-numbing, poorly paid and politically impotent jobs in the so-called 'service sector'—a rapidly growing section of unorganized and vulnerable workers that especially included women and minorities.

Union membership declined precipitously. The demise of the USSR and China's turn to capitalism had a dual effect: it eliminated collectivist (socialist) pressure for social welfare and opened up their markets—with their cheap, disciplined workers—to foreign manufacturers. The US Federal Reserve and President 'Bill' Clinton deregulated financial capital, leading to a frenzy of speculation. Congress wrote laws that permitted overseas tax evasion—especially in Caribbean tax havens. Regional free trade agreements, like NAFTA, spurred the relocation of jobs abroad. De-industrialization accompanied the decline of wages, living standards and social benefits for millions of American workers.

The New Abolitionists: The Trillionaires

The New Deal, the Great Society, trade unions and the anti-war and urban movements were in retreat and primed for abolition.

Wars without welfare (or guns without butter) replaced earlier 'social imperialism', with a huge growth of poverty and homelessness. Domestic labor was now exploited to finance overseas wars, not vice versa. The fruits of imperial plunder were not for sharing.

As the working and middle classes drifted downward, they were used up, abandoned and deceived on all sides—especially by the Democratic Party. They elected militarists and demagogues as presidents.

President 'Bill' Clinton ravaged Russia, Yugoslavia, Iraq and Somalia and liberated Wall Street. His regime gave birth to the prototype billionaire swindlers: Michael Milken and Bernard 'Bernie' Madoff.

Clinton converted welfare into cheap 'workfare', exploiting the poorest and most vulnerable and condemning the next generations to grinding poverty. Under Clinton the prison population of mostly African Americans expanded and the break-up of families ravaged the urban communities.

Provoked by an act of terrorism (9/11), President G. W. Bush, Jr. launched the 'endless' wars in Afghanistan and Iraq and deepened the police state (Patriot Act). Wages for American workers and profits for American capitalist moved in opposite directions.

The Great Financial Crash of 2008–2011 shook the paper economy to its roots and led to the greatest shakedown of any national treasury in history directed by the first black American president. Trillions of public wealth were funnelled into the criminal banks on Wall Street, considered 'just too big to fail'. Millions of American workers and homeowners, however, were 'just too small to matter'.

The Age of Demagogues

President Obama transferred two trillion dollars to the ten biggest bankers and swindlers on Wall Street and another trillion to the Pentagon to pursue the Democrats' version of foreign policy: from Bush's two overseas wars to Obama's seven.

Obama's electoral 'donor-owners' stashed away two trillion dollars in overseas tax havens and looked forward to global free trade pacts—pushed by the eloquent African American president.

Obama was elected to two terms. His liberal Democratic Party supporters swooned over his peace and justice rhetoric while swallowing his militarist escalation into seven overseas wars as well as the foreclosure of two million American householders. Obama completely failed to honour his campaign promise to reduce wage inequality between black and white wage earners while continuing to moralize to black families about 'values'.

Obama's war against Libya led to the killing and displacement of millions of black Libyans and workers from Sub-Saharan Africa. The smiling Nobel Peace Prize president created more desperate refugees than any previous US head of state—including millions of Africans flooding Europe.

'Obamacare', his imitation of an earlier Republican governor's health plan, was formulated by the private corporate health industry (private insurance, Big Pharma and the for-profit hospitals) to mandate enrolment and ensure triple-digit profits with double-digit increases in premiums. By the 2016 presidential elections, Obamacare was opposed by a 43–45 percent margin of the American people. Obama's propagandists could not show any improvement in life expectancy or decrease in infant and maternal mortality as a result of his healthcare reform. Indeed, the opposite occurred among the marginalized working class in the old 'rust belt' and in rural areas. This failure to show any significant health improvement for the masses of Americans is in stark contrast to LBJ's Medicare program of the 1960s, which continues to receive massive popular support.

Forty years of anti-welfare legislation and pro-business regimes paved a golden road for the election of Donald Trump.

Trump and the Republicans are focusing on the tattered remnants of the social welfare system: Medicare, Medicaid, social security. The remains of FDR's New Deal and LBJ's Great Society are on the chopping block.

The moribund (but well-paid) leadership has been notable by its absence in the ensuing collapse of the social welfare state. The liberal left Democrats embraced the platitudinous Obama/Clinton team as the Great Society's gravediggers, while wailing at Trump's allies for shoving the corpse of the welfare state into its grave.

Conclusion

Over the past forty years the working class and the rump of what was once referred to as 'the movement' has contributed to the dismantling of the social welfare state, voting for 'strike-breaker' Reagan, 'workfare' Clinton, 'Wall Street crash' Bush, 'Wall Street savior' Obama and 'Trickle-down' Trump.

Gone are the days when social welfare and profitable wars raised US living standards and transformed American trade unions into an appendage of the Democratic Party and a handmaiden of empire. The Democratic Party rescued capitalism from its collapse in the Great Depression, incorporated it into the war economy and the post- colonial global empire, and resurrected Wall Street from the 'Great Financial Meltdown' of the 21st century.

The war economy no longer fuels social welfare. The military-industrial complex has found new partners on Wall Street and among the globalized multinational corporations. Profits rise while wages fall. Low-paying workfare lopped off state transfers to the poor. Technology—IT, robotics, artificial intelligence and electronic gadgets—has created the most class-polarized social system in history. The first trillionaire and multi-billionaire tax evaders rose on the backs of a miserable standing army of tens of millions of low-wage workers, stripped of rights and representation. State subsidies eliminate virtually all risk to capital. The end of social welfare coerced workers (including young mothers with children) to seek insecure low-income employment while slashing education and health—cementing the feet of generations into poverty. Regional wars abroad have depleted the US Treasury and robbed the country of productive investment. Economic imperialism exports profits, reversing the historic relationship of imperialist booty to the state.

To escape from Reagan and the strike breakers, the working class embraced the promises of Clinton for improved conditions and a better life; black and white workers united to elect Obama who expelled millions of immigrant workers, pursued seven wars, abandoned black workers and enriched the already filthy rich. Deception and demagogy of the democrats and liberals bred the ugly and unlikely plutocrat-populist demagogue, leading many workers to vote for Trump.

The demise of welfare and the rise of the opioid epidemic that has killed close to one million (mostly working-class) Americans mostly occurred under Democratic regimes. The collaboration of liberals and unions in promoting endless wars opened the door to Trump's mirage of a stateless, tax-less, ruling class.

Who will the Democrats choose as their next demagogic champion to challenge 'Donald'? One who will speak to the 'deplorables' and work for the trillionaires?

Chapter 13

Imperial Recovery and Disappearing Workers

Nero played his fiddle, Obama shot baskets and Trump twittered while their empires burned. What makes empire decay and what makes empires expand has everything to do with the relations between rulers and the ruled. Several factors are decisive. These include: (1) rent, land and housing, (2) the direction of living standards, (3) the rise or fall of mortality rate, (4) decline or rise of families.

Throughout history, rising empires bring their population on side for the task of empire by distributing a portion of their plunder to the masses—providing them with land, low rents and housing. Large-scale landlords facing the return of young war veterans reduced excessive land concentration to avoid domestic unrest.

Rising empires raised living standards, with salaried employees, workers and artisans, merchants and scribes finding employment as the oligarchies expanded conspicuous consumption and the state bureaucracy running the empire.

A prosperous empire is cause and consequence of increases in the population and the growth of healthy and educated plebeians who service and serve the rulers. In contrast, declining empires plunder the domestic economy, without regard to the negative social consequences that include a reduction in life expectancy, which in the US is among the lowest of all advanced industrialized countries—even lower than in Cuba. As a result, deteriorating empires experience a declining rate of mortality; home-ownership and land is concentrated in the hands of an elite of renters living off unearned wealth via inheritance, speculation and rents, which degrades productive work based on skill and knowledge.

Declining empires are cause and consequence of vulnerable families composed of opioid-addicted workers suffering from rising inequality between rulers and ruled.

The US imperial experience over the past century embodies the trajectory of the rise and fall of empires. The past quarter-century describes the relations between rulers and ruled at a time of declining empire.

Living standards of Americans have declined precipitously. Employers have ceased paying for pensions; reduced or eliminated health coverage; and reduced corporate taxes, thus lowering the quality of public education.

Over the past two decades, the wages and salaries of the majority of households have stagnated or declined; education and health expenses have bankrupted many and reduced university graduates to long-term debt peonage.

Access to home ownership for Americans under the age of forty-five has fallen dramatically from 24 percent in 2006 to 14 percent in 2017. At the same time, rents have skyrocketed, especially in large cities across the country, in most cases absorbing between a third and a half of monthly income.

Business elites and their housing experts divert attention to 'intergenerational' inequalities between pensioners and younger wage and salaried employees and away from rising income inequality between CEOs and both workers and pensioners, which has risen from 100 to 400 to one over the past three decades.

Mortality rates between the business elite and workers have widened as the wealthy live longer and healthier lives while workers experience declining life expectancy, the first time in American history! As the business elites' income from profits, dividends and interest increases they can afford high-cost private medical care that prolongs life, while millions of workers are prescribed opioids to 'reduce pain' that precipitate premature deaths.

Births are declining as a result of the high cost of medical care and the absence of day care and paid maternal/paternal leave. The most recent studies reveal that 2017 experienced the fewest babies in thirty years. The so-called 'economic recovery' following the financial collapse of 2008/9 was class based: real estate and financial elites received over two trillion dollars in bailouts while over three million working-class households were evicted by financial mortgage holders. The result was a rapid rise in homeless people, especially in cities with the highest rate of recovery from the crisis.

Homelessness and crowded, overpriced rentals and minimum wages are likely causes of declining birth rates and increasing mortality rates.

Imperialism Expands, Living Standards Fall

Unlike the earlier, post-World War II decades when overseas expansion was accompanied by low-cost higher education, accessible low-cost mortgages and increasing home ownership and employer-paid pensions and health coverage, over the past two decades imperial expansion has been based on forced reductions in living standards.

The empire grew and living standards declined because the capitalist class evaded trillions of taxable income via overseas tax havens, transfer pricing and tax exemptions. Moreover, capitalists received massive state subsidies for infrastructure, and cost-free transfers of publically funded technological innovations.

Imperial expansion is now based on the relocation overseas of multi-national manufacturing corporations to lower costs, increasing the percentage of low-wage service workers in the US. The decline of living standards for the majority is a result of the restructuring of the empire, the advent of the regressive tax system, the redistribution of state welfare transfers from public social spending to private finance and real estate subsidies and bailouts.

Conclusion

In the beginning, imperialism involved an explicit social contract with overseas expansion, shared profits, taxes and income exchanged for workers' political support for imperial overseas economic exploitation and resource plundering as well as service in the imperial armed forces.

The social contract was conditioned by a relative balance of power: unionized workers represented the majority of manufacturing, public sector and skilled workers. But this balance of power in class relations was based on the capacity of workers to engage in class struggle and influence the state. In other words, the entire imperialism and welfare configuration was based on a particular set of conditional relations intrinsic to the social pact.

Over time, imperial expansion faced overseas constraints from rising national and socialist opposition that forced or encouraged corporations to relocate capital abroad. Imperial rivals in Europe and Asia competed for overseas markets, forcing the US to increase productivity, lower costs, relocate abroad.

Unions divorced from the broader community movements and lacking an independent political movement, corrupted from within and committed to a disappearing social compact, declined in number and capacity to formulate a new combative post-social pact strategy. The capital class gained total control over class relations and, therefore, unilaterally set the terms of taxation, employment, living standards and, most importantly, state expenditure.

Imperial military and economic expenditures grew in direct proportions to the decline of social welfare payments. Rival power groups fought over the share of capitalist budgets and political-military priorities. Economic imperialists competed with or converged with military imperialists; free market neoliberals competed for overseas markets with national militarists pursuing territorial occupations, conquests, closed markets and submissive clients. Rival political power configurations competed over imperial priorities—powerful Zionist configurations sought regional wars for Israel, while multinationals looked to advance their political-economic expansion in Chinese, Indian and Southeast Asian markets.

Competing elite factions monopolized budgets, taxes and expenditures, driving living standards downward. Imperialist classes formed pacts—though only amongst themselves—but the quality and quantity of workers decreased through impoverished healthcare and educational systems. In contrast, elite offspring attended the best schools and secured the highest posts in government and the economy.

Privilege and power did not produce imperial triumphs. China harnessed educational programs and skilled workers to productive work. In contrast, privileged US university graduates sought employment in lucrative but parasitical financial services rather than in science, engineering or social welfare. Military academy graduates joined networks of 'commanders' who condoned sexual abusers, trained and promoted officers who sent missiles which targeted military bases and bombed population centers and trained naval captains specializing in own-ship collisions.

Ivy League graduates secured high government positions, leading the US into endless Middle East wars, multiplying adversaries, antagonizing allies and spending trillions on wars for Israel, not social welfare and higher wages for American workers. Oh yes, the *economy* is recovering ... only the people are doing worse.

Chapter 14

Global Empire and Internal Colonialism

The dynamic of contemporary US imperialism is built around two structural features: the drive toward global military expansion, conquest and occupation backed by the intensification of exploitation of domestic and pillage of the domestic economy.

In this essay we challenge the notion that overseas economic exploitation has transferred income to 'buy off' the domestic working and middle classes in the course of consolidating imperial hegemony. We argue that the empire is no longer based on robust overseas growth but rather that empire today is a costly and declining proposition. We then proceed to outline the costs of militarized imperialism and the relative economic decline of the empire.

We will then turn to analyzing how the US imperial state has resorted to financing the empire through its regressive tax, regulator and budgetary policies.

We will conclude by refuting the notion that the US turn to protectionism will revive the US economic empire.

Empire: Past and Present

From the end of World War II to the end of the Cold War, the US empire was driven by the wealth and power of the multinational corporations to extract and transfer profits to the domestic economy and sustain a 'trickle down' effect on a partially unionized force and fund its military guardians of global capital.

The US dominated world trade and led global investments, as well as being the leading force behind the creation of international financial institutions (the World Bank and IMF). Free trade and neoliberal doctrine flowed from the 'Washington Consensus', prescriptions designed to induce the denationalization and privatization of the targeted national economies around the world.

The US empire secured further global ascendance with the demise of the USSR, the absorption of the ex-Soviet client states and the pillage of the Russian economy. Washington declared that the world had become a 'unipolar state' in which the US was the sole dominant power, free to invade, conquer and exploit at will.

To sustain and further its global military dominance, Washington declared a worldwide 'war on terrorism' which accentuated the military dimensions of 'unipolarity'. The US empire was redefined through its military capacity to overthrow independent regimes, carry on multiple wars and simultaneously fund overseas economic conquests while maintaining dynamic domestic growth.

The empire builders pillaged Russia but failed to build a viable productive satellite. Instead they poured billions of dollars into expanding NATO to Russian borders. In contrast, Germany profitably incorporated the post-communist economies into the European Union.

The empire builders' unipolar vision led them to endless billion-dollar wars, which did not finance themselves and reduced the US global economic presence and source of profit. The empire's pursuit of a unipolar world, through global wars 'on terror', led to a highly militarized imperial state that greatly reduced US economic competitiveness and the exponential growth of commercial deficit.

In response to military demands for state financing, MNCs sought low-tax, cheap, high-profit overseas markets. The industrialization was accompanied by the financialization of the US economy.

The imperial state was a two-faced Janus: militarized foreign policy and financialized domestic policy. Military deficits and multiple and inconclusive wars led empire builders to make further demands on the economy.

Financialization led a trillion-dollar crisis in 2008/9 and a decade-long trillion-dollar bailout.

The empire was a cost not a benefit to the economic empire and few overseas 'partners' were willing or able to share the costs. The empire builders turned to intensifying the exploitation of the domestic/market, reallocating the federal budget and reducing taxes for the economic elite. The US redefined empire building as exploiting the domestic economy to militarize the empire.

Washington debated two parallel options: one based on further internationalizing the US economy hoping to regain markets and capital; the second option was turning the US into a 'fortress Americana' by creating walls around a protectionist state and preparing for a 'trade war'. Both options depended on lowering costs, concentrating wealth and reducing welfare.

President Obama opted for 'internationalization', linking economic and military imperialism. President Trump chose a protectionist-militarist strategy designed to bring overseas capital to the US domestic market by intimidating adversaries through military trade threats. Both approaches were basically premised on domestic colonialism.

The Dynamics of Internal Colonialism

The run-up to the financial crises of 2008/9 and the trillion-dollar bailout led to the pillage of the state and deepened the financialization of the economy. The large-scale transfer of profits from domestic manufacturing to overseas markets and to banking, real estate and insurance (FIRE) sectors contributed to the growing polarization of the economy and bargaining social inequalities.

These shifts in the economy were accompanied by regressive changes in the tax burden: the multinationals avoided hundreds of billions in taxes through overseas tax havens (*Financial Times*, 3/12/18, p. 1) and paid less domestic taxes as the effective tax rate declined (*Financial Times*, 3/12/18, p. 3).

National states competed to lower taxes for the elite, which led to reduced welfare spending; deregulation of the banking and energy sector led to the rise of speculative capital.

Global capital grew at the expense of the domestic economy; the growth of financial capital reduced the income of the working and middle class; costly imperial wars increased the commercial deficit; low-paid, temporary employment in the services became the norm.

Health and environmental conditions deteriorated. Empire builders intensified under development to finance a rising commercial deficit and a declining empire. Popular dissent grew.

The imperial state faced two choices: to further marginalize the majority or to turn toward a protectionist policy, which in effect sought to direct mass discontent toward outside economic and military competitors.

The Democrats sought to blame Russia, the Republicans pointed to China and the EU.

The election of Trump led to the adoption of a policy of deepening deregulation, increasing the concentration of wealth, massive tax reductions for MNCs and a trade war for local capital protectionist policy—plus a war policy to satisfy the ideological warlords.

The Obama regime's resort to military and financial imperialism based on internal colonialism had reached its limits; the Trump regime sought to externalize enemies —first and foremost directing its 'national imperialism' against China.

President Trump: China and the Commercial Deficit

The Trump regime backed by the Democrats sought to sustain a militarized imperialism by fabricating a Russian war threat in Syria, Ukraine, the UK (the poisoned spy caper) and the US elections.

Trump sought to avoid facing the impending failure of his trickle-down economic policy by accusing China of unfairly exploiting the US via one-sided trade, investment and technology relations—all leading to large trade deficits.

Contrary to Trump's view, the trade imbalance has everything to do with the perverse economic structure and policies of the US and the elites who created and rule it.

The US trade deficit is a result of MNCs moving to China and exporting back to the US. US exports from China account for nearly a third of the deficit. Washington appears unable or unwilling to attract the MNCs back to the US with generous tax incentives.

Second, the trade deficit is a result of growing military spending in multiple and continuing wars rather than increasing investment in export sectors. In contrast, China increases its public investments in high-growth export sectors that add value and secure new markets.

Third, the US restricts exports of high tech and military goods to further the interests of the warlord economy, leading to loss of markets and less ability to lower the deficits.

Fourth, the US restricts Chinese investment in sectors that could finance export industries able to rebalance trade, using the fake argument of 'national security'.

Fifth, US MNCs are allowed—and even incentivized by the state—to retain 2.5 trillion dollars abroad, thus reducing the capacity of the US to finance its export sector and balance trade with China (and the rest of the world).

Sixth, the US accuses Beijing of insisting that US corporations that invest in China transfer technology. But this is a win-win situation: US MNCs reap profits, China gains know-how. If the US invested these profits in constantly upgrading its technology it could continue to retain its export advantages and markets—and its profits.

In a word, China is not 'cheating'; it is learning and growing. It is now up to the US to do the same, instead of channeling the profits derived from the productive sector of the economy into the financial sector—into unproductive financial instruments or tax havens.

The US threat of a trade war against China will devastate US exports in technology, transport, agriculture and advanced industries while undermining domestic consumption.

The net result will be the reduction of employment, income and trade. The US will have to squeeze domestic income to sustain the primary of its military-financial elite—provoking greater domestic discontent.

One thing is clear: China will adapt to its global infrastructure investment and trade—it will survive a trade war with alternative partners.

Conclusion

US military and financial imperialism was a temporary, short-lived success based on the demise of the USSR and a mono-polar world, the launch of a global war on terror and the financial bubble. With the military rise of Russia and China's dynamic economic growth, these short-term advantages have disappeared and the vulnerability revealed. Trillion-dollar bank bail-outs and prolonged military losses have undercut whatever temporary advantages existed. The pillage of the domestic economy has deepened domestic discontent. Trump-style 'national' imperialism has increased profits but lost trade wars.

A speculative economy, plundered public treasury and militarized empire cannot restructure the economy, not even with trade war rhetoric and trillion-dollar tax handouts. Time is running out for President Trump: the economy is preparing to plunge and the voters are turning their backs.

Chapter 15

Immigration
Western Wars and Imperial Exploitation Uproot Millions

Immigration has become the dominant issue dividing Europe and the US, yet the main driver of immigration is overlooked: war. In this chapter we expand on this issue with a central focus on imperial wars as a fundamental cause—one of many that we cannot get into at this point—of the explosive growth of international migration and associated pressures on the US administration, in recent years. We then proceed by identifying the major countries affected by these imperial wars and the resulting forced migration flows, before showing how western powers have compelled economic and political refugees to follow the trail of corporate profit.

Imperial Wars and Mass Immigration

The US invasions of and wars in Afghanistan and Iraq uprooted several million people, destroying their lives, families, livelihood, housing and communities and undermining their security.

As a result, most victims faced a choice of resistance or flight. Millions chose to flee to the West since at least NATO countries would not bomb their residence in the US or Europe. Others who fled to neighbouring countries in the Middle East or to Latin America were persecuted or ended up in countries too poor to offer them employment or opportunities to earn a livelihood. Some Afghans fled to Pakistan or the Middle East but discovered that these regions too were subject to armed attack from the West.

Iraqis were devastated by the Western sanctions, invasion and occupation and fled to Europe and, to a lesser degree, the US, the Gulf states and Iran.

Libya, prior to the US-EU invasion, was a 'receiver' country, accepting and employing millions of Africans, providing them with citizenship and a decent livelihood. After the US-EU air and sea attack and the arming and financing of terrorist gangs, hundreds of thousands of sub-Saharan emigrants were forced to flee to Europe. Most crossed the Mediterranean to the West via Italy and Spain and headed toward precisely the affluent European countries that had savaged their lives in Libya.

The US-EU financed and armed client terrorist armies that assaulted the Syrian government and forced millions of Syrians to flee across the border to Lebanon, Turkey and Europe, causing the so-called 'immigration crises' and the rise of right-wing anti-immigrant parties. This led to divisions within the established social democratic and conservative parties, as sectors of the working class turned anti-immigrant.

Europe is reaping the consequences of its alliance with US militarized imperialism, with the US uprooting millions of people and the EU spending billions of euros to cover the cost of immigrants fleeing Western wars.

Most of the immigrants' welfare payments are no match for the losses incurred in their homeland. Their jobs, homes, schools and civic associations in the EU and US are far less valuable and accommodating than what they possessed in their original communities.

Economic Imperialism and Immigration in Latin America

From 1960, in the wake of the Cuban Revolution, to 2000, almost two decades into a 'new world order' and the neoliberal era of capitalist development, Nicaragua, El Salvador, Guatemala and Honduras, countries in the immediate backyard of US imperialism, engaged in a series of popular struggles for socioeconomic justice and political democracy—i.e. liberation from US imperialism in the form of military intervention and the invasion of US-based multinational corporations—forcing millions of Latin Americans to emigrate to the United States. Popular insurgencies on the verge of victory over landed oligarchs and multinational corporations were blocked by Washington spending billions of dollars on arming, training and advising the countries' military and paramilitary forces. Land reform was aborted; trade unionists were forced into exile and thousands of peasants fled the marauding terror campaigns.

US-backed oligarchic regimes forced millions of displaced and uprooted or unemployed and landless workers to flee to the US.

US-supported coups and dictators resulted in 50,000 refugees in Nicaragua, 80,000 in El Salvador and 200,000 in Guatemala. President Obama and Hillary Clinton supported a military coup in Honduras that overthrew liberal President Zelaya and led to the killing and wounding of thousands of peasant activists and human rights workers and the return of death squads, resulting in a new wave of immigrants to the US.

The US-promoted free trade agreement (NAFTA) drove hundreds of thousands of Mexican farmers into bankruptcy and low-wage maquiladoras; others were recruited by drug cartels, but the largest group was forced to emigrate across the Rio Grande.

The US 'Plan Colombia' launched by President Clinton established seven US military bases in Colombia and provided a billion dollars in military aid between 2001 and 2010. Plan Colombia, under US-backed President

Alvaro Uribe, doubled the size of the military, resulting in the assassination of over 200,000 peasants, trade union activists and human rights workers by Uribe-directed narco-death squads. Over two million farmers fled the countryside and migrated to the cities or across the border.

At a different level, US business secured low wages for hundreds of thousands of Latin Americans. Although they paid tax on these minimum wages, almost all agricultural and factory workers were without health insurance or benefits. In this context, immigration doubled profits, undermined collective bargains and lowered US wages. Unscrupulous US 'entrepreneurs' recruited immigrants into drugs, prostitution, the arms trade and money laundering.

As for the politicians in this context many of them exploited the immigration issue for political gain, blaming the immigrants for the decline of working class living standards distracting attention from the real source: wars, invasions, death squads and economic pillage.

Conclusion

The US overthrow of progressive leaders like Libyan president Gaddafi and Honduran president Zelaya and destruction of the lives of innumerable working people overseas saw millions forced to become immigrants. Iraq, Afghanistan, Syria, Colombia and Mexico witnessed the flight of millions of their population—all victims of US and EU wars. Washington and Brussels blamed the victims and accused the migrants of illegality and criminal conduct.

The West debates expulsion, arrest and jail instead of reparation for crimes against humanity and violations of international law.

To restrain immigration the first step would be to end imperial wars, withdraw troops and cease financing paramilitary and client terrorists. And the second would be to establish a long-term, multi-billion-dollar fund for reconstruction and recovery of the economies, markets and infrastructure they bombed.

The demise of the peace movement allowed the US and EU to launch and prolong serial wars which led to massive immigration—the so-called refugee crisis and the flight to Europe. There is a direct connection between the conversion of liberals and social democrats to war parties and the forced flight of immigrants to the EU.

The decline of the trade unions and, worse, their loss of militancy has led to the loss of solidarity with people living in the midst of imperial wars. Many workers in the imperialist countries have directed their ire to those 'below'—the immigrants—rather than to the imperialists who directed the wars that created the immigration problem.

Immigration, war, the demise of peace and workers' movements and parties of the left has led to the rise to power of militarists and neoliberals throughout the West. However, their anti-immigrant politics has provoked new contradictions within regimes between business elites and among popular movements in the EU and US. The elite and popular struggles can go in at least two directions: toward fascism or toward radical social democracy.

Chapter 16

Imperialists' Fear and Loathing ... of Being Colonized

For decades and longer, the United States and Europe lectured and encouraged countries in Latin America, Africa and Asia to welcome and accept foreign investment as the virtuous path to modernization, growth and prosperity.

With few notable exceptions, Western leaders and academics promoted unlimited flows of capital (and the outflows of profits). No section of the targeted economies was off-limits—agriculture, mining, manufacturers, utilities, transport and communication were to be 'modernized' through US and European ownership and control.

Third World leaders who abided by the 'open markets' doctrine and 'invited' foreign ownership—whether generals, bankers or landowners, whether dictators or elected by hook or by crook—were praised. Nationalism and nationalists were condemned as restricting the wheel of progress and blocking the 'march of history'.

To be fair, the Western regimes encouraged all countries to open their doors to capital flows—but of course only the imperial countries had the capital, technology and political power to do so.

Economists preached the doctrine of specialization in 'comparative advantage': for the West this meant investing in, profiting from and dominating markets; for the South it meant accepting low wages, a junior partnership role and dependent industries.

This system worked very well for countries in the West as long as they were the dominant power and shaped the markets, flows of capital and terms of exchange.

Nationalist leaders were condemned, sanctioned, ousted and demonized throughout the era of Anglo-American ascendancy.

In time and with effort, Third World countries began to follow another path—through revolution or reform, state direction or national entrepreneurs, they invested, innovated, borrowed and transformed their economies. Some, like China, began to successfully compete with Western powers for markets, minerals and technology.

Role Reversal: Imperial Washington Denounces China for Colonizing the Economy

As the US empire failed to out-compete China, not only in overseas markets but also in sectors of the domestic economy, local manufacturers relocated to China and Mexico or went bankrupt or merged or were acquired by foreign capital—notably Chinese.

Nationalism replaced neoliberalism and globalism among sectors of the ruling class, especially among political ideologies grouped around President Trump. The nationalists forged a national pluto-populist alliance, linking Wall Street, backward sectors of the capitalist class with displaced and under- and unemployed workers under the umbrella of 'protectionist rhetoric': massive business tax cuts and tariffs, quotas and taxes on European, Asian and North American competitors. Gone were Washington lectures on free markets and the virtues of globalization and multi-lateral trade agreements.

The new protectionism echoed the rhetoric of 18th and 19th-century America and the Great Depression-era Smoot-Hawley tariff. Earlier, the US claimed that tariffs were necessary to protect and foster so-called 'infant' industries; 21st-century protectionism claims it about 'national security', i.e. protecting against cross-oceanic (China) and cross-border (Canada, Mexico) mortal military threats … .

President Trump adopted the ideology of Third World national liberation governments to undermine its imperial competitors. Washington's ersatz 'nationalist' empire builders were assisted by their media allies, who spilled tons of ink attacking 'imperial' China's overseas investments for 'plundering' Africa, Latin America and Asia.

Washington projected an image of the US surrounded by enemies who were taking advantage of their privileged position to exploit a 'weak America'. President Trump transformed the nationalist slogans of Third World liberation into imperialist calls to 'Make America's Empire Strong'.

Third World nationalism is an ideology that aims to create domestic markets and industries in largely agro-mineral economies through public-private investment and state ownership, oversight, regulation and subsidy. Nationalism of declining empires is the ideology of authoritarian militarists and fascist regimes that can no longer compete in the market place.

But imperial countries in decline have several options:

1   They can adapt to the new realities by upgrading their economies, reducing overseas military commitments, reallocating budgets and investments and educating their labor force for productive activity.
2   They can form partnerships with emerging competitors via power sharing, innovations, joint ventures and multilateral trade agreements.
3   They can engage in trade wars and overseas military conquests or encircle emerging rivals through sanctions, tariffs and protectionist fiats.

Nostalgia for the past 'glory' of unipolarity, economic supremacy and unquestioned ideological superiority is a formula for losing wars and a Hobbesian world of all against the predator.

Conclusion

In the beginning a nationalist-populist revival can stimulate growth as rivals will appease the aggressor; the imperial classes will prosper through lower taxes; and the 'deplorables' may glory in the rhetoric of nationalism and the expectation that 'great things are coming'.

But tax gains mean bigger debts; appeaser nations in the face of perma-nent losses of vital exports will retaliate and succumb to the protectionist contagion. Imperial globalists will turn into nationalists.

Nationalists will also replace impotent neoliberal social democrats. Workers will turn to nationalists to recover their lost workplaces and neighborhood solidarity; nationalists will exploit downward mobility and appeal to images of past prosperity.

National plutocrats will turn to authoritarians who speak to popular grievances in order to deflect class antagonism. Nationalists will gain a popular audience in the face of a left that avoids, dismisses or rejects the shared values of local communities. Liberal and progressive support of overseas wars that increase the flow of immigrants alienates working- and middle-class taxpayers.

A declining empire will not die early.

The nationalist revival can revive an imperial last hurrah. A fear and loathing of being colonized is the driving force for imperial revival. The lies and hypocrisy that accompanied the older imperial claims of conquest in the name of 'defending Western values' no long works. A consequential opposition can only emerge if it links class and nationalist appeals to com-munity values and social solidarity.

Part IV

Geopolitics of Empire

Dis-Accumulation on a World Scale

Pillage, Plunder and Wealth

Over the past thirty years wealth has grown exponentially and has become increasingly concentrated, mostly in the hands and banks of the top 1 percent of income 'earners'. The concentration of wealth has continued through booms and busts of the real economy and financial and IT crises. Wealth has grown despite long-term economic recessions and stagnation because the so-called recovery programs imposed austerity on 80 percent of the households while transferring public revenues to the rich.

The so-called 'crisis of capitalism' has neither reversed nor prevented the emergence of an international class of billionaires who acquire, merge and invest in each other's activities. The growth of wealth has been accompanied by the pillage of accumulated profits from productive sectors that are stored as wealth rather than investment capital.

The dispossession of capital and its conversion to private wealth has led to the rapid expansion of the financial and real estate sectors. Capital accumulation of profits has been the source of private accumulation of wealth at the expense of wages, salaries, public welfare and state revenues.

The growth of private wealth at the expense of productive investments is a worldwide phenomenon that has been facilitated by an international network of banks, political leaders and 'regulators' centered in the United States and England.

The single most important aspect of private wealth accumulation on a world scale is criminal behaviour by the elites in multiple locations and involves the violation of multiple laws and regulations.

The Chain of Illegality: From Exploitation to the Pillage of the Nation's Wealth

The original source of private wealth is the exploitation by capital, with a small percentage of the profits reinvested in expanding production in the 'home market' or overseas. The bulk of the profits are transferred into financial networks that in turn illicitly channel the funds into overseas accounts.

The movement of profits 'overseas' takes multiple forms (transfer pricing, phony invoices, etc.) and they are primarily converted into private wealth. These 'international movements' of profits are largely composed of mega-thievery or plunder by political and business leaders from 'developing' countries. According to the *Financial Times* (17/11/14, p. 2), 'Up to $1 trillion is being taken out of developing countries every year through a web of corrupt activities involving anonymous shell companies that typically hide the identity of their true owners.'

The one trillion dollars of stolen profits and revenues from the developing countries (Africa, Asia, South America) are part of a corruption chain that is organized, managed and facilitated by the major financial institutions in the US and UK. According to a World Bank report in 2011, '70 percent of the biggest corruption cases between 1980 and 2010 involved anonymous shell companies. The US and the UK were among the jurisdictions most frequently used to incorporate legal entities that held proceeds of corruption' (*Financial Times*, 17/11/14, p. 2).

This process of plunder or pillage of developing countries feeds into rent seeking, conspicuous consumption and other non-productive activity in 'developed' countries or, more accurately, the imperialist states. The principal beneficiaries of the pillage of developing countries by the local elites are their counterparts in the top 1 percent of the imperial countries, who control, direct and manage the financial, real estate and luxury sectors of their economies.

The very same financial institutions in the imperial countries (and their related accountancy, legal and consultancy arms) facilitate the pillage of trillions from the developed countries to offshore sites, via massive tax evasion operations, hoarding wealth instead of investing profits or paying taxes to the public treasury.

Large-scale pillage and tax evasion depend on the central role of the financial sector at both ends of the world economy. This results in an 'imbalance of the economy'—the predominance of finance capital as the final arbiter on how profits are disposed.

The extremely narrow membership in the dominant financial sectors means that its growth will result in greater inequalities between classes. A disproportionate share of wealth will accrue to those who pillage the revenues and profits of the productive sector. As a result, so-called 'productive capitalists' hasten to join and lay claim to membership in the financial sector.

The links between 'productive' and 'fictitious' (or financial swindle) capital defy any attempt to find a progressive sector within the dominant classes. But efforts to enter the charmed circle of the dominant financial 1 percent are fraught with danger and risk because the financial sector has a highly dynamic and super-active capacity for swindles.

The entire process of decapitalizing the economy is underwritten in the US by the financial elite's controls over the executive branch of government, especially the regulatory and enforcement agencies—the Security Exchange Commission, the Treasury and Justice departments.

Financial institutions facilitate the inflow of trillions of dollars from the kleptocrats in developing countries as well as the outflow of trillions of dollars by multi-nationals to offshore tax havens. In both instances the banks are key instruments in the process of dis-accumulation of capital by dis-possessing nations and treasuries of revenues and productive investments.

The hoarding of MNC profits in offshore shell companies does not in any way prevent speculative activity and large scale swindles in the for-ex, equity and real estate markets. On the contrary, the boom in high-end real estate in London, New York and Paris, and the high growth of luxury goods sales, reflects the concentration of wealth in the top .01 percent, 0.1 percent and 1 percent. They are the beneficiaries of 'no risk' pillage of wealth in developing countries, receiving lucrative commissions and fees in laundering the illicit inflows of wealth and outflows by tax-dodging multinationals.

The Inverted Pyramid of Wealth

A small army of accountants, political fixers, corporate lawyers, publicists, financial scribblers, consultants and real estate promoters make up the next 15 percent of the beneficiaries of the pillage economies. The 30 percent below them comprises upper and lower middle classes who experience tenuous affluence subject to the economic shocks, market volatility and risks of downward mobility. In the bottom 30 percent, waged, salaried and small business classes experience declining incomes, downward mobility and rising risk of mortgage foreclosure, job losses and destitution.

Despite wide variations in the class structure between 'developing' neo-colonial and 'developed' imperial states, the top 1 percent across national boundaries has forged economic, personal, educational and social ties. They attend the same elite schools, own multiple private residences in similar high-end neighbourhoods and share private bankers, money launderers and financial advisors. Each elite group has its own national police and military security systems, as well as political influentials who also cooperate and collaborate to ensure impunity and defend the illegal financial flows for a cut of the wealth ... .

The investigatory authorities of each developed country tend to specialize in prosecuting rival financial institutions and banks, occasionally levying fines—never imprisonment—for the most egregious swindles that threaten the confidence of the defrauded investors.

Yet the basic structure of the pillage economy continues unaffected—in fact thrives—because the 'show' of oversight and judicial charges neutralizes public indignation and outrage.

The Decisive Role of Dis-Accumulation in the World Economy

While orthodox economists elaborate mathematical models that have no relationship to the operations, agencies and performance of the economy and ignore the real elite actors which operate the economy, leftist economists similarly operate with theoretical premises about capital, profits and capital accumulation, crises and stagnation that ignore the centrality of pillage, dis-accumulation and the dynamic growth of wealth by the international 1 percent.

The research center, the Capital Financial Integrity Group, provides a vast array of data documenting the trillion-dollar illicit financial flows that now dominate the world economy.

US MNCs have 'hoarded' over $1.5 trillion dollars in overseas shell companies, 'dead capital', to avoid taxes and speculate in stocks, bonds and real estate.

Mexico's ruling elite organizes massive illicit financial flows, mostly laundered by US banks, ranging from $91 billion in 2007 to $68.5 billion in 2010. The massive increase in illicit financial flows is greatly facilitated by the deregulation of the economy resulting from the North American Free Trade Agreement (NAFTA). Contrary to the view of most leftist critics the main beneficiaries of NAFTA are not Canadian mine owners or US agrobusiness or auto manufacturers but North American financial and real estate money launderers.

Between 1960 and 2010 the Brazilian 1 percent pillaged over $400 billion dollars. These illicit financial flows were laundered in New York, Miami, London, Switzerland and Montevideo. In recent years the rate of pillage has accelerated: between 2000 and 2012 illicit financial flows averaged $14.7 billion a year. And under the self-styled 'Worker's Party' (PT) regime of Lula Da Silva and Dilma Rousseff, $33.7 billion in illicit outflows were laundered annually—1.5 percent of GDP. Much of the pillage is carried out by private and public 'entrepreneurs' in the so-called 'dynamic' economic sectors of agro-minerals, energy and manufacturing via trade 'mispricing', import overpricing and export underpricing invoices.

According to a study published in the *Wall Street Journal* (10/15/12), China's elite's illicit financial flows top $225 billion a year—3 percent of national economic output. China's 1 percent, the business-political elite, finance their children's overseas private education, providing them with half-million-dollar condos. Illicit flows allow Chinese 'investors' to dominate the luxury real estate markets in Toronto, Vancouver, New York and London. They hoard funds in overseas shell companies. Chinese corporate kleptocrats are leaders in the drive to deregulate China's financial markets—to legalize the outflows.

The scale and scope of China's elite pillage has provoked popular outrage that threatens the entire capitalist structure, prompting a major anti-corruption campaign spearheaded by China's president Xi Jinping. Thousands of millionaire officials and business people have been jailed, causing a sharp decline in the sales of the world's luxury manufacturers.

India's capitalist kleptocrats have long played a major role in de-capitalizing the economy. According to the *Financial Times* (11/24/14, p. 3), the Indian elite's illicit financial flows totalled $343 billion dollars between 2002 and 2011. The Indian finance ministry immediately threw up a smoke screen on behalf of the 1 percent, claiming the Indian elite had only $1.46 billion in Swiss accounts. Most of India's wealthy have taken to holing up their illicit wealth in Dubai, Singapore, the Cayman and Virgin Islands as well as London.

India's neoliberal policies eased the illegal outflows. Massive corruption accompanied the privatization of public firms and the allocation of multi-billion-dollar assets such as mobile phones, coal fields and energy.

Indonesia, percentage-wise, is the leader in the outflow of illicit flows: fully 23 percent of annual output. The 1 percent elite of foreign and domestic capitalists plunders agriculture and natural resources such as timber and metals and dis-accumulates. Profits flow to foreign accounts in Tokyo, Hong Kong, Singapore, Sydney, Los Angeles, London and Amsterdam.

Ethiopia, with a per capita income of $365 dollars, is the site of vast pillage by its ruling elite. From 2000 to 2009, over $11.7 billion dollars in illicit financial flow was laundered, mostly by US banks. These outflows enriched the Ethiopian and US 1 percent and triggered famine for Ethiopia's 90 percent.

Conclusion

Illicit financial flows surpass the capital invested in productive activity. The process of dis-accumulation of capital through relocation is channelled to overseas shell corporations and private bank accounts and beyond into financial holdings and real estate. The accumulation of private wealth exceeds the sums invested in productive activity generating investments and wages. Massive perpetual tax evasion means higher regressive taxes on consumers (VAT) and wage and salaried workers, reductions in social services, and austerity budgets targeting food, family and fuel subsidies.

The past thirty years of deregulated capitalism and financial liberalization is a product of the financial takeover of state regulatory agencies. The signing of free trade agreements has provided the framework for large-scale, long-term illicit financial flows.

While illicit financial flows have financed some productive activities, the bulk has just vastly expanded the financial sector. The absorption of illicit flows by the financial elite has led to greater inequalities of wealth between the 1–10 percent and the rest of the workforce.

Illicit earnings via mega-swindles among the largest and most respected US and EU banks has curtailed the amount of capital that is available for production, profits, wages and taxes. The circuits of illicit capital flows militate against any form of long-term economic development—outside of the wealth-absorbing elites who control both the financial and political centers of decision-making.

The growth and ascendancy of financial elites that pillage public treasuries, resources and productive activity is the result of an eminently political process. The origins of deregulation, free trade and the promotion of illicit flows are all made possible by state authorities.

First and foremost, finance capital conquered state power—with the cooperation of 'productive capital'. The peaceful transition reflected the interlocking directorates between banks and industry, aided and abetted by public officials rotating between government and investment houses.

The entire African continent was pillaged by billionaire rulers, many former nationalist politicians (South Africa) and ex-guerilla and 'liberation leaders' (Angola, Mozambique, Guinea Bissau) in collaboration with US, EU, Chinese, Russian and Israeli oligarchs. Trillions of dollars were laundered by bankers in London, New York, Zurich, Tel Aviv and Paris. Growth of the commodity sector bolstered Africa's decade-long expanding GDP—and the mega-outflows of illicit earnings.

Worldwide, billionaires multiplied profits 'received' while wages, salaries, pensions and health coverage declined. Swindles multiplied as outflows accelerated in both directions. The higher the growth in China, India, Indonesia and South Korea, the bigger and more pervasive the corruption and outflows of wealth-led by 'communist' neoliberals in China, Indian 'free marketeers' and Russian 'economic reformers'.

The economic 'reforms' proposed by the World Bank and IMF freed the incipient political kleptocrats from controls and unleashed two-sided illicit financial flows—laundered funds from abroad and trillion-dollar offshore tax-dodging citadels. In the process illicit swindles dwarfed earnings from capital accumulation. Relations between capital and labor were framed by the organization and policies dictated by the directors and operators of the trillion-dollar financial networks based on the pillage of treasuries and the wealth of nations.

The center of China's growth is shifting from manufacturing and the exploitation of labor to real estate and 'financial services', as workers demand and secure double-digit increases in wages. The exploiters of labor have turned into predators to sack the national treasury. Under the pretext of 'stimulating' construction, real estate speculators in league with Communist Party officials absconded with over a trillion dollars between 2009 and 2014 (*Financial Times*, 28/11/14, p. 1).

Factories still produce, agro-business still exports, the paper value of high tech companies has risen to the high billions, but the ruling 1 percent of the system stand or fall with the illicit financial flows drawn from the pillage of treasuries. To replenish these treasuries, regimes insist on perpetual austerity for the 90 percent: greater pillage for the 1 percent, less public revenues for health care, which results in more epidemics. Fewer funds and less funding for pensions means later retirement: work till you die.

The plunder of the economy is accompanied by unending wars—because war contracts are a major source of illicit financial flows. Plundering oligarchs share with militarists a deep and abiding belief in the pillage of countries and destruction of productive resources. The one reinforces the other in an eternal embrace—defied only by insurgents who embrace a moral economy and proclaim the need for a total change: a new civilization.

Chapter 18

Washington's Two-Track Policy
Marines to Central America and Diplomats to Cuba

Everyone, from political pundits in Washington to the Pope in Rome, and including most journalists in the mass media and the alternative press, during Obama's presidency—especially in 2015—focused on US moves toward ending the economic blockade of Cuba and gradually opening diplomatic relations. Talk at the time was rife regarding a 'major shift' in US policy toward Latin America, with an emphasis on diplomacy and reconciliation. Even the most progressive commentators and journals ceased writing about US imperialism. However, there was also mounting evidence that Washington's negotiations with Cuba were merely one part of a two-track policy begun under Clinton's administration. Also there was clearly a major US build-up in Latin America, with increasing reliance on 'military platforms' designed to facilitate direct military interventions in strategic countries. Moreover, US policymakers were actively involved in promoting 'client' opposition parties, movements and personalities to destabilize independent governments, intent on re-imposing US domination.

In this essay we will start our discussion with the origins and unfolding of this 'two-track' policy, its current manifestations, and projections into the future. We will conclude by evaluating the possibilities of re-establishing US imperial domination in the region.

Origins of the Two-Track Policy

Washington's pursuit of a 'two-track policy', based on combining 'reformist policies' toward some political formations while working to overthrow other regimes and movements by force and military intervention, was practiced by the early Kennedy administration following the Cuban revolution. Kennedy announced a vast new economic program of aid, loans and investments—dubbed the 'Alliance for Progress'—to promote development and social reform in Latin American countries willing to align with the US. At the same time the Kennedy regime escalated US military aid and joint exercises in the region. Kennedy sponsored a large contingent of Special Forces—'Green Berets'—to engage in counter-insurgency warfare. The

Alliance for Progress was designed to counter the mass appeal of the social-revolutionary changes underway in Cuba with its own program of 'social reform'. While Kennedy was promoting watered-down reforms in Latin America, he launched the 'secret' CIA invasion of Cuba in 1961 ('Bay of Pigs') and the naval blockade in 1962, leading to the so-called 'missile crisis'. The two-track policy ended up sacrificing social reforms and strengthening military repression. By the mid-1970s the 'two tracks' became one. The US invaded the Dominican Republic in 1965. It backed a series of military coups throughout the region, effectively isolating Cuba. As a result, Latin America's workforce experienced nearly a quarter-century of declining living standards.

By the 1980s US client-dictators had lost their usefulness and Washington once again took up a dual strategy: On one track, the White House whole-heartedly backed their military-client rulers' neoliberal agendas and sponsored them as junior partners in Washington's regional hegemony. On the other track they promoted a shift to highly controlled electoral politics, which they described as a democratic transition', in order to 'decompress' mass social pressures against its military clients. Washington secured the introduction of elections and promoted client politicians willing to continue the neoliberal socioeconomic framework established by the military regimes.

By the turn of the new century, the cumulative grievances of thirty years of repressive rule, regressive neoliberal socioeconomic policies and the denationalization and privatization of the national patrimony had caused an explosion of mass social discontent. This led to the overthrow and electoral defeat of Washington's neoliberal client regimes.

Throughout most of Latin America, mass movements were demanding a break with US-centered 'integration' programs. Overt anti-imperialism grew and intensified. The period saw the emergence of center-left governments in Venezuela, Argentina, Ecuador, Bolivia, Brazil, Uruguay, Paraguay, Honduras and Nicaragua. Beyond the regime changes, world economic forces had altered: growing Asian markets, their demand for Latin American raw materials and the global rise of commodity prices helped to stimulate the development of Latin American-centered regional organizations—outside of Washington's control.

Washington was still embedded in its twenty-five-year single-track policy of backing civil-military authoritarian and imposing neoliberal policies and was unable to present a reform alternative in response to the anti-imperialist, center-left challenge to its dominance. Instead, Washington worked to reverse the new party-power configuration. Its overseas agencies—the Agency for International Development, the Drug Enforcement Agency—and embassies worked to destabilize the new governments in Bolivia, Ecuador, Venezuela, Paraguay and Honduras. The US 'single track' of intervention and destabilization failed throughout the first decade of the new century (with the exception of Honduras and Paraguay).

In the end Washington remained politically isolated. Its integration schemes were rejected. Its market share in Latin America declined. Washington not only lost its automatic majority in the Organization of American States (OAS) but became a distinct minority.

Washington's single-track policy of relying on the 'stick' and holding back on the 'carrot' was based on several considerations. The Bush and Obama regimes were deeply influenced by the US's twenty-five-year domination of the region (1975–2000) and the notion that the uprisings and political changes in Latin America in the subsequent decade were ephemeral, vulnerable and easily reversed. Moreover, Washington, accustomed to over a century of economic domination of markets, resources, policies and politics and took for granted that its hegemony was unalterable. The White House failed to recognize the power of China's growing share of the Latin American market. The State Department ignored the capacity of Latin American governments to integrate their markets and exclude the US.

US State Department officials never moved beyond the discredited neoliberal doctrine they had successfully promoted in the 1990s. The White House failed to adopt a *reformist* turn to counter the appeal of radical reformers like Hugo Chávez, the Venezuelan president. This was most evident in the Caribbean and the Andean countries where President Chávez launched his two 'alliances for progress': 'Petro-Caribe' (Venezuela's program of supplying cheap, heavily subsidized, fuel to poor Central American and Caribbean countries and heating oil to poor neighborhoods in the US) and 'ALBA' (Chávez' political-economic union of Andean states, plus Cuba and Nicaragua, designed to promote regional political solidarity and economic ties). Both programs were heavily financed by Caracas. Washington failed to come up with a successful alternative.

Unable to win diplomatically or in the 'battle of ideas', Washington resorted to the 'big stick' and sought to disrupt Venezuela's regional economic program rather than compete with Chávez' generous aid packages. The US's 'spoiler tactics' backfired. In 2009, the Obama regime backed a military coup in Honduras, ousting the elected liberal reformist president Zelaya and installed a bloody tyrant, a throwback to the 1970s when the US-backed Chilean coup brought General Pinochet to power. Secretary of State Hilary Clinton, in an act of pure political buffoonery, refused to call Zelaya's violent ouster a coup and moved swiftly to recognize the dictatorship. No other government backed the US on its Honduras policy. There was universal condemnation of the coup, highlighting Washington's isolation.

Washington tried repeatedly to use its card of hegemonic power but was roundly out-voted at regional meetings. At the Summit of the Americas in 2010, Latin American countries overrode US objections and voted to invite Cuba to its next meeting, defying a fifty-year-old US veto. The US was left alone in its opposition.

The position of Washington was further weakened by the decade-long commodity boom (spurred by China's voracious demand for agro-mineral products). The 'mega-cycle' undermined US Treasury and State Department's anticipation of a price collapse. In previous cycles, commodity 'busts' had forced center-left governments to run to the US-controlled International Monetary Fund (IMF) for highly conditional balance of payment loans, which the White House used to impose its neoliberal policies and political dominance. The 'mega-cycle' generated rising revenues and incomes. This gave the center-left governments enormous leverage to avoid the 'debt traps' and marginalize the IMF. This virtually eliminated US-imposed conditionality and allowed Latin governments to pursue populist-nationalist policies. These policies decreased poverty and unemployment. Washington played the 'crisis card' and lost. Nevertheless, Washington continued working with extreme right-wing opposition groups to destabilize the progressive governments, in the hope that 'come the crash', Washington's proxies would waltz right in and take over.

The Re-introduction of the Two-Track Policy

After a decade and a half of hard knocks, repeated failures of its 'big stick' policies, rejection of US-centered integration schemes and multiple resounding defeats of its client-politicians at the ballot box, Washington finally began to rethink its one-track policy and tentatively explore a limited two-track approach.

The two tracks, however, encompassed polarities clearly marked by the recent past. While the Obama regime opened negotiations and moved toward establishing relations with Cuba, it escalated the military threats toward Venezuela by absurdly labeling Caracas a 'national security threat to the US's.

Washington had woken up to the fact that its bellicose policy toward Cuba had been universally rejected and had left the US isolated from Latin America. The Obama regime decided to claim some reformist credentials by showcasing its opening to Cuba. The 'opening to Cuba' is really part of a wider policy of a more active political intervention in Latin America. Washington will take full advantage of the increased vulnerability of the center-left governments as the commodity mega-cycle comes to an end and prices collapse. It applauds the fiscal austerity program pursued by Dilma Rousseff's regime in Brazil. It wholeheartedly backs newly elected Tabaré Vázquez's 'Broad Front' regime in Uruguay with its free market policies and structural adjustment. It publicly supports Chilean president Bachelet's recent appointment of center-right, Christian Democrats to Cabinet posts to accommodate big business.

These changes within Latin America provide an opening for Washington to pursue a dual-track policy. On the one hand Washington is increasing political and economic pressure and intensifying its propaganda campaign against state-interventionist policies and regimes in the immediate period. On the other hand, the Pentagon is intensifying and escalating its presence in Central America and its immediate vicinity. The goal is ultimately to regain leverage over the military command in the rest of the South American continent.

The *Miami Herald* (5/10/15) reported that the Obama administration had sent 280 US marines to Central America without any specific mission or pretext. Coming so soon after the Summit of the Americas in Panama (April 10–11, 2015), this action had great symbolic importance. While the presence of Cuba at the Summit may have been hailed as a diplomatic victory for reconciliation within the Americas, the dispatch of hundreds of US marines to Central America suggests another scenario in the making.

Ironically, at the Summit meeting, the Secretary General of the Union of South American Nations, former Colombian president (1994–1998) Ernesto Samper, called for the US to remove all its military bases from Latin America, including Guantanamo: 'A good point in the new agenda of relations in Latin America would be the elimination of the US military bases.'

The point of the US 'opening' to Cuba is precisely to signal its greater involvement in Latin America, one that includes a return to more robust US military intervention. The strategic intent is to restore neoliberal client regimes, by ballots or bullets.

Conclusion

Washington's current adoption of a two-track policy is a cheap version of the John F. Kennedy policy of combining the velvet glove of the Alliance for Progress with the iron fist of the Green Berets. However, Obama offered little in the way of financial support for modernization and reform to complement his drive to restore neoliberal dominance.

After a decade and a half of political retreat, diplomatic isolation and relative loss of military leverage, the Obama regime has taken over six years to recognize the depth of its isolation. When Assistant Secretary for Western Hemisphere Affairs, Roberta Jacobson, claimed she was 'surprised and disappointed' when every Latin American country opposed Obama's claim that Venezuela represented a 'national security threat to the United States', she exposed just how ignorant and out of touch the State Department had become with regard to Washington's capacity to influence Latin America in support of its imperial agenda of intervention.

With the decline and retreat of the center-left, the Obama regime has been eager to exploit the two-track strategy. As long as the FARC president Santos peace talks in Colombia advance, Washington is likely to recalibrate its military presence in Colombia to emphasize its destabilization campaign against Venezuela. The State Department will increase diplomatic overtures to Bolivia. The National Endowment for Democracy will intensify its intervention in this year's Argentine elections.

Varied and changing circumstances dictate flexible tactics. Hovering over Washington's tactical shifts is an ominous strategic outlook directed toward increasing military leverage. As the peace negotiations between the Colombian government and FARC guerrillas advance toward an accord, the pretext for maintaining seven US military bases and several thousand US military and Special Forces troops diminishes. However, Colombian president Santos has given no indication that a peace agreement would be conditional on the withdrawal of US troops or the closing of its bases. In other words, the US Southern Command would retain a vital military platform and infrastructure capable of launching attacks against Venezuela, Ecuador, Central America and the Caribbean. With military bases throughout the region, in Colombia, Cuba (Guantanamo), Honduras (Soto Cano in Palmerola), Curacao, Aruba and Peru, Washington can quickly mobilize interventionary forces. Military ties with the armed forces of Uruguay, Paraguay and Chile ensure continued joint exercises and close co-ordination of so-called 'security' policies in the Southern Cone of Latin America. This strategy is specifically designed to prepare for internal repression against popular movements, whenever and wherever class struggle intensifies in Latin America. The two-track policy in force today plays out through political-diplomatic and military strategies.

In the immediate period throughout most of the region, Washington pursues a policy of political, diplomatic and economic intervention and pressure. The White House is counting on the right-wing swing of former center-left governments to facilitate the return to power of unabashedly neoliberal client regimes in future elections. This is especially true with regard to Brazil and Argentina.

This political-diplomatic track is evident in Washington's moves to re-establish relations with Bolivia and strengthen allies elsewhere in order to leverage favourable policies in Ecuador, Nicaragua and Cuba. Washington proposes offering diplomatic and trade agreements in exchange for a toning down of anti-imperialist criticism and weakening of 'Chávez era' programs of regional integration.

The two-track approach, as applied to Venezuela, has a more overt military component than elsewhere. Washington will continue to subsidize violent paramilitary border crossings from Colombia. It will continue to encourage domestic terrorist sabotage of the power grid and food distribution system. The strategic goal is to erode the electoral base of the Maduro government, in preparation for the legislative elections in the fall of 2015. When it comes to Venezuela, Washington is pursuing a four-step strategy:

1   Indirect violent intervention to erode the electoral support of the government
2   Large-scale financing of the electoral campaign of the legislative opposition to secure a majority in Congress
3   A massive media campaign in favour of a Congressional vote for a referendum impeaching the president
4   A large-scale financial, political and media campaign to secure a majority vote for impeachment by referendum.

In the likelihood of a close vote, the Pentagon would prepare a rapid military intervention with its domestic collaborators—seeking a 'Honduras-style' overthrow of Maduro.

The strategic and tactical weakness of the two-track policy is the absence of any sustained and comprehensive economic aid, trade and investment program that would attract and hold middle-class voters. Washington is counting more on the negative effects of the crisis to restore its neoliberal clients. The problem with this approach is that pro-US forces can only promise a return to orthodox austerity programs, reversing social and public welfare programs while making large-scale economic concessions to major foreign investors and bankers. The implementation of such regressive programs inevitably ignite and intensify class, community-based and ethnic conflicts.

The electoral transition strategy of the US is a temporary expedient given the highly unpopular economic policies, which it would surely implement. The complete absence of any significant US socioeconomic aid to cushion the adverse effects on working families means that US client-electoral victories will not last long. This is why and where the US strategic military build-up comes into play: the success of track one, the pursuit of political-diplomatic tactics, will inevitably polarize Latin American society and heighten prospects for class struggle. Washington hopes that it will have its political-military client-allies ready to respond with violent repression. Direct intervention and heightened domestic repression will come into play to secure US dominance.

The two-track strategy will, once again, evolve into a one-track strategy designed to return Latin America to a satellite region, ripe for pillage by extractive multinationals and financial speculators.

As we have seen over the past decade and a half, one-track policies lead to social upheavals. And the next time round the results may go far beyond progressive center-left regimes toward truly social-revolutionary governments!

Epilogue

US empire builders have demonstrated throughout the world their inability to intervene and produce stable, prosperous and productive client states (Iraq and Libya are prime examples). There is no reason to believe that, even if the US two-track policy leads to temporary electoral victories, Washington's efforts to restore dominance will succeed in Latin America, least of all because its strategy lacks any mechanism for economic aid and social reform that could maintain a pro-US elite in power. For example, how could the US possibly offset China's $50 billion aid package to Brazil—except through violence and repression.

It is important to understand how the rise of China, Russia, strong regional markets and new centers of finance have severely weakened efforts by client regimes to realign with the US. Military coups and free markets are no longer guaranteed formulas for success in Latin America. Their past failures are too recent to ignore.

Finally, the financialization of the US economy, what the International Monetary Fund itself describes as the negative impact of 'too much finance' (*Financial Times*, 5/13/15, p. 4), means that the US cannot allocate capital resources to develop productive activity in Latin America. The imperial state can only serve as a violent debt collector for its banks in the context of large-scale unemployment. Financial and extractive imperialism is a politico-economic cocktail for detonating social revolution on a continent-wide basis—far beyond the capacity of the US marines to prevent or suppress.

Chapter 19

The United States' Grand Strategy Toward China
Mistaken Assumptions and Prescriptions

> We will have a very strong (military) presence, very strong continued pos-
> ture throughout the region to back our commitments to our allies, to protect
> and work with our partners and to continue ensuring peace and stability in
> the region, as well as back our diplomacy vis-à-vis China on the South
> China Sea.
> David Shear, US Department of Defense's Assistant Secretary for Asian and
> Pacific Security Affairs

> [Indian president Modi] seals $22 billion of deals on China visit … China
> had already promised $20 billion of infrastructure investment during [Chi-
> nese president] Xi's visit to India last year.
> *Financial Times* (5/18/15, p. 4)

The Council on Foreign Relations, a highly influential imperial policy
forum, in May 2015 published a Special Report entitled 'Revising US
Grand Strategy Toward China'[1] co-authored by two of its Senior Fellows,
Robert Blackwill and Ashley Tellis, which proposes a re-orientation of US
policy toward China. The report proposes and outlines a policy for buttressing 'US primacy in Asia' and countering what they describe as 'the
dangers that China's geo-economic and military power pose to US national
interests in Asia and globally'. The report concludes by listing seven
recommendations that Washington should follow to re-assert regional
primacy.

The essay begins by discussing the basic fallacies, which include outdated
and dangerous presumptions about US power and presence in Asia today,
that underpin the report. It then proceeds with an analysis of the authors'
incoherent, contradictory and unrealistic prescriptions.

Mistaken Assumptions About Past and Present US Policies Toward China

Blackwill and Tellis (hereinafter B & T) start out with the preposterous
claim that contemporary US policy toward China has been driven by its

positive 'effort to "integrate" China into the liberal international order'. This is a gross misrepresentation of Washington's past and current efforts to subvert the Chinese communist government and undermine its state-directed transition to capitalism.

Ever since the end of the Second World War, and especially since the Chinese Civil War (1945–1949) that brought the Chinese Communist Party to power, the US has poured billions of dollars in military aid to the retreating Nationalist regime and to finance the bloody Korean War (1950–1953)—with the open goal of overthrowing the Chinese communist government. When US forces briefly reached the Chinese-Korean border, provoking a Chinese response, Washington threatened to unleash nuclear weapons on the Chinese. For the next two decades, the US maintained a naval and air embargo against the world's most populous state, an insane policy that was only reversed by President Nixon's re-establishment of diplomatic and commercial relations in 1973.

When the veteran Chinese leader, Deng Xiaoping, embarked on a state-managed transition to capitalism, Washington adopted a two-track policy of encouraging China's rulers to 'open their markets' to US multinational corporations while financing and backing pro-US liberal activists seeking to overthrow the communist government (culminating in, for example, the so-called Tiananmen Square Uprising), as well as secessionist Tibetan and Uyghur insurgencies in western China.

Far from trying 'to integrate China into the liberal international order', Washington attempted to replicate the decade-long chaotic and destructive 'transition to capitalism' that took place with the dissolution of the USSR under Mikhail Gorbachev. During the disastrous US-backed regime of Russian president Boris Yeltsin—the 'lost decade' (1990–1999)—living standards for the average citizen plunged 70 percent and Russia was transformed from an advanced superpower to a ravaged vassal state. Beijing's rulers took careful stock of the grotesque pillage of the former USSR and rejected US plans to replicate their 'Russian success' and integrate China as a vassal state within the international capitalist system.

Following the defeat of its Tiananmen Square proxies, Washington's sanctions and boycott policy was of no avail, failing to stop the massive influx of US multinational corporations into China. Its punitive measures had no impact on China's political stability and unprecedented economic growth.

Washington's policy supporting China's entry into the World Trade Organization encouraged China to open up to US investors, but US policymakers did not understand how the Chinese state's carefully calibrated mix of dependence on foreign capitalist investment and technology alongside the adoption and assimilation of this technology and the autonomous expansion of endogenous Chinese expertise would create a such a massive independent economic superpower.

Washington's strategy of penetration and conquest, dubbed by B & T as 'integration into the international order', ultimately failed, despite frequent attempts to undermine Chinese state regulations and controls on foreign capital. US efforts to subordinate ('integrate') China into its burgeoning Asian empire was unsuccessful.

During this period, China expanded into world markets, harnessing Western capital to its national goals. It borrowed and improved on US technology to develop a high-growth model, exceeding US growth rate by 600 percent!

For over two decades China grew exponentially, accumulating hundreds of billions of dollars in foreign reserves, while the US economy ran up monstrous trade deficits with Beijing. The US had embarked on a series of prolonged wars while converting its economy from productive to finance capitalism, and it needed to borrow vast sums from China in the form of sales of Treasury notes or face a major domestic financial crisis.

Although not noted by B & T, China was 'integrated' into the international economic order as a productive, creditor state, at the same time as the US was reduced to debtor status and lost its global economic primacy while pursuing unpopular wars in the Middle East.

It was not the failure of liberal US market policies that propelled China forward to primacy in Asia, as B & T argue in their essay, but rather the fact that Washington's multi-trillion-dollar wars in South Asia, the Middle East and North Africa and its wholesale conversion to Wall Street speculation caused the US to lose its primacy in Asia. B & T's claim that US 'market liberalism' helped China emerge as the economic superpower in Asia is a flimsy pretext for ignoring real causes and now prompting an even greater level of US militarism in the region. Unfortunately, their muddle-headed diagnoses and militarist proposals strongly influence the Obama administration's policy decisions.

Blackwill and Tellis's unwillingness to recognize China's peaceful rise to economic supremacy in Asia leads them to rely on a purely ideological construct to bolster their militaristic argument for intensifying 'the US naval and air presence in the South and East China Seas and accelerating the US ballistic-missile defense [sic] posture' in the Pacific. B & T's a priori ideological presumptions lead them to declare that 'China is a danger to US Asian interests', ignoring China's obvious vital national interests in having open and secure access to vital waterways leading to their Asian markets and sources of raw materials. At no point do B & T identify a single move implemented by China that has threatened the open seaways. Nor do they identify a single overt or covert threat by China toward the US. While B & T fantasize about China's military threats, they suffer a severe case of amnesia with regard to overt US attacks, invasions and occupations of China's Asian neighbors. Over a dozen such military assaults, which B & T conveniently omit to mention, have been launched by Washington in the region.

B & T's evocation of a 'China threat' is a crude ploy to justify further US military encirclement of China, in line with their policy recommendations. The US has recently dispatched B-1 bombers and surveillance planes to Australia and threatens to attack China's base and port construction on its offshore shoals and island territories. Equally ominous, US officials arrested a visiting Chinese academic attending a conference, claiming he was part of a plot stealing 'dual purpose' high-tech secrets.

Contradictions and Incoherence of B & T's Policy Recommendations

B & T's policy recommendations for securing US primacy in Asia are contradictory and incoherent. For example, they recommend that the US 'revitalize the economy' and promote 'robust growth' as a first priority, but then demand a 'substantial increase' in the enormous US military budget. They advocate limits on the sale of civilian technology (so-called 'dual' use) and the exclusion of China from US-sponsored Asian trade networks like the 'Trans-Pacific Partnership' (TPP).

Most experts openly acknowledge that the huge US ten-trillion-dollar military spending over the past two decades has destroyed any possibility for 'robust growth' of the US economy. B & T's recommendations for even more military spending can only make matters worse by diverting public and private capital away from economic growth. This is what undermines the United States strategic future in Asia!

B & T advise Washington 'to expand Asian trade networks' by excluding China ... the largest investment site and market for the leading '500' US multinational corporations! In fact, when Obama, in line with B & T's recommendations, loudly refused to participate in the Chinese-sponsored Asian Infrastructure Investment Bank (AIIB), all of the US's major Asian partners' except Japan ignored Washington and joined the AIIB! China is unquestionably the leading economic partner for all Asian countries and none of the bellicose rhetoric that B & T spout is going to erode those essential realities.

In fact, B & T's proposal to eliminate from ongoing trade with China so-called 'dual purpose' technological exports will further isolate the US from its much ballyhooed Asian partners, who are especially eager to 'add value' to their exports. In short, B & T's recommendations to US policymakers will guarantee anemic, not 'robust', growth.

Contrary to advancing US trade networks, B & T proposals are guided by a strictly military logic. They (and the Obama regime) propose the reinforcement of what they call the Indo-Pacific partnership via a 'build-up (of) the power-political capabilities of its friends and allies on China's periphery'. Whatever B & T meant by 'power-political capabilities', they certainly did not take into consideration India's drive for economic development and long-term, large-scale investment and trade agreements. In terms of trade and development deals, the meager results on the heels of Obama's recent visit to India demonstrate just how shallow the administration's policy towards the subcontinent really is.

The Indo-Chinese economic and development partnership far surpassed in size and scope any of the vacuous proposals put forward by B & T to the Obama administration. In mid-May 2015, Indian president Modi signed a twenty-two-billion-dollar business deal with China on top of the massive twenty-billion-dollar Chinese infrastructure investment agreement in 2014. Forty-two-billion dollars of Chinese investment and trade deals with India have pulled the rug out from under any Obama regime plans to enlist India into its anti-China campaign and military provocations. The reality of Indian-Chinese economic deals shows just how absurd B & T policy recommendations are.

President Modi put the nail in the coffin of B & T's 'US Grand Strategy toward China' in his final speech in China at the end of his most successful visit: 'I strongly believe that this century belongs to Asia'. Lest it be thought by any other Kissinger protégé (Blackwill is a Henry Kissinger Senior Fellow) that the deepening Indo-China relationship is a mere passing phenomenon, their agreements involve the most advanced sectors of their economies, including telecommunication and energy, as well as the development of a solar photovoltaic industrial park.

As for B & T's proposal to block 'dual use' technology transfers to China, the Indian government has openly rejected that line of unreason by calling on countries to accelerate technology transfers.

Together with the entire crowd of armchair warmongers at the Council on Foreign Relations (CFR), B & T have misread the most basic economic developments of our time. US economic growth is becoming increasingly dependent on large-scale, long-term foreign capital inflows from 'emerging economies'—especially China! Developing Asian nations accounted for 440 billion dollars in outward investment, greater than North America or Europe, as the largest source for foreign direct investment. China's 266 billion dollars accounted for most outgoing FDI from Asia.

China's importance as a source of investment can only expand, especially through its newly founded Asian Infrastructure Investment Bank and its plans to promote the multi-billion Silk Road linking Beijing through Central Asia to European markets. China's financial role is going to be crucial in the new BRICS (Brazil, Russia, India, China and South Africa) bank—developed to counter the IMF.

Nothing that the Obama regime and its advisers from the Council on Foreign Relations have proposed can possibly balance the rise of China, because their policies include the boycott of large-scale, long-term Chinese economic initiatives which Washington's 'allies' are eager to join. Virtually all have rushed to sign up with the AIIB, leaving a sour-faced Obama administration totally isolated. The Council on Foreign Relations' proposal for Obama to form anti-Chinese networks with its allies is pointless when such hostile networks are clearly not going to undermine their most lucrative economic deals with China.

After running through a laundry list of hostile policies toward China, based on a strategy of escalating military encirclement, B & T conclude their essay with a bizarre call for Washington to 'energize high-level diplomacy with Beijing' and do 'everything it can to avoid a confrontation with China'.

This piece of 'expert' idiocy could only have been written by a former lecturer from the Harvard Kennedy School.

Policies designed to surround China with US military installations and naval vessels threaten China's vital maritime routes. Measures to restrict the sale of 'dual use' (civilian) technology and efforts to build hostile regional networks and military partnerships are hardly conducive to energizing high-level diplomacy with Beijing. B & T's proposals and Obama's policies are designed to confront, provoke and undermine China. That is one very obvious reason why China pursues such favorable economic agreements with its neighbours.

B & T policy proposals are doomed to fail because the US has not and cannot match China's robust economic growth. Washington cannot compete with Beijing's open and flexible large-scale economic agreements with all Asian countries (except the US vassal, Japan).

Most Asian powers have rejected the ideological message peddled by the Obama administration that China is a danger. They see China as a partner, a source of capital and easy finance for vital projects without the onerous conditions that the US-controlled IMF imposes. They are not interested in big, wasteful spending on costly weapons systems pushed by US war industries, which have no productive value.

An Alternative 'Grand Strategy' Toward China

If one were to propose a realistic and reasonable 'Grand Strategy' one would have to start by shedding all the false assumptions and bellicose proposals put forward by the CFR and the authors of the report under review.

First and foremost, the US would have to give up its self-appointed role as global policeman, reallocate its bloated Pentagon budget to finance vital domestic economic development, while rebalancing the US economy away from Wall Street speculation in the FIRE (finance, insurance real estate) sector and toward producing goods, providing quality services and financing long-overdue infrastructure development projects.

Second, Washington would have to expand and promote long-term, large-scale exports of its advanced technology to compensate for the loss of low-value exports.

Third, it should join with China in its new infrastructure bank, securing contracts via aid packages; it should look at China's export of capital as an opportunity to improve the US's deteriorating infrastructure. Washington would need to increase and expand its cyber-technical ties with China via joint ventures. It would need to replace its military bases surrounding China with industrial parks, commercial ports and regional 'Silicon Valleys' and promote co-operative ventures that allow the US to ride the wave of Chinese dynamism. Since the US cannot (and should not) curtail or compete with China's growth it should join them and share it.

The US should not attempt to block China's growth and expansion; it should assist and share in its ascendancy, especially in the face of great global climate and energy challenges. Washington is much more likely to strengthen its Asian–Pacific partnership and succeed in its diplomacy if it replaces its military posturing with robust economic growth.

Note

1 Council on Foreign Relations (2015). 'Revising US Grand Strategy Toward China'. Council on Foreign Relations, New York.

Chapter 20

Re-mapping the Middle East

The US has spent several trillion dollars over the past two decades in the Middle East, North Africa and West Asia. US interventions, from Libya, South Sudan and Somalia across to Syria, Palestine, Iraq, Iran and Afghanistan, have resulted in enormous costs and dubious advances. The results are meager except in terms of suffering. The US has spread chaos and destruction throughout Libya and Syria but failed to incorporate either into an enlarged empire. The Middle Eastern wars, initiated at the behest of Israel, have rewarded Tel Aviv with a sense of invulnerability and a thirst for more while multiplying and unifying US adversaries.

Empires are not effectively enlarged through alliances with armed tribal, sectarian and separatist organizations. Empires allied with disparate, fractured and self-aggrandizing entities do not expand or strengthen their global power.

The US has waged war against Libya and lost the political leverage and economic resources it enjoyed during the Gaddafi regime. It intervened in Somalia, South Sudan and Syria and gained enclaves of warring, self-serving 'separatists' and subsidized mercenaries. The war in Afghanistan, the longest in US history, is an unmitigated military disaster. After seventeen years of warfare and occupation, the US is holed up in the walled enclaves of the capital, Kabul. Meanwhile, the puppet regime feeds on multi-billion-dollar monthly subsidies.

Iraq is a 'shared' imperial outpost—the result of fifteen years of military intervention. Kurdish clients, Sunni-Saudi warlords, Shia militia, Baghdad kleptocrats and US contractor-mercenaries compete for control and a larger piece of the pillage. Every square meter of contested territory has cost the US 500 million dollars and scores of casualties.

Iran remains forever under threat but retains its independence outside of the US-Saudi-Israeli orbit. The US geo-political map has been reduced to dubious alliances with Saudi Arabia and its micro-clients among the Emirate statelets—which are constantly fighting among themselves—and Israel, the 'client' that openly revels in leading its patron by the nose!

Compared to the period before the turn of the millennium, the US imperial map has shrunk and faces further retrenchment.

The US-NATO-EU Map

Russia has reduced and challenged the US pursuit of a unipolar global empire following the recovery of its sovereignty and economic growth after the disaster of the 1990s. With the ascent of President Putin, the US–EU empire lost their biggest and most lucrative client and source of naked pillage.

Nevertheless, the US retains its political clients in the Baltic, the Balkans and Eastern and Central European regimes. However, these clients are unruly and often eager to confront a nuclear-armed Russia, confident that US-NATO will intervene, in spite of the probability of being vaporized in a nuclear Armageddon.

Washington's efforts to recapture Russia and return it to vassalage have failed. Out of frustration Washington has resorted to a growing series of failed provocations and conflicts—between the US and the EU, within the US between Trump and the Democrats, and among the warlords controlling the Trump cabinet.

Germany has continued lucrative trade ties with Russia, despite US sanctions, underscoring the decline in US power to dictate policy to the European Union. The Democratic Party and the ultra-militaristic Clinton faction remained pathologically nostalgic for a return to the 1990s' Golden Age of Pillage (before Putin). Clinton's faction was fixated on the politics of revanchism. As a result they vigorously fought against candidate Donald Trump's campaign promises to pursue a new realistic understanding with Russia. The 'Russiagate' investigation is not merely a domestic electoral squabble led by hysterical 'liberals'. What is at stake is nothing less than a profound conflict over the remaking of the US global map. Trump recognized and accepted the re-emergence of Russia as a global power to be 'contained', while the Democrats campaigned to roll back reality, overthrow Putin and return to the robber baron orgies of the Clinton years. As a result of this ongoing strategic conflict, Washington is unable to develop a coherent global strategy, which in turn has further weakened US influence in the EU in Europe and elsewhere.

Nevertheless, the intense Democratic onslaught against Trump's initial foreign policy pronouncements regarding Russia succeeded in destroying his 'pivot to realism' and facilitated the rise of a fanatical militaristic faction within his cabinet, which intensified the anti-Russia policies of Clintonite Democrats. In less than a year, all of Trump's realist advisers and cabinet members were purged and replaced by militarists. Their hard-core confrontational anti-Russia policy has become the platform for launching a global military strategy based on vast increases in military spending, demands that EU nations increase their military budgets, and open opposition to an EU-centered military alliance, such as the one recently proposed by French president Emmanuel Macron.

Despite President Trump's campaign promises to 'pull back', the US has re-entered Afghanistan, Iraq and Syria in a big way. The Trump shift from global containment and realism to rollback and aggression against Russia and China has failed to secure a positive response from either past or present allies.

China has increased economic ties with the EU. Russia and the EU share strategic gas and oil trade ties. Domestically, the US military budget deepens the fiscal deficit and drastically threatens social spending. This creates a scenario of increasing US isolation, its futile aggression pitched against a dynamic and changing world.

Conclusion

The Trump remaking of the global empire has had uneven results, which are mostly negative from a strategic viewpoint.

The circumstances leading to new clients in Latin America is significant but has been more than countered by retreat in Asia, divisions in Europe, turmoil domestically and strategic incoherence.

Remaking global empires requires realism—the recognition of new power alignments, accommodation with allies and, above all, domestic political stability balancing economic interests and military commitments.

The key shift from realism toward a recovered Russia to militarization and confrontation has precipitated the breakdown of the US as a unified coherent leader of a global empire.

The US embraces prolonged losing wars in peripheral regions alongside destructive trade wars in strategic regions. It has budgeted vast sums on non-productive activities while impoverishing state and local governments via sweeping tax 'reforms' that favor oligarchs.

Global remapping now involves a volatile and impulsive US-driven empire incapable of succeeding, while emerging powers are immersed in regional power grabs.

There is no longer a coherent imperial empire controlling the fate of the globe. We live in a world of political maps centered on regional powers and unruly clients, while incompetent, gossip-mongering politicians in Washington compete with an arrogant, benighted President Trump and his fractured regime.

Chapter 21

The Offensive Against Venezuela

Venezuela today leads the anti-imperialist struggle in Latin America. This struggle, in the current form of the Bolivarian Revolution, according to President Maduro, can be traced back twenty-six years to the popular rebellion against the neoliberal policies of the Carlos Andrés Pérez government that produced the Caracazo (February 27–28, 1989)—the massacre by government security forces of at least 3,000 protesters. 'This was,' he noted (in a telephone conversation with the governor of the state Aragua), 'the beginning of the Bolivarian Revolution to escape the mistreatment [of the people], the pillaging and neocolonialism, [and] the false democracy' [of the republic] (*El Jorope*, 2/28/15). In a televised broadcast of around the same time, Maduro pointed out that, under the leadership of Hugo Chávez, Venezuela was the first country in the region to say 'no' to the concerted effort of imperialist forces to convert the countries of the region into 'colonies of the IMF' and to reject 'savage capitalism and neoliberalism'.

In this televised broadcast Maduro also alluded to the form that the anti-imperialist struggle would take under Chávez's leadership, that of the Bolivarian Revolution, or, as he had it, the miracle of the socialist revolution and the *misiones*—the social programs of the government's national executive.

The course of this open-ended and ongoing revolutionary process has been anything but smooth and far from consolidated—indeed, it is currently in jeopardy, assailed as it is by forces of opposition from both within and outside the country. The aim of this chapter is to elucidate some of the political dynamics of this revolutionary process and the efforts of the US imperialist state to derail it.

First, we outline some of the critical features of Chávez's political project to bring about, by means of the Bolivarian Revolution, what he described as 'the socialism of the 21st century', an antidote to both capitalism in its neoliberal form and US imperialism. Our main focus here is on the strategic response of the US to Chávez's political project and the political dynamics of class struggle associated with it.

Second, we trace the changes in the correlation of force in the class and anti-imperialist struggle subsequent to Chávez's death and the transition to the Madero regime. Our main concern here is to establish the diverse forms taken by the class struggle and US imperialism in this conjuncture and the conditions of a failed attempted coup against a democratically elected regime.

Chávez and the Anti-Imperialist Struggle

The Chávez years witnessed the thwarting of US efforts to restore client regimes in Latin America and the growth of anti-imperialist movements in the region. However, Colombia remained the lynchpin of US foreign policy in the region—with seven US military bases—and principal adversary of Chávez's anti-imperialist struggle.

The anti-imperialist struggle from the 1950s to the 1970s predominantly took the form of armed movements of national liberation, which combined anti-imperialist struggles with movements for revolutionary change in the direction of socialism. In the new century under Chávez's leadership the anti-imperialist struggle took the form of the Bolivarian Revolution, which involved mobilizing the resistance against imperialist exploitation, made tangible with two projects: (i) building a movement towards the socialism of the 21st century and (ii) pushing for Latin America's integration, which has taken various forms including UNASUR, CELA and ALBA, conceived and led by Hugo Chávez and excluding Washington.

Needless to say, both projects converted Chávez into US enemy number one in the region. In response Venezuela mobilized its power to deepen its commitment to Latin American-centered trade and diplomatic blocs.

With the defeat of US efforts to oust Chávez in 2002, considerable advances were made to further the Chávez project to socialize the economy and develop a comprehensive welfare state. In turning the society towards socialism, the government proposed to nationalize production, placing decisions in the hands of elected community councils; join the PWC in progressive extractivism using oil resources to reduce poverty; and promoting ALBA as a counterweight to the US-dominated OAS.

The approach adopted by Chávez to bring about 21st-century socialism was what might be termed 'progressive extractivism', or even the 'new developmentalism' based on a post-Washington consensus on the need for a inclusive development, an approach focused on reducing poverty through the use of oil rents and promoting forms of social ownership. This strategy, considered by some economists as the 'new developmentalism', points to the need to bring the state back into the development process and increase social expenditures as a more inclusive form of economic growth. This strategy of 'progressive extractivism' was also pursued in Bolivia and Ecuador. In Venezuela, however, the government went much further, moving beyond the institutional pillars of the new developmentalism by redistributing the proceeds, socialising the means of production and purporting to put the economy in the hands of the workers. This approach took the form of nationalizing enterprises as a first step. The second step would involve instituting communal councils where decisions regarding production and marketing would be made at the local level—development from below, it could be argued.

Maduro and US Imperialism

Over the past few years Venezuela has been in a state of permanent and worsening crisis, reflected in conditions of hyper-inflation, economic stagnation and scarcity of basic consumer goods. Although the crisis has been exacerbated by policy measures (such as devaluation) that the government was forced to take in order to deal with a serious external imbalance, the major reason for the crisis was the fall in the world price for oil, the source of 95 percent of the country's export and fiscal revenues for financing its social programs. Equally important, the crisis has resulted from a concerted strategy of economic and political destabilisation engineered by the US imperial state. Acting through local supermarket owners and distributers organizing large-scale hoarding, Washington created a scarcity of products needed to meet the basic needs of the population. This resulted in increased prices and then hyper-inflation that has eroded the living standards of the population and undermined the poverty-reduction impact of the government's progressive social policies. The economic crisis created conditions for two coups, including the failed attempt in February 2015 (see discussion below).

The crisis is also a result of serious imbalances in the economy, to some extent provoked by the destabilizing efforts of the US but also because of structural contradictions in the economic model, including the reliance on extractivism and oil rents. Up to 95 percent of exports take the form of oil, exposing Venezuela to what has been described as a 'resource curse', distorting the exchange rate and placing enormous pressures on non-petroleum exporters. When the world price of oil fell, the problems inherent in extractivism as a development strategy became evident. The US took advantage of this vulnerability by pressuring Saudi Arabia not to cut back and indeed to increase production, placing enormous pressures on the economies of the US's main enemies: Russia, Iran and Venezuela. Oil price manipulation became a weapon in the Venezuelan class war.

The US Strategy Versus Maduro

The US has escalated its efforts to overthrow the government using all the mechanisms at its disposal, including violent street mobs, the so-called *guarimbas,* as well as the mobilization of large retailers to provoke artificial shortages. With the aid of local and international mass media and corporate-funded NGOs, it accuses the Maduro government of being 'authoritarian'. Self-styled human rights groups have launched a virulent propaganda campaign against the government for jailing oppositionists who have been exposed as plotting terrorist activity and military coup oppositionists like the mayor of Caracas Antonio Ledesma, who, it was revealed, signed a document endorsing a coup programmed for February 2015. The staged propaganda campaign is designed to take advantage of the crisis to discredit the government by exaggerating the deterioration and labeling the government as incompetent.

The US propaganda campaign has not worked in the region, where it is the US that is isolated—its actions almost universally denounced. The formation of a new political bloc inclusive of all governments in the region with the exception of the two imperial powers, the US and Canada, has rejected Washington's intervention and the anti-Venezuelan propaganda of the mass media—the BBC, NYT, WP.

All countries in the region and non-aligned countries beyond—the group is now well over a hundred—and organizations such as CARICOM have supported and continue to support the Maduro government in diverse international forums against the transparent efforts of the US government to wield its formidable state power. Unfortunately, none of this appears in the North American mass media, which continue to present Venezuela's actions in defense of the constitutional order as undemocratic ... as constituting a threat to the security of the region and thus to the US.

Anatomy of a Failed Coup (February 2015)[1]

February 22, 2015, saw a serious attempt to provoke a coup in the context of Operation Jericó, a US operation supported by Germany, Canada, Israel and the UK.

The plan for this operation kicked in on February 12, 2015. A plane owned by Academi (formerly Blackwater), disguised by the insignia of the armed forces of Venezuela, would bomb the presidential palace in Caracas and kill President Nicolas Maduro. The conspirators planned to put into power former congressional deputy Maria Corina Machado and seek the support of several former Latin American presidents who would acclaim the necessity and legitimacy of the coup as an act of restoring democracy.

President Obama had issued a clear warning. He put it in writing in his new defense doctrine (National Security Strategy): 'We are on the side of citizens whose full exercise of democracy is in danger, as in the case of Venezuelans.' In reality, Venezuela, since the adoption of the 1999 Constitution, is one of the most democratic states in the world. Obama's bellicose rhetoric presaged a worst-case scenario in terms of US government attempts to impede Venezuela's march along the road to national independence and the redistribution of national wealth—toward a socialism of the 21st century. By February 6, 2015, Washington was in the process of finalizing its plans for the overthrow of Venezuela's democratic institutions. The coup was planned for February 12.

Operation Jericho had the oversight of the National Security Council, under the responsibility of Ricardo Zuñiga. This 'diplomat' is the grandson of another Ricardo Zuñiga, president of the National Party of Honduras, who organized the military coups of 1963 and 1972 on behalf of General López Arellano. The Ricardo Zuñiga who now works in the White House directed the CIA station in Havana 2009–2011, where he recruited agents and funded a feeble opposition to Fidel Castro.

In such operations, Washington strives not to appear involved in the events that it leads. The CIA organizes and directs a coup through supposedly 'nongovernmental' organizations or 'civil society': the NED (National Endowment for Democracy) and its two tentacles on the right and left, the International Republican Institute (IRI) and the National Democratic Institute (NDI); Freedom House and the International Center for Non-Profit Law. Moreover, the US always uses its domestic clients as contractors in organizing or conducting certain aspects of the coup. This time at least Germany was an active participant, charged with ensuring the protection of citizens of NATO countries during the coup. As for Canada, an avid supporter of Obama's campaign against Venezuela, it was assigned control over Caracas International Airport. Israel was put in charge of ensuring the murder of several Chavista personalities, while the UK was put in charge of propaganda for the coup—putting a 'democratic' spin on it. Finally, the US government planned to mobilize its political networks in securing recognition of the coup: in Washington, Senator Marco Rubio; in Chile, former president Sebastián Piñera; in Colombia, former president Álvaro Uribe Vélez; in Mexico, former presidents Felipe Calderon and Vicente Fox; and in Spain, the former prime minister José María Aznar.

To justify the planned coup, the White House encouraged large Venezuelan companies to hoard their store of staples and sabotage the economy. The non-distribution of these products was intended to cause large queues at the shops followed by the outbreak of riots prompted by provocateurs infiltrated among disgruntled consumers. But the maneuver failed because, despite the artificially induced scarcity during January and February and the queues at the shops, Venezuelans did not riot or attack the shops as was hoped.

To strengthen the planned economic sabotage, on December 18, 2014, President Obama signed a law imposing sanctions against Venezuela and several of its leaders. Officially Washington said it wanted to punish the persons responsible for the 'repression' of student demonstrations. But in actual fact, since the beginning of the year Washington had been paying a salary—four times the average income of Venezuelans—to gang members to engage them in assaulting the police. The pseudo student riot led to the killing of 43 people, mostly police and regime supporters, and spread terror in the streets of Caracas.

The military action was put under the supervision of General Thomas W. Geary, from SOUTHCOM headquarters in Miami, and Rebecca Chávez, from the Pentagon. The actual military operation was subcontracted to Academi (formerly Blackwater), currently administered by Admiral Bobby R. Inman (former head of the NSA) and John Ashcroft (former Attorney General of the Bush administration).

According to this part of the plan, a Super Tucano military aircraft, with the registration N314TG, purchased by Academi in Virginia in 2008, was to be used. The plane, to be falsely given the insignia of the armed forces of Venezuela, would bomb the Miraflores presidential palace and other targets such as the headquarters of the Ministry of Defense, the intelligence directorate and the headquarters of Telesur, a multinational television channel created by the ALBA. The plane was parked in Colombia, the headquarters of the coup-makers, who were installed in the US embassy in Bogota with the participation of US ambassador Kevin Whitaker and his deputy, Benjamin Ziff.

Several senior officers, active and retired, had prepared a pre-recorded message to the nation announcing that they had seized power to restore order in the country. They were also expected to underwrite the Transition Plan, drafted by the Department of State and published on the morning of February 12, 2015 in *El Nacional*. The plan included the formation of a new government led by former deputy Maria Corina Machado, president of Súmate, the association that organized and lost the recall referendum against President Hugo Chávez in 2004. Machado's funds came from the National Endowment for Democracy. Maria Corina Machado was received with honours by President George W. Bush in the Oval Bureau of the White House on March 21, 2005. After being elected in 2011 as a representative from the State of Miranda, on March 21, 2014, Maria Corina Machado appeared before the Organization of American States as head of the delegation of Panama to the continental forum and was immediately dismissed from her post as deputy for having violated articles 149 and 191 of the Constitution of Venezuela.

Unfortunately for the coup-makers, Venezuelan military intelligence had under surveillance individuals suspected of having fomented a previous plot to assassinate President Maduro. In May 2014, the prosecutor of Caracas accused María Corina Machado, Governor Henrique Salas Romer, the former diplomat Diego Arria, the lawyer Gustavo Tarre Birceño, the banker Eligio Cedeño and businessman Pedro M. Burelli of an active role in a planned coup. By tracking the conspirators, military intelligence discovered Operation Jericho. On the night of February 11, the main leaders of the conspiracy and an agent of the Israeli Mossad were arrested and aerial protection of the Venezuelan capital was reinforced. Others involved were arrested on February 12. On the 20th, the confessions of those arrested led to the arrest of another accomplice, the mayor of Caracas, Antonio Ledezma, a liaison officer with Israel. The coup had totally unravelled (but not without attempts by the White House to accuse the Maduro regime of actions to subvert democracy).

Obama's Imperialist Offensive Against Venezuela

When the plan of the 'opposition' forces to overthrow the democratically elected Maduro government, by diverse measures including destabilizing the economy, was discovered and made public, the *Washington Post* (February 23) and *New York Times* (February 14) published editorials denouncing the discovered 'conspiracy' as a 'distraction' engineered by the government to divert attention from the growing economic crisis and calling the government's response (i.e. the arrest of the plotters) 'repressive'. They called on the government to resign and supported the 'coupster' opposition's call for Maduro to step down in favour of a regime that would implement the 'transition government program' created and presented by the clearly undemocratic opposition forces.

On March 9, 2015, Obama signed an executive order declaring Venezuela to be a threat to national security and US foreign policy. Why did Obama make this claim, declare a 'national emergency', assume executive prerogatives and decree sanctions against top Venezuelan officials in charge of national security, at this time?

First, the White House presented no evidence whatsoever because there was nothing to present! There were no Venezuelan missiles, fighter planes, warships, Special Forces, secret agents or military bases poised to attack US domestic facilities or its overseas installations. On the other hand, the US has warships in the Caribbean, seven military bases just across the border in Colombia manned by over two thousand US Special Forces, and Air Force bases in Central America. And Washington has financed proxy political and military operations in Venezuela intended to overthrow the legally constituted and elected government.

Obama's claims resemble a ploy that totalitarian and imperialist rulers frequently use: accusing their imminent victims of the crimes they are preparing to perpetrate against them. No country or leader, friend or foe, has supported Obama's accusations against Venezuela. His charge that Venezuela represents a 'threat' to US foreign policy requires clarification. First, which elements of US foreign policy are threatened? Venezuela has successfully proposed and supported several regional integration organizations, which are voluntarily supported by their fellow Latin American and Caribbean members. These regional organizations replace, in large part, US-dominated structures that served Washington's imperial interests. In other words, Venezuela supports alternative diplomatic and economic organizations that its members believe will better serve their economic and political interests than those promoted by the Obama regime. Petrocaribe, a Central American and Caribbean association of countries supported by Venezuela, addresses the development needs of their members better than US-dominated organizations like the Organization of American States or the so-called 'Caribbean Initiative'. And the same is true of Venezuela's support of CELAC (Community of Latin American and Caribbean States) and UNASUR (Union of South American Nations). These are Latin American organizations that exclude the dominating presence of the US and Canada and are designed to promote greater regional independence. Both CELAC and UNASUR, together with the G77 within the UN and China, denounced the Obama government's decree regarding Venezuela as a threat to regional and national security.

Obama's charge that Venezuela represents a threat to US foreign policy was an accusation directed at all governments that have freely chosen to abandon US-centered organizations and reject US hegemony. In other words, what aroused Obama's ire and motivates his aggressive threats toward Venezuela was Caracas's political leadership in challenging US's imperialist foreign policy.

Venezuela does not have military bases in other parts of Latin America nor has it invaded, occupied or sponsored military coups in other Latin American countries like Obama and his predecessors. Venezuela condemned the US invasion of Haiti, the US-supported military coups in Honduras (2009), Venezuela (2002, 2014, 2015), Bolivia (2008) and Ecuador (2010). Evidently, Obama's 'emergency' decree and sanctions against Venezuela were directed at maintaining unchallenged US imperial supremacy in Latin America and degrading Venezuela's independent, democratic foreign policy. So, to understand Obama's policy toward Venezuela we have to analyze why he chose overt, unilateral bellicose threats at this time?

Obama's War Threat a Response to Political Failure

The principal reason why Obama intervened so directly in Venezuelan politics is that his other efforts to oust the Maduro government had failed. In 2013, Obama relied on US financing of an opposition presidential candidate, Henrique Capriles, to oust the incumbent. President Maduro defeated Obama's choice and derailed Washington's 'via electoral' to regime change. Subsequently, Obama attempted to boycott and discredit the Venezuelan voting process via an international smear campaign. The White House boycott lasted six months and received no support in Latin America or from the European Union, since scores of international election observers, ranging from former president James Carter to representatives of the Organization of American States, certified the outcome.

In 2014, the Obama regime backed violent large-scale riots that left 43 persons dead and scores wounded (most victims were pro-government civilians and law enforcement officers) and millions of dollars' worth of damage to public and private property, including power plants and clinics. Scores of vandals and right-wing terrorists were arrested, including Harvard-educated terrorist Leopoldo Lopez. However, the Maduro government released most of the saboteurs in a gesture of reconciliation. Obama, on his part, escalated the terror campaign of internal violence. He recycled his operatives and, in February 2015, backed a new coup. Several US embassy personnel (the US had at least 100 stationed in their embassy) turned out to be intelligence operatives using diplomatic cover to infiltrate and recruit Venezuelan military officials to plot the overthrow of the elected government and assassinate President Maduro by bombing the presidential palace.

But President Maduro and his national security team discovered the coup plot and arrested both its military and political leaders, including the mayor of Caracas. Obama, furious at having lost major internal assets and proxies, turned to his last resort: the threat of direct US military intervention.

The Purpose of Obama's 'national Emergency' Declaration

Obama's declaration of a national security emergency has psychological, political and military objectives. His bellicose posture was designed to bolster the spirit of his jailed and demoralized operatives and let them know that they still have US support. To that end, Obama demanded that President Maduro free the terrorist leaders. Washington's sanctions were primarily directed against the Venezuelan security officials who upheld the constitution and arrested Obama's hired thugs. The terrorists in their prison cells can console themselves with the thought that, while they serve 'hard time' for being US shock troops and puppets, their prosecutors will be denied visas by President Obama and can no longer visit Disneyland or shop in Miami ... . Such are the consequences of the current US 'sanctions' in the eyes of a highly critical Latin America.

The second goal of Obama's threat is to test the response of the Venezuelan and Latin American governments. The Pentagon and CIA seek to gauge how Venezuela's military, intelligence and civilian leaders will deal with this new challenge in order to identify the weak links in the chain of command, i.e. those officials who wil run for cover, cower or seek to conciliate by giving in to Obama's demands.

It should be remembered that during the US-backed April 2002 coup, many self-styled 'Chavista revolutionaries' went into hiding, some holing up in embassies. In addition, several military officials defected and a dozen politicians curried favour with the coup leaders, until the tide turned and over a million ordinary Venezuelans, including slum dwellers, marched to surround the presidential palace and, with the backing of loyalist paratroopers, ousted the golpistas (coup-makers) and freed their president. Only then did the fair-weather Chavistas come out from under their beds to celebrate the restoration of Hugo Chávez and the return of democracy.

In other words, Obama's bellicose posture is part of a 'war of nerves' to test the resistance, determination and loyalty of government officials when their positions are threatened, US bank accounts frozen, visas denied and access to Disneyland cut. Obama is putting the Venezuelan government on notice: a warning this time, an invasion next time.

The White House's openly thuggish rhetoric is also intended to test the degree of opposition in Latin America—and the kind of support Washington might expect in Latin America and elsewhere.

Cuba responded forcefully with unconditional support for Venezuela. Ecuador, Bolivia, Nicaragua and Argentina repudiated Obama's imperial threats. The European Union did not adopt the US sanctions, although the European Parliament did echo Obama's demand for the jailed terrorists to be freed. Initially, Brazil, Uruguay, Chile and Mexico backed neither the US nor the Venezuelan government. Uruguayan vice president Raul Sendic was the only official in Latin America to deny US intervention. However, on March 16 at an emergency meeting of UNASUR in Quito, Ecuador, the foreign ministers of Argentina, Bolivia, Chile, Colombia, Ecuador, Guyana, Peru, Surinam, Uruguay and Venezuela unanimously denounced US sanctions and military intervention.

But what was most important was that President Maduro stood firm. He declared a national emergency and asked for special powers. He called for two weeks of nationwide military exercises involving 100,000 soldiers, beginning March 14. He made it clear to the Pentagon and White House that a US invasion would meet resistance. That confronting millions of Venezuelan freedom fighters would not be a 'cake walk'—that there would be US casualties, body bags and new US widows and orphans to mourn Obama's imperial schemes.

Conclusion

Although his coup operatives failed in two consecutive years, Obama neither prepared an immediate invasion nor gave up on regime change. His militarist posture was designed to polarize Latin America: to divide and weaken the regional organizations; to separate the so-called 'moderates' in Mercosur (Brazil/Uruguay/Paraguay) from Venezuela and Argentina. Despite his failures, Obama pressed on, activating opposition to Venezuelan security policies among the Chilean, Peruvian, Mexican, and Colombian neoliberal regimes.

Washington built pressure externally and prepared for a new round of violent unrest internally to provoke a robust government response. In other words, Obama's military invasion followed the well-rehearsed scenario of 'humanitarian intervention' orchestrated in Yugoslavia, Libya and Syria—with such disastrous consequences for the people of those countries. At the time, Obama lacked the international political support from Europe and Latin America that might have provided the fig leaf of a multilateral coalition and he had lost his key internal operatives. He could not risk a bloody unilateral US invasion and prolonged war in the immediate future, but even so he inexorably moved in that direction.

Obama seized executive prerogatives to attack Venezuela. He alerted and mobilized US combat forces in the region. He understood that his current teams of operatives in Venezuela had demonstrated that they were incapable of winning elections or seizing power without major US military backing. He subsequently engaged in psychological as well as physical warfare, designed to run down the Venezuelan economy, intimidate the faint-hearted, and exhaust and weaken the militants through constant threats and ever-widening sanctions.

The Maduro government accepted the challenge. Maduro mobilized the people and the armed forces: his democratically elected regime did not surrender. The national resistance were fighting in their own country for their own future. They fought an invading imperial power. They represented millions and they had a 'world to lose' should the *squalidos* (the domestic fifth column) ever take power: if not their lives, their livelihoods, their dignity and their legacy as a free and independent people.

Note

1   This section is a summary and paraphrase of the analysis made by Thierry Meyssan (2015). Our translation.

Chapter 22

The Sun Never Sets but a Mote Remains

Post-colonial empires are complex organizations. They are organized on a multi-tiered basis, ranging from relative autonomous national and regional allies to subservient vassal states, with variations in between.

In the contemporary period, an empire does not operate as a stable global structure, though it may aspire and strive to do so. Though the US is the major imperial power, it does not dominate all leading global political-economic and military powers, like Russia and China.

Imperial powers have, like the US, established regional satellites but suffered setbacks and retreats from independent local economic and political challengers.

Empire is not a fixed structure embedded in military or economic institutions. It contains sets of competing forces and relations that can change over time and according to circumstances. Moreover, imperial followers do not pursue fixed lines of submission. For example, submission to general agreements on ideology, military doctrine and economic policy that are identified with imperial rulers can also find vassal states pursuing links with non-imperial markets, investors and exporters.

If the global world of imperial powers is complex and indeterminate to some degree, so is the internal political, economic, administrative and military structure of the imperial state. The imperial political apparatus has become heavily weighted on the side of security institutions, over and above diplomatic and representative bodies. The economic institutions are organized for overseas markets organized by multinational corporations, over and against local markets and producers. To speak of market economies is a misnomer.

The military institutions have absorbed the bulk of state functionaries and resources. They subordinate economic markets and diplomatic institutions to military priorities. Even as imperial state operations function through their military and civilian administrative apparatus, it is subject to competitive influential socio-political class, ethnic and military configurations.

In analyzing the effective or 'real power' of the principle institutions of the imperial state one must distinguish between goals and achievements, purpose and performance. All too often commentators make grand statements of imperial power and especially of dominance when, in fact, their engagement leads to costly losses, and retreats inflicted by national, local or regional alignments. Hence, understanding the imperial interaction between its various tiers of allies and adversaries is crucial in analyzing the immediate and long-term structures and direction of imperial state policy.

We will first discuss the leader–follower imperial relationships in four zones, the West, East, Middle East and Latin America, and identify the terrain of struggles and conflict. This will allow us to examine the contemporary 'map of empire'. We will then contrast the alignment of forces between Western imperial allies and their adversaries.

In the final section we will look at the sources of fragmentation between the imperial state and economic globalization, as well as the fissures and fallout between imperial allies and followers.

Tiers of Imperial Allies in the West

Western imperialism is a complex pyramidal structure in which the dominant United States interacts with a multiple five-tier system.

Western imperialism takes the form of a vertical and horizontal structure of leader and follower states that cannot be understood with reference to the metaphor of center, semi-periphery and the periphery.

Western imperial power extends from the first to the second tier, from the United States to France, England, Germany, Italy and Canada. The scope and depth of US military, bureaucratic, political and economic institutions form the framework within which the followers operate.

The second tier of empire acts as the link between the top and bottom tiers. It provides military backing and economic linkages while securing autonomous levers to enlarge their geo-political spheres.

The third tier of the empire, which includes Poland and the Nordic, Low and Baltic countries, are geographically and economically proximate to Western Europe and militarily dependent on US-NATO military dominance. The third tier is a heterogeneous grouping, from highly advanced economic countries like Sweden, Norway and Denmark to relatively backward Baltic dependencies like Latvia, Estonia and Lithuania. They rarely engage in independent power initiatives and depend for backing from the tier 1 and 2 imperial centers. Tier four countries, which include Greece, Spain, Hungary, Czech and Slovakia, the Balkans (Bulgaria and Romania), are essentially satellite nations that follow the leader imperial countries, providing bases, troops and tourist resorts. Except in isolated instances they have no independent voice or presence in regional or global conflicts in the context of NATO.

The recently fabricated tier five satellites are mini-states like Albania, Kosovo, Macedonia, Slovenia and Croatia, which act as military bases, tourist havens and economic dependencies. They are outgrowths from tier one and the result of two wars designed to demolish Russian influence in Serbia.

Mapping the leader-follower structure of the Western empire depends on the distribution of military resources and their location on the frontiers of Russia. The US-EU empire faces the dilemma of the rising economic demands of the multi-tiered empire exceeding its capacity, leading to shifting trading alliances and independent pressure to 'go beyond' the imperial leaders.

Imperial states have economic and ideological control over their followers, especially when the military consequences of empire have disrupted everyday life and the economy. For example, US imperial wars have set in motion a massive invasion of Europe by refugees from the Middle East. Likewise, US sanctions on European exports, which accompanied the US putsch in the Ukraine, provoked rivalry to secure Russian petroleum resources.

The Eastern Imperial Empire

US imperial design in East Asia is vastly different in structure, adversaries and allies from that in the West. The leaders and followers are distinct in the East. The multi-tiered US empire is designed to block, undermine and dominate China and North Korea.

Since the Second World War, the US has been the centerpiece of the Pacific empire. But it has also suffered serious military setbacks, in Korea and Indo-China. Overtime, however, with the aid of its multi-tiered auxiliaries, it has recovered influence in the Indo-Chinese and South Korean peninsulas.

US dominance at the top is sustained by second-tier imperial allies that include Australia, New Zealand, India and Japan.

These second-tier allies are diverse entities. For example, the Indian regime is a reticent latecomer to the US empire and one that still retains a higher degree of autonomy in dealing with China. In contrast, although Australia and New Zealand retain their dependent military ties with the US, they are increasingly dependent economically on Chinese commodity markets and investments.

Japan, a powerful traditional economic ally of the US, remains a military satellite of the US's Asian empire.

In the third tier are South Korea, Taiwan, the Philippines, Malaysia, Thailand and Indonesia. South Korea is the US's most important military dependency. Nevertheless, it has moved steadily closer to the Chinese market, as has Indonesia. Taiwan, likewise, is a military dependency of the US. However, its economic links have moved it closer to China than the US. The Philippines is a US military vassal-state, which retains its legacy as an imperial colonial enclave against China. Thailand and Malaysia remain third-tier imperial auxiliaries, subject to nationalist or democratic upsurges.

The fourth-tier countries of the Eastern empire are the least reliant because of their relatively new associations. Vietnam, Cambodia, Laos and Myanmar have converted from the status of independent statist economies to US-Japanese and Chinese market, financial and military dependencies.

The US empire has concentrated on militarily confronting China, controlling its South China trading routes and forming economic trading agreements that exclude China. However, the imperial multi-tiered structure has remained largely a US military operation with minimal economic input from even their closest allies.

The US Eastern empire has lost significant economic counterparts to China. Its trade-pacts have failed to undermine China's economic advances.

The US Eastern empire may lead and militarily dominate its multi-tiered allies, vassals and recent converts. It may generate military tensions with China. But it has failed to establish an Asian economic structure to sustain US imperial superiority.

China is the Asian power that drives the growth and dynamism of Asia. China is the vital market and supplier of minerals, agricultural products and industrial, high-tech and service activity for Asia.

The US imperial resort to 'fifth tier' allies in Tibet, Hong Kong and the Islamic hinterland of China plays a propaganda role but is ineffective in weakening China to imperial advantage.

The Eastern empire has little of the economic leverage in China that the Western empire has with Russia. China has established far more effective economic influence in Asia than Russia has in the West. Russia has greater military capacity to contain Western imperial military threats than China, but the latter has accelerated its high-tech military capabilities. Moreover, the joint military-economic linkages between Russia and China are formidable counterweights to the multi-tiered alliances linking the US and EU to Japan, Australia and South Korea. In other words, the diverse geographic multi-tiered US imperial structures in the East do not, and cannot, dominate the top-tier alliance of Russia and China, despite the paucity of their multiple military allies.

If we look beyond European and Asian spheres of empire to the Middle East and Latin America, the US imperial presence is subject to rapidly evolving relations of power. We cannot simply add or subtract from the US and Russian and Chinese rivalry because they do not necessarily add up to a new 'imperial' or 'autonomous' center of power.

Imperial Power in the Middle East: The Multi-Tiered Empire in Retreat

The US imperial empire in the Middle East occupies a pivotal point between West and East; between the top and secondary tiers of empire; between Islamic and anti-Islamic alliances.

If we extend the 'Middle East' to include South Asia and North Africa we capture the dimensions of the Western imperial quest for supremacy.

The imperial empire in the Middle East reflects US and Western European tiers of power interacting with local counterparts and satellite states.

The US-EU top tiers link their military encirclement of Russia and regional adversaries like Iran with their NATO ally—the Turkish state.

International imperial powers rely on Middle Eastern allies, auxiliaries and satellites, which share and compete for territorial fragments of power among regional adversaries.

In the top tier is the United States, accompanied, at second-tier level, by the European Union, Israel, Turkey and Saudi Arabia.

In the third tier are the Egyptian, Tunisian, Iraqi and Jordanian states which are financial and political dependencies of the empire.

The fourth tier includes the Gulf states, the Kurds, the Lebanese and Yemeni satellites of Saudi Arabia, and the satellite Palestinian Bantustan of Israel in the West Bank.

The terrorist enclaves backed by the Western empire are located in Syria, Iraq and Libya. They have a 'specific and multi-purpose' role in undermining adversaries in order to restore imperial dominance.

The Middle East empire is the least stabilized region and the most susceptible to internal rivalries.

Israel exercises a powerful voice in securing US financial and military resources and political support for its colonial control over Palestine and Syrian territories and population. Saudi Arabia finances and arms autonomous Islamic armed terrorist detachments to pursue its political-territorial designs in Pakistan, Yemen, Afghanistan, Iraq, Syria, Iran and the Gulf Coast. The US empire competes with its auxiliaries for control over the same Middle East vassalage entities.

The Middle East empire is fraught with powerful adversaries in each of its points of contention. Iran stands as a counterweight in opposition to the West, Saudi Arabia and Israel for influence among satellites in the Gulf, Yemen, Iraq and Syria. Hezbollah stands in defense of Syria and in alliance with Iran against Israel. Russia stands in military alliance with Syria and Iran in opposition to the Western imperial alliance. The US imperial satellite states of Afghanistan, Iraq, Libya and Egypt are rapidly disintegrating in the face of gross corruption, Islamic resurgence, policy incompetence and economic crises.

To speak formally of a Western imperial empire in vast sections of the Middle East is a misnomer for several reasons. In Afghanistan, the National-Islamic Taliban and its allies control most of the country except for garrison cities. Yemen, Libya and Iraq are battleground states, uncontested terrain in which nothing remotely resembling an imperial domain is visible. Iraq is under siege from the north by Kurds, the center by ISIS, the south by nationalist Shi'a in contention with corrupt US empire-backed auxiliaries.

The US–EU mercenaries in Syria have been defeated by Syrian-Russian-Hezbollah-Iranian forces aided by Kurds.

Israel is a regional predator—usurper of Palestine—more than an imperial collaborator. The Middle East is the costliest and least advantageous Western imperial region. First and foremost, the Middle East imperial debacle resulted because top-tier leaders followed policies and strategies which were incompatible with imperial precepts that guide empires.

The top tier of the US imperial elite is directed by Israeli military prerogatives, dictated by the Zionist power configuration embodied in the US state apparatus. Their policy is to destroy Islamic structures and institutions of power, not reconfigure them in the image of Western imperial institutions ... as the US was able to do in Asia and Europe.

The multiple tiers of the Western empire, from the US and Western Europe at the top to Kosovo at the bottom, followed imperial imperatives. In contrast, Israel directs US military power at perpetual conflict in the Middle East.

This divergent path has contributed to disastrous defeats, which have repercussions throughout the global empire—especially freeing up competitors and rivals in Asia and Latin America.

Tiers of Empire in Latin America

The US imperial empire reigned supreme in Central America and the Caribbean for most of the first half of the 20th century in the era of British imperial rule—Pax Britannica. Subsequently the British empire was replaced by the US empire, which established a dominant position in the region in the wake of the Second World War.

There were several major challenges to US imperial dominations in the middle of the 20th century. The centerpiece of anti-imperial opposition was the Cuban Revolution in 1959, which provided political, ideological and material backing to a continental challenge throughout Latin America. Earlier, in 1953, a socialist government took power in Guyana and was defeated.

In 1956 the Dominican Revolution challenged a US-backed dictatorship but was defeated by a US invasion.

In 1970–1973 a democratic socialist government was elected in Chile and overthrown by a CIA coup.

In the same year a workers and peasants' coalition backed a nationalist military government in Bolivia and was ousted by a US-backed military coup.

In Argentina (Perón), Brazil (Goulart) and Peru (Alvarez), national-popular governments that opposed US imperialism rose to power between the mid-1960s and mid-1970s. They were overthrown by US military coups. Other than in the Cuban Revolution, the US empire counter-attacked, relying on US and local business elites to back imperial-directed military juntas in overthrowing their anti-imperialist adversaries.

The US empire re-established hegemony based on a multi-tiered military and market directorate headed by the US and followed at second-tier level by Argentina, Brazil and Chile, which engaged in large-scale state and death squad exterminations, exile and jailings.

The third tier was based on US surrogates, generals and oligarchical associates in Colombia, Venezuela, Peru, Bolivia, Paraguay and Uruguay.

The fourth tier of satellite regimes included the countries of Central America—apart from Nicaragua—and all of the Caribbean, apart from Cuba and Grenada.

The US empire ruled with predator allies and satellite oligarchs, aiming to impose a uniform imperial structure based on neoliberal policies. US-centered regional trade, investment and military pacts ensured US imperial supremacy, through which the country sought to 'blockade' the Cuban Revolution.

The US imperial system reached its high point between the mid-1970s and late 1990s. It then faced a new wave of challenges from popular uprisings, electoral changes and the demise of the auxiliary neoliberal regimes.

The US empire faced powerful challenges from popular-nationalist regimes between 1999 and 2006 in Venezuela, Argentina, Brazil, Bolivia and Ecuador. It was challenged by dissident liberal-nationalist governments in Uruguay, Honduras and Paraguay.

The US empire was unable to engage in military interventions in Latin America because multiple imperial wars in the Middle East (Iraq, Libya, Syria), Asia (Afghanistan) and Europe (Ukraine, Serbia) undermined its imperial capacity.

Cuba, the center of anti-imperialist politics, was fortified by economic aid from Venezuela and diplomatic alliances with the anti-interventionist center-left.

The US imperial empire in Latin America was in retreat and disarray but did not suffer a strategic defeat because the powerful business, political and state auxiliaries it retained were intact, able to regroup and counter-attack. By the end of the first decade of the 21st century the imperial empire counter-attacked, relying on its political-military satellites, which seized power in the weakest links, Honduras and Paraguay.

Subsequently, neoliberal extremists took power in Argentina; ousted the president of Brazil; and prepared the terrain to seize control in Venezuela.

The US empire re-emerged in Latin America after a decade-long hiatus with a new multi-tier structure. At the top was the US, dependent on satellite military and business elites within the second tier of Colombia, Argentina, Brazil and Mexico. The third tier linked Chile, Peru, Venezuela and Uruguay to the US in tier two. The fourth tier was dominated by weak submissive regimes in Central America (Panama, Guatemala, Honduras and

El Salvador), the Caribbean (especially Santo Domingo, Haiti and Jamaica) and Paraguay.

Although the US re-mounted its imperial ensemble rapidly, it was extremely fragile, incoherent and subject to disintegration.

Argentina, the centerpiece of the empire, faced the triple threat of mass unrest, economic crises and a regime under siege.

Brazil's new US neoliberal constellation was rife with regime corruption, judicial trials, economic recession and social polarization.

Venezuela's right-wing auxiliaries lacked the economic resources to escape the demise of the oil economy, hyper-inflation and the virulent internecine conflicts within the right.

The US empire in Latin America could best operate through links with the Asian-Pacific trade pact. However, even with Asian ties the Latin satellites exhibit none of the stability that their Asia counterparts exhibit. Moreover, China's dominant economic role in both regions has limited US hegemony over the principal props of the empire.

The Myth of a US Global Empire

The construction of a narrative of a US global empire is based on several profound misconceptions, which have distorted the capacity of the US to dominate world politics. The US's regional empires operate in contested universes in which powerful counterforces limit imperial dominance.

In Europe, Russia is a powerful counterforce, aided and abated by its allies in Asia (China), the Middle East (Iran) and, to a limited extent, by the BRIC countries.

Moreover, the multi-tiered allies of the US in Europe have exhibited, at times, autonomous policies. For example, Germany's oil-gas agreements with Russia have undermined US sanctions aimed at isolating Russia.

While it may appear that the imperial military, banking, multi-national corporate structure shares, at a high level of abstraction, a common imperial enterprise, when it comes to everyday policy making, budget making, war policies, trade agreements, diplomacy/subversion and the capitalist marketplace there are countervailing forces.

Multi-tiered allies of the empire make claims on as well as sacrifices for the US imperial center. Internal members of the imperial structure define competing priorities via domestic power wielders. The US empire has widened its military operations to over seven hundred bases across the world, but each operation has been subject to restraints and reversals. US multinationals have multi-billion operations but they adjust to the demands of counter-imperial powers (China). They evade trillion-dollar tax returns to the US. They absorb assets from the US Treasury. In short, the sun may never set on the empire, but the emperors have lost sight of the empire.

Chapter 23

The Emperor's Rage

Chaos reigns and spreads as enraged leaders in the US and Europe and their clients and allies pursue genocidal wars. Mercenary wars in Syria; Israel's terror bombing on Gaza; proxy wars in the Ukraine, Pakistan, Iraq, Afghanistan, Libya and Somalia. Tens of millions of refugees flee scenes of total destruction. Nothing is sacred. There are no sanctuaries. Homes, schools, hospitals and entire families are targeted for destruction.

Chaos by Design

At the center of chaos, the wild-eyed President Obama strikes blindly, oblivious of the consequences, willing to risk a financial debacle or a nuclear war. He enforces sanctions against Iran; imposes sanctions on Russia; sets up missile bases five launch minutes from Moscow; sends killer drones against Pakistan, Yemen and Afghanistan; arms mercenaries in Syria; trains and equips Kurds in Iraq and pays for Israel's savagery against Gaza.

Nothing works.

The Chaos President is blind to the fact that starving one's adversaries does not secure submission: it unites them to resist. Regime change, imposing proxies by force and subterfuge, can destroy the social fabric of complex societies: million of peasants and workers become uprooted refugees. Popular social movements are replaced by organized criminal gangs and bandit armies.

Central America, the product of decades of US direct and proxy military interventions that prevented the most basic structural changes, has become a chaotic, unliveable inferno for millions. Tens of thousands of children flee from their 'free market'-induced mass poverty and militarized state and gangster violence. Children refugees at the US border are arrested en masse and imprisoned in makeshift detention camps, subject to psychological, physical and sexual abuse by officials and guards on the inside. On the outside, these pitiful children are exposed to the racist hatred of a frightened US public unaware of the dangers these children are escaping and the US government's role in creating these hells.

The US-backed Kiev aviation authorities re-directed international passenger airlines to fly over war zones bristling with anti-aircraft missiles while Kiev's jets bombed the rebellious cities and towns. One flight was shot down and nearly 300 civilians perished. Immediately, an explosion of accusations from Kiev blaming Russian president Putin flooded Western media, with no real facts to explain the tragedy/crime. War-crazy President Obama and the slavering prime ministers of the EU ejaculated ultimatums, threatening to convert Russia into a pariah state. 'Sanctions, sanctions, everywhere—but first … France must complete its $1.5 billion sale to the Russian navy.' And the City of London exempts the Russian oligarchs from the sanctions, embedded as they are in London's money laundering, parasitical FIRE (Fire, Insurance and Real Estate) economy. The Cold War has returned and taken an ugly turn—with exceptions … for business.

Confrontation among nuclear powers is imminent—and the maniacal Baltic states and Poland bray the loudest for war with Russia, oblivious to their position on the front lines of incineration … .

Each day Israel's war machine chews up more bodies of Gaza's children while spitting out more lies. Cheering Israeli Jews perch on their fortified hills to celebrate each missile strike on the apartments and schools of the densely populated Shejaiya neighbourhood of besieged Gaza. A group of orthodox and secular entrepreneurs in Brooklyn have organized group tours to visit the holy sites by day and enjoy the Gaza pyrotechnics by night … night goggles to view the fleeing mothers and burning children are available at a small extra charge … .

Again, the US Senate votes unanimously in support of Israel's latest campaign of mass murder; no crime is depraved enough to ruffle the scruples of America's leaders. They hew close to a script from the fifty-two presidents of the major American Jewish organizations. Together they embrace a Beast from the Apocalypse gnawing on the flesh and bones of Palestine.

But, Sacré Bleu! France's Zionists have prevailed on 'President-Socialiste' Hollande. Paris bans all anti-Israel demonstrations despite the clear reports of genocide. Demonstrators supporting the Gazan resistance are gassed and assaulted by special riot police; 'Socialist' Hollande serves the demands of powerful Zionist organizations while trashing his country's republican traditions and sacred 'Rights of Man'.

The young protestors of Paris fought back with barricades and paving stones in the finest traditions of the Paris Commune, waving the flags of a free Palestine. Not a single 'red banner' was in sight: members of the French 'left' were under their beds or off on vacation.

There are ominous signs away from the killing fields. The stock market is rising while the economy stagnates. Wild speculators have returned in their splendour, widening the gap between the fictitious and real economy before the 'deluge', the chaos of another inevitable crash.

In industrial America's once great Detroit, clean water is shut off to tens of thousands of poor citizens unable to pay for basic services. In the middle of summer, urban families are left to defecate in hallways, alleyways and empty lots. Without water the toilets are clogged and children not washed. Roscoe, the master plumber, says the job is way beyond him.

According to our famed economists, the economy of Detroit is 'recovering … profits are up, it's only the people who are suffering'. Productivity has doubled, speculators are satisfied; pensions are slashed and wages are down. But the Detroit Tigers are in first place.

Public hospitals everywhere are being closed. In the Bronx and Brooklyn, emergency rooms are overwhelmed. Chaos! Interns work thirty-six-hour shifts … and the sick and injured take their chances with a sleep-deprived medic. Meanwhile, in Manhattan, private clinics and 'boutique' practices for the elite proliferate.

Scandinavians have embraced the putschist power grab in Kiev. The Swedish foreign minister Bildt bellows for a new Cold War with Russia. The Danish emissary and NATO leader, Rasmussen, salivates obscenely at the prospect of bombing and destroying Syria in a replay of NATO's 'victory' over Libya.

The German leaders endorse the ongoing Israeli genocide against Gaza; they are comfortably protected from any moral conscience by their nostalgic blanket of guilt over Nazi crimes seventy years ago.

Saudi-funded Jihadi terrorists in Iraq showed their 'infinite mercy' by … driving thousands of Christians from ancient Mosul. Nearly 2,000 years of a continuous Christian presence was long enough! At least most escaped with their heads still attached.

Chaos Everywhere

Over one hundred thousand agents of the US National Security Agency are paid to spy on two million Muslim citizens and residents in the United States. But for all the tens of billions of dollars spent and tens of millions of conversations recorded, Islamic charities are prosecuted and philanthropic individuals are framed in 'sting operations'.

Where the bombs fall no one knows, but people flee. Millions are fleeing the chaos.

But there is no place to go! The French invade half a dozen African countries but the refugees are denied refuge in France. Thousands die in the desert or drown crossing the Med. Those who do make it are branded criminals or relegated to ghettos and camps.

Chaos reigns in Africa, the Middle East, Central America and Detroit. The entire US frontier with Mexico has become a militarized detention center, a multinational prison camp. The border is unrecognizable to our generation.

Chaos reigns in the markets. Chaos masquerades as trade sanctions: Iran yesterday, Russia today and China tomorrow. Washington, watch out! Your adversaries are finding common ground, trading, forging agreements, building defenses; their ties are growing stronger.

Chaos reigns in Israel. War-obsessed Israelis discover that the Chosen People of God can also bleed and die, lose limbs and eyes in the alleyways of Gaza where poorly armed boys and men stand their ground. When the cheers turn to jeers, will they re-elect Bibi, their current kosher butcher? The overseas brethren, the fundraisers, the lobbyists and the armchair verbal assassins will automatically embrace some new face, without questions, regrets or (god forbid!) self-criticism: if it's good for Israel and the Jews, it's got to be right!

Chaos reigns in New York. Judicial rulings favor the pirates and their vulture funds demanding 1,000 percent returns on old Argentine bonds. If Argentina rejects this financial blackmail and defaults, shock waves will ripple throughout global financial markets. Creditors will tremble in uncertainty. Fears will grow over a new financial crash. Will they squeeze out another trillion-dollar bailout?

But where's the money? Printing presses are working day and night. There are only a few lifeboats, enough for the bankers and Wall Street; the other 99 percent will have to swim or feed the sharks.

The corrupted financial press now advises warlords on which country to bomb and politicians on how to impose economic sanctions; they no longer provide sound economic information or advise investors on markets. Their editorial rants will incite an investor flight to buy king-sized mattresses for stuffing as the banks fail.

The US president is on the verge of a mental breakdown: he's a liar of Munchausen proportions with a bad case of political paranoia, war hysteria and megalomania. He's gone amok, braying, 'I lead the world: it's US leadership or chaos.' Increasingly the world has another message: 'It's the US *and* chaos.'

Wall Street is abandoning him. The Russians have double-crossed him. The Chinese merchants are now doing business everywhere we used to be and ought to be. They're playing with loaded dice. The stubborn Somalis refuse to submit to a Black President: they reject this 'ML King with drones' ... . The Germans suck on their thumbs in total stupor as Americans monitor and record their every conversation ... for their own safety! 'Our corporations are ingrates after all we have done for them,' the First Black President whines. 'They flee from our taxes while we subsidize their operations!'

Final Solutions: The End of Chaos

The only solution is to move on: chaos breeds chaos. The president strives to project his 'leadership'. He asks his close advisers hard questions:

Why can't we bomb Russia, just like Israel bombs Gaza? Why don't we build an 'Iron Dome' over Europe and shoot down Russian nuclear missiles while we fire upon Moscow from our new bases in Ukraine? Which countries will our 'Dome' protect? I am sure that the people of East Europe and the Baltic States will gladly make the supreme sacrifice. After all, their leaders were at the very front frothing for a war with Russia. Their reward, a nuclear wasteland, will be a small price to ensure our success!

The Zionist lobby will insist our 'Iron Dome' covers Israel. But the Saudis may try to bribe the Russians to spare the oil fields as Moscow targets the US missile bases near Mecca. Our radioactive allies in the Middle East will just have to relocate to a new Holy Land.

Do Obama and his advisers imagine reducing the Asian population by a billion or two? Do they plan several hundred Hiroshimas because the Chinese crossed the president's 'red lines': China's economy and trade grew too fast, expanded too far, it was too competitive, too competent, too successful at gaining market shares, and they ignored our warnings and our unparalleled military might.

Most of Asia will inhale nuclear dust, millions of Indians and Indonesians will perish as collateral damage. Their survivors will feast on radiated fish in a glowing sea.

Beyond Chaos: The New American Way

Because our Iron Dome will have failed us, we will have to re-emerge out of toxic ashes and crawl from our bunkers, dreaming of a new America free from wars and poverty. The Reign of Chaos will have ended. The peace and order of the graveyard will reign supreme.

The emperors will be forgotten.

And we never will have found out who fired that missile at the doomed Malaysian airliner with its 300 passengers and crew. We will have lost count of the thousands of Palestinian parents and children slaughtered in Gaza by the Chosen People of Israel. We will not know how the sanctions against Russia panned out.

It won't matter in the post-nuclear age, after the Chaos ... .

Part V

Ideology of Empire

Chapter 24

The Harvard School of Empire Building

Harvard professor Joseph Nye, a former senior Pentagon functionary, is one of the longest serving and most influential advisers to US empire-building officials. Nye has recently re-affirmed the primacy of the US as a world power in his latest book, *Is the American Century Over?*[1] and in his article, 'The American Century Will Survive the Rise of China' (*Financial Times*, 3/26/15, p. 7). These publications are in line with his earlier book, *Bound to Lead*, and his longstanding view that the US is not a declining world power, that it retains 'supremacy' even in the face of China's rise to global power.

Nye's views of US world supremacy have served to encourage Washington to wage multiple wars; his sanguine view of US economic power has allowed policymakers to ignore fundamental weaknesses in the US economy and to overestimate US power, based on what he dubs 'soft' and 'military' power.

In tackling Professor Nye's work, we are not dealing with a 'detached academic in the ivory tower'; we are taking on a high-level political influential, a hard-line military hawk, whose views are reflected in the forging of strategic decisions and whose arguments serve to justify major government policies.

First, we will proceed with a critical analysis of his theoretical assumptions, historical arguments and conceptual framework. In the second part of this essay, we will consider the political consequences, which have flowed from his analysis and prescriptions. In the conclusion I propose an alternative, more realistic, analysis of US global power, one more attuned to the real international position of the US in the world today.

Ossified in a Distorted Time Warp

Nye's segmentation of power into three spheres—economic, military (hard) and diplomatic/cultural (soft)—overlooks the inter-relation between them. What he dubs as 'soft power' usually relies on 'hard power', either before, during or after the application of 'soft power'. Moreover, the capacity to influence by 'soft power' depends on economic promise or military coercion to enforce 'persuasion'. Where economic resources or military threats are not present, soft power is ineffective.

Nye's argument that military power is co-equal with economic power is a very dubious proposition. Over the medium run, economic power buys, expands and increases military power. In other words, economic resources are convertible into military as well as 'soft' power. It can influence politicians, parties and regimes via trade, investments and credit in many ways that military power cannot. Over time, economic power translates into military power. Nye's claims of persistent US military superiority in the face of its admitted economic decline is ephemeral or time bound.

Nye's argument about the continued ascendancy of US global power 'for the next few decades' is a dubious, static view—ignoring a long-term and large-scale historical trajectory. Lifelong shibboleths never die! By all empirical indicators—economic, political and even military—the US is a declining power. Moreover, what is important is not where the US is at any given moment but where it is moving. Its declining share of Latin American, African and Asian markets clearly points to a downward trajectory.

Power is a political relation. By definition it means a country's capacity to make other countries or political entities do what they otherwise would not do. To consider the US as the dominant world power, we cannot, as Nye proposes, look at its 'reputation' as a world power or cite its 'military capacity' or willingness to project military force. We need to look at military and political outcomes in multiple key issue areas in which US policymakers have sought to establish regional or local dominance.

Nye's discussion fails to look at the negative cumulative effects of US policy failures in multiple regions over time to determine whether the US retains its global supremacy or is a declining power.

To preach that 'the American century is not over' simply because some critics in the past mistakenly thought that the USSR in the 1970s or Japan in the 1980s would displace the US as the global power is to overlook the foundational weakness and repeated failures of US policymakers to impose or persuade other nations to accept US supremacy over the past decade and a half.

If, as Nye grudgingly concedes, China has replaced the US as the leading economic power in Asia, he does not understand the dynamic components of Chinese economic power, especially its accumulation of large-scale foreign reserves and rapidly growing technical knowhow. Even worse, Nye ignores how the military dimension of world power has actively undermined US economic supremacy.

It is precisely Nye's belief, shared by other Pentagon advisers, that US military supremacy make it a 'world power' which has led to catastrophic, prolonged and costly wars. These wars have degraded and undermined US pretensions of 'world leadership' or, more accurately, *imperial supremacy*.

While the US has spent trillions of dollars of public money on prolonged and losing wars in Afghanistan, Iraq and Somalia, as well as ongoing military interventions in Libya, Syria, Ukraine and Yemen, China and other emerging powers have engaged in large long-term economic expansion, increasing market shares, acquiring productive enterprises and expanding their sources of capital accumulation in dynamic regions.

Repeated US projections of military power have not created new sources of wealth. The US capacity and willingness to engage in multiple disastrous wars has led to a greater loss of military influence.

Consequences of High Military Capacity and Declining Economic Performance

The consequence of utilizing its great storehouse of military capacity so disastrously has degraded and weakened the US military as well as its imperial economic reach. Repeated US military defeats, its inability to secure its goals or impose its dominance in Lebanon, Syria, Iraq and Afghanistan has severely weakened the domestic political foundations of global military power, to the point where the US public is averse to sending American ground troops into combat.

Nye's inventory of military resources—the stockpile of up-to-date bombers, nuclear weapons, fighter planes, military bases, special forces operations—and its vast spy ('intelligence') apparatus—in other words, the US's supreme military 'capacity'—has not resulted in the establishment of a prosperous, stable and submissive empire (the goal that Nye euphemistically dubs 'world supremacy'). US military engagements, both high- and low-intensity wars, have resulted in costly defeats and retreats as adversaries advance into the vacuum. Superior material capacity has not translated into US dominance because nationalist, anti-imperialist consciousness and movements based on mass armed resistance have demonstrated superiority in countering foreign (US) invasions, occupations and satellite building.

Nye ignores a decisive 'military resource' that the US does not have and its adversaries have in abundance—nationalist consciousness. Here, Nye's notion of US supremacy in 'soft power' has been terribly wrong-headed. According to Nye, the US superiority in the use and control of mass media, films, news and cultural organizations and educational institutions continues and has allowed the US to retain its global supremacy.

No doubt the US global propaganda apparatus and networks are formidable, but they have not been successful—at least, not as a bulwark of US global supremacy. Once again Nye's inventory of soft power assets relies exclusively on quantitative, contemporary, material structures and ignores the enormous counter-influence of historical legacies and nationalist, cultural, religious, ethnic, class, race and gender consciousness, which rejects US dominance in all of its forms. US 'soft power' has not conquered or gained the allegiance of the people in Afghanistan, Iraq, Syria or Yemen. Nor has it convinced the billions of Chinese, Latin American or Islamic peoples to embrace American 'leadership'.

No doubt 'soft power' has worked to a limited extent, especially among sectors of the educated classes and the local political elite, converting them into imperial collaborators. No doubt elements of the educated elite have been co-opted by US-funded 'non-governmental organizations' that engage in grassroots counter-insurgency as the counterpart to the drone attacks from above. But, once again, Nye relies on quantitative rather than qualitative measures of influence. Despite an army of NGOs and the budgeting of billions of dollars, US imperial conquests, coups, occupations, rigged elections and puppet regimes are highly unpopular. As a result, US troops need to diminish their presence, and the country's overseas and visiting diplomats require a squadron of security officials and operate out of armed fortresses.

Professor Nye's treatment of what he calls 'soft power' is reduced to an inventory of propaganda resources, developed and/or cultivated by the imperial state (the US) to induce submission to and acceptance of the global supremacy of the US. However vast the spending and however broad the scope of this soft power, Nye fails to recognize the ineffectiveness of the US's soft power apparatus in the face of systemic crimes against humanity, which have decisively turned world opinion and particular national publics against the US. Specifically, Washington's practice of torture (Abu Ghraib), kidnapping (rendition) and prolonged jailing without trial (Guantanamo), its global spy network monitoring hundreds of millions of citizens in the US and the countries of its allies, and its use of drones, killing more non-combatant (innocent) citizens than armed adversaries, have severely weakened, if not undermined, the appeal of US 'soft powers'. Nye is oblivious to the ways in which US projections of military power have led to the precipitous long-term decline of soft power as well as the way in which that decline has resulted in the greater reliance on military power ... in a vicious circle.

Nye ignores the changing composition of the strategic decision-makers who decide where and when military power will be exercised. He blandly assumes that policy is directed by and for enhancing US 'global supremacy'. But as Mearsheimer and Walt (*The Israel Lobby*)[2] and Petras (*The Power of Israel in the United States*)[3] have demonstrated, powerful, organized lobbies like AIPAC and Israel First officials in the Executive branch have taken military decisions to focus on the Middle East at the behest of Israel in order to enhance its power. These decisions have had an enormous cost in terms of loss of human and financial resources and have contributed to the decline of US global supremacy. Nye fails to recognize how the ascendancy of his militarist colleagues in the Pentagon and the Zionists in Congress and the Executive have drastically changed the way in which hard power (military) is exercised.

And how it has weakened the composition and use of soft power and provoked greater imbalances between economic and military power.

Nye's argument is further weakened by his incapacity to 'problematize' the changing content of military power, its shift from tool of economic expansion, directed by US empire builders, to end in itself, exploiting economic resources to enhance Israeli hegemony in the Middle East. This weakness is exacerbated by his failure to recognize the changing nature of economic power—the shift from manufacturing to finance capital—and the negative consequences resulting from the projection of US economic power and dominance.

Finally, Nye totally ignores the moral dimension of the US drive for world dominance. At worst, he blithely assumes that destructive US wars are, by their nature, virtuous. Nye's political commitment to the 'American Century' and total belief in its benignancy blind him to the killing and displacement of millions of Iraqis, Syrians, Afghans, Somalis, Libyans and now Ukrainians, among others. Nye's assumption of the beneficial effects of the US-NATO-EU expansion into former Warsaw Pact countries—especially Russia—ignores the vast impoverishment of 70 percent of the Ukrainian population, the outward flight of twenty million skilled professionals and workers, and the subsequent militarization of Eastern Europe and East Germany via its incorporation in NATO. According to Nye's moral calculus, any policy that enhances US global power is virtuous, no matter how it impacts the recipient population. These are not only Nye's views, they provide the ideological underpinning of the official 'soft power' propaganda accompanying past, present and near-future wars of mass destruction.

Nye is not your typical garden variety Ivy League-ideologue-for-US-and-Israeli-dominance (and there are many in US academia). Nye has been an important theoretical architect and strategic planner responsible for US global wars and the accompanying crimes against humanity. His global fantasies of US ascendancy have led to the parlous state of the US domestic economy, multiple unwinnable wars overseas and the eclipse of any strategic thinking about reversing the economic decline of the US in the world economy. If Professor Nye were employed as a CEO in the private sector, a cost-benefit analysis applied to his policies would long ago have resulted in his being fired and dispatched to a prestigious business school to teach 'ethics'. Since he is already tenured at Harvard and employed by the Pentagon he can continue to churn out his irresponsible 'manifestos' of US global leadership and not be held to account for the disasters.

In Joseph Nye we have our own American version of Colonel Blimp surveying his colonial projects: he has exchanged his pith helmet, short britches and walking stick for a combat helmet and boots and limited his 'reviews' of the empire to secure zones, surrounded by an entourage of combat-ready leathernecks or mercenaries, circling helicopter warships and super-vetted local military toadies.

Historical Fallacies

Even at its zenith of 'global power' during the 1940s, 1950s and 1960s, US military performance was the least effective component of world power. Two major wars, in Korea and Indo-China, speak against Nye's formula. The US military failed to defeat the North Korean and Chinese armies; Washington had to settle for a compromise. And the US was militarily defeated and forced to withdraw from Indo-China. Success in securing influence came afterwards, via economic investments and trade, accompanied by political and cultural influences.

Today, Nye's reliance on the superior military resources of the US to project the continuance of the 'American Century' rests on very shaky historical foundations.

Military Metaphysics as Crackpot Realism

The US has declined as a world power because of its 'military pivot'—following Nye's military metaphysics and 'soft power' psychobabble. In every practical situation, where the US has attempted to secure its dominance by relying on its superior 'military capacity' against its competitors' reliance on economic and political resources, Washington has lost.

China has set in motion the Asian Infrastructure Investment Bank (AIIB)—with an initial offering of fifty billion dollars. The US is staunchly opposed to the AIIB because it clearly represents an alternative to the US-dominated International Monetary Fund (IMF). Despite Washington's pressure to reject membership, its 'allies', led by the UK and followed by all major powers (except Japan for now), have applied for membership. Even Israel has joined!

Washington sought to convince leading 'emerging economies' to accept US-centered economic integration, but, instead, Brazil, Russia, India, China and South Africa (BRICS) founded the BRICS bank.

The US engineered the overthrow of the elected government in the Ukraine and set up a puppet regime to incorporate it as a NATO client and military platform on Russia's border. But the Ukraine turned into an economic basket case, run by kleptocratic oligarchs, defended by openly neo-Nazi brigades and incapable of defeating federal autonomist rebels in the industrialized east.

The US and EU imposed economic sanctions on Russia and federal autonomist rebels of the Donbass in eastern Ukraine. This has become another example of projecting political power to enlarge the scope of military operations at the cost of devastating losses in trade and investment, in this case between Moscow and the European Union, not to speak of the Ukraine, whose economy was dependent on trade with Russia.

The decline of US world power is, in part, a result of the dynamism and economic growth of emerging powers such as China and the relative decline of US market shares and inferior rates of growth.

In one of his more egregiously foolish efforts to puff up US economic superiority and downgrade China's economic rise, Nye argues that China's growth rate is 'likely to slow in the future'. Dear Joe ... don't you know that a Chinese 'slow down' from double-digit growth to 7 percent is still triple the rate of growth of the US today and for the foreseeable future?

Moreover, China's economy, balanced between production and finance, is less crisis-prone than the lopsided growth of the corrupt US financial sector. Nye's economic calculus ignores the qualitative, as well as quantitative, dimensions of economic power.

Conclusion

The dubious intellectual value of Joseph Nye's writings would not merit serious consideration except for the fact that they have a deep and abiding influence on US foreign policy. Nye is an ardent advocate of empire building and his arguments and prescriptions carry weight in the White House and Pentagon. His normative bias and his love of empire building blinds him to objective realties. The fact that he is a failed policy adviser who refuses to acknowledge the defeats, decline and destruction resulting from his world view has not lessened the dangerous nature of his current views.

Nye's attempt to justify his vision of continuing US world supremacy has led him to blame his critics. In his latest book he rants that predictions of US decline are 'dangerous' because they could encourage countries such as China to pursue more aggressive policies. In other words, Nye, having failed, through logic and facts, to sustain his assertions against his better-informed critics, questions their loyalty—evoking a McCarthyite spectre of intellectuals critical of US global power ... stabbing the country in the back.

Nye tries to deflect attention from the fragile material foundations of US power to disembodied 'perceptions'. According to Nye, it's all perceptions (or illusions!): if the world leaders and public believe that 'the American century is set to continue for many decades', that faith will, in itself, help to sustain America's superiority! Nye's fit of irrationality, his reliance on Harry Houdini-style political analysis ('Now you see US global power, now you don't!') is unlikely to convince any serious analyst beyond the halls of the Pentagon and Harvard University's John F. Kennedy School.

What matters is that the US, while it is a declining world power, is still militarily powerful, dangerous and destructive, even as its empire building is weakening and its forces are in retreat. As Mahatma Gandhi once stated about the declining British empire, 'It's the aging tiger that becomes the man-eater.'

As an alternative, we can follow two lines of inquiry: one is to question the entire imperial enterprise and focus on our return to republican values and domestic social and democratic reconstruction. That is a necessary but prolonged struggle under present circumstances. In the meantime, we can pursue policies that emphasize the importance of shifting from destructive military expansionism toward constructive economic engagements, flexible cooperation with emerging competitors, and diplomatic agreements with adversaries. Contrary to Nye's assertions, militarism and economic expansion are not compatible. Wars destroy markets and occupations provoke resistance, which frighten investors. 'Soft power' and NGOs that rely on manipulation, lies and the demonization of critics gain few adherents and multiple adversaries.

The US should increase its ties and co-operation with BRICS and China's AIIB. It should reach out to sign trade deals with Iran, Syria and Lebanon. It should cut off aid to Israel because of that country's bellicose posture toward the Arab East and its brutal colonization of Palestine. Washington should end its support of violent coups and engage with Venezuela. It should lift sanctions against Russia and eastern Ukraine and propose joint economic ventures. By ending colonial wars we can increase economic growth and open markets. We should pursue economic accommodation not military occupation. The former leads to prosperity, the latter to destruction.

Notes

1 Nye, Joseph (2015). *Is the American Century Over?* Hoboken, NJ: Wiley.
2 Mearsheimer, John and Stephen Walt (2006). 'The Israel Lobby', *Middle East Policy*, Vol. 13, No. 3, Fall.
3 Petras, James (2006). *The Power of Israel in the United States*. Blackpoint, NS: Fernwood Publications / Atlanta: Clarity Press.

Chapter 25

Lies and Deceptions on the Left

In 2014 and 2015 what appeared as hopeful signs, i.e. left-of centre governments that emerged as powerful alternatives to right-wing pro-US regimes in a progressive cycle of regime change,[1] is turning into a historic rout that will relegate them to the dustbin of history for many years to come. The rise and rapid decay of left-wing governments in France, Greece and Brazil is not the result of military coups, nor is it due to the machinations of the CIA. The debacle of left governments is a result of deliberate political decisions that break decisively with the progressive programs, promises and commitments that political leaders had made to the great mass of working- and middle-class voters who elected them.

Increasingly, the electorate views the leftist rulers as traitors who have betrayed their supporters at the beck and call of their most egregious class enemies: the bankers, the capitalists and the neoliberal ideologues.

Left Governments Commit Suicide

The self-destruction of the left is an unanticipated victory for the most retrograde neoliberal political forces. These forces have sought to destroy the welfare system, impose their rule via non-elected officials, widen and deepen inequalities, undermine rights and privatize and denationalize the most lucrative sectors of the economy.

Three cases of left regime betrayal serve to highlight this process: the French socialist regime of President Francois Hollande governing in the second leading power in Europe (2012–2015); Syriza, the left regime in Greece elected on January 25, 2015, portrayed as a sterling proponent of an alternative policy to 'fiscal austerity'; and the Workers' Party of Brazil, governing the biggest Latin American country (2003–2015), which is also a leading member of the BRICS group.

French Socialism: The Great Leap Backward

In his presidential campaign, Francois Hollande promised to raise taxes on the rich up to 75 percent; lower the retirement age from sixty-two to sixty years; launch a massive public investment program to reduce unemployment; vastly increase public spending on education (hiring 60,000 new teachers), health and social housing; and withdraw French troops from Afghanistan as a first step toward reducing the role of Paris as an imperialist collaborator.

From 2012, when he was elected, to the present (March 2015), Francois Hollande has betrayed each and every political commitment: public investments did not materialize and unemployment increased to over three million. His newly appointed economic minister Emmanuel Macron, a former partner of Rothschild Bank, sharply reduced business taxes by fifty billion euros. His newly appointed prime minister Manuel Valls, a neoliberal zealot, implemented major cuts in social programs, weakened government regulation of business and banking and eroded job security. Hollande appointed Laurence Boone from Bank of America as his top economic adviser.

The French 'socialist president' sent troops to Mali, bombers to Libya, military advisers to the Ukraine junta and aided the so-called Syrian 'rebels' (mostly Jihadist mercenaries). He signed off on billion-euro military sales to the Saudi Arabian monarcho-dictatorship and reneged on a contracted sale of warships to Russia.

Hollande joined with Germany in demanding that the Greek government comply with full and prompt debt payments to private bankers and maintain its brutal 'austerity program'.

As a result of defrauding French voters, betraying and embracing bankers, big business and militarists, less than 19 percent of the electorate has a positive view of the 'socialist' government, placing it in third place among the major parties. Hollande's pro-Israel policies and his hard line on US-Iranian peace negotiations, Minister Vall's Islamophobic raids in French Muslim suburbs and the support of military interventions against Islamic movements have increasingly polarized French society and heightened ethno-religious violence in the country.

Greece: Syriza's Instant Transformation

From the moment Syriza won the Greek elections on January 25, 2015, to the middle of March, Alexis Tsipras, the prime minister, and Yanis Varoufakis, his appointed finance minister, reneged in rapid order on every major and minor electoral program. They embraced the most retrograde measures, procedures and relations with the 'Troika' (the IMF, the European Commission and the European Central Bank), which Syriza had denounced in its Thessaloniki program a short time earlier.

Tsipras and Varoufakis repudiated the promise to reject the dictates of the 'Troika'. In other words, they accepted colonial rule and continued vassalage.

Typical of their demagogy and deceit, they sought to cover up their submission to the universally hated Troika by dubbing it 'the Institution'—fooling nobody but themselves—and becoming the butt of cynical cackles from their EU overseers.

During the campaign, Syriza had promised to write off all or most of the Greek debt. In government, Tsipras and Varoufakis immediately assured the Troika that they recognized and promised to meet all of their debt obligations.

Syriza had promised to prioritize humanitarian spending over austerity—raising the minimum wage, rehiring public employees in health and education and raising pension payments. After two weeks of servile groveling, the 're-formed' Tsipras and Varoufakis prioritized austerity: making debt payments and 'postponing' even the most meagre anti-poverty spending. When the Troika lent the Syriza regime two billion dollars to feed hungry Greeks, Tsipras lauded his overseers and promised to submit a multi-billion-euro list of regressive 'reforms'.

Syriza had promised to re-examine the previous right-wing regime's dubious privatization of lucrative public enterprises and to stop ongoing and future privatizations. In government, Tsipras and Varoufakis quickly disavowed that promise. They approved past, present and future privatizations. In fact, they made overtures to procure new privatization 'partners', offering lucrative tax concessions in selling-out more public firms.

Syriza promised to tackle the depression-level unemployment (26 percent national, 55 percent youth) via public spending and reduced debt payments. Tsipras and Varoufakis dutifully met debt payments and did not allocate any funds to create jobs!

Not only did Syriza continue the policies of its right-wing predecessors, it did so in a ludicrous style and substance: adopting ridiculous public postures and demagogic inconsequential gestures.

One day Tsipras would lay a wreath at the gravesite of 200 Greek partisans murdered by the Nazis during World War II. The next day he would grovel before the German bankers and concede to their demands for budget austerity, withholding public funds from two million unemployed Greeks.

One afternoon, Finance Minister Varoufakis would pose for a photo spread for *Paris Match* depicting him, cocktail in hand, on his penthouse terrace overlooking the Acropolis; and several hours later he would claim to speak for the impoverished masses!

Betrayal, deceit and demagogy all during the first two months in office, Syriza has established a record in its conversion from a leftist anti-austerity party to a conformist, servile vassal of the European Union.

Tsipras' call for Germany to pay reparations for damages to Greece during World War II—a long overdue and righteous demand—is another phony demagogic ploy designed to distract the impoverished Greeks from Tsipras and Varoufakis sell-out to German contemporary austerity demands. A cynical European Union official told the *Financial Times* (12/3/15, p. 6), 'He's [Tsipras] giving them [Syriza militants] a bone to lick on.'

No one expects German leaders to alter their hard line because of past injustices, least of all because they come from interlocutors on bended knees. No one in the EU takes Tsipras' demand at face value. They see it as more empty 'radical' rhetoric for domestic consumption.

Talking up seventy-year-old German reparations avoids taking practical action today repudiating or reducing payments on illegitimate debt to German banks and repudiating Merckel's dictates. The transparent betrayal of their most basic commitments to the impoverished Greek people has already divided Syriza. Over 40 percent of the central committee, including the president of the Parliament, repudiated the Tsipras-Varoufakis agreements with the Troika.

The vast majority of Greeks who voted for Syriza expected some immediate relief and reforms. They are increasingly disenchanted. They did not expect Tsipras to appoint Yanis Varoufakis, a former economic adviser to the corrupt neoliberal PASOK leader George Papandreou, as finance minister. Nor did voters abandon PASOK, en masse, over the past five years only to find the same kleptocrats and unscrupulous opportunists occupying top positions in Syriza thanks to Alexis Tsipras' index finger.

Nor could the electorate expect any fight, resistance or willingness to break with the Troika from Tsipras' appointments of ex-pat Anglo-Greek professors. These armchair leftists ('Marxist seminarians') neither engaged in mass struggles nor suffered the consequences of the prolonged depression.

Syriza is a party led by affluent, upwardly mobile professionals, academics and intellectuals. They rule over (but in the name of) the impoverished working and salaried lower middle class but in the interests of the Greek and, especially, German bankers.

They prioritize membership of the EU over an independent national economic policy. They abide by NATO by backing the Kiev junta in the Ukraine, EU sanctions on Russia and NATO intervention in Syria/Iraq and maintain a loud silence on US military threats to Venezuela.

Brazil: Budget Cuts, Corruption and the Revolt of the Masses

Brazil's self-styled Workers' Party government, in power an unlucky thirteen years, has been one of the most corruption-ridden regimes in Latin America. Backed by one of the major confederations and several landless rural workers' organizations, and sharing power with center-left and center-right parties, it was able to attract tens of billions of dollars of foreign extractive, finance and agro-business capital. Thanks to a decade-long commodity boom in agro-mineral commodities, easy credit and low interest rates, it raised income, consumption and the minimum wage while multiplying profits for the economic elite.

Subsequent to the financial crisis of 2009 and the decline of commodity prices, the economy stagnated, just as the new president Dilma Rousseff was elected. The Rousseff government, like that of her predecessor, Lula Da Silva, favoured agribusiness over the rural landless workers' demands for land reform. Her regime promoted the timber barons and soya growers encroaching on Indian communities and the Amazon rain forest.

Elected to a second term, Rousseff faced a major political and economic crisis: a deepening economic recession, a fiscal deficit, and the arrest and prosecution of scores of corrupt Workers' Party and allied congressional deputies and Petrobras oil executives.

Workers' Party leaders and the party's campaign treasury received millions of dollars in kickbacks from construction companies securing contracts with the giant semi-public petroleum company. During her election campaign, President Rousseff promised to 'continue to support popular social programs' and 'root out corruption'. However, immediately after her election she embraced orthodox neoliberal policies and appointed a cabinet of hard-right neoliberals, including Bradesco banker Joaquin Levy as finance minister. Levy proposed to reduce unemployment payments, pensions and public salaries. He argued for greater deregulation of banks. He proposed to weaken job protection laws to attract capital. He sought to achieve a budget surplus and attract foreign investment at the expense of advancing social development.

Consistent with her embrace of neoliberal orthodoxy, Rousseff appointed Katia Abreu, a right-wing senator, life-long leader of agro-business interests and sworn enemy of land reform, as the new agricultural minister. Crowned 'Miss Deforestation' by Greenpeace, Senator Abreu was vehemently opposed by the Landless Rural Workers' Movement (MST) and the confederation, but to no avail. With Rousseff's total backing Abreu set out on a course of ending even the minimal land redistribution carried out during Rousseff's first term in office (establishing land settlements benefiting less than 10 percent of the landless squatters). Abreu endorsed regulations facilitating the expansion of genetically modified crops and promises to forcefully evict Amazonian Indians occupying productive land in favor of large-scale agro-business corporations. Moreover, she promises to vigorously defend landlords from land occupations by landless rural workers.

Rousseff's incapacity and/or unwillingness to fire and prosecute the Workers' Party treasurer, involved in a decade-long billion-dollar kickback and bribery scandal, deepened and widened mass opposition.

On March 15, 2015, over a million Brazilians filled the streets across the country, led by rightist parties but drawing support from the popular classes, demanding immediate anti-corruption trials and stern sentences and the revocation of Levy's cuts in social expenditures.

The counter demonstration in support of Rousseff by the CUT (the Central Unica dos Trabalhadores) and the MST drew one-tenth that number—about 100,000 participants.

Rousseff responded by calling for 'dialogue' and claiming to be 'open to proposals' on the issue of corruption, but she explicitly rejected any changes in her regressive fiscal policies, neoliberal cabinet appointments and embrace of their agro-mineral agenda.

In less than two months, the Workers' Party and its president has indelibly stained its leaders, policies and backers with the brush of corruption and socially regressive policies.

Popular support has plummeted. The right wing is growing. Even the authoritarian, pro-military coup activists were present in the mass demonstrations, carrying signs calling for 'impeachment' and a return to military rule.

As in most of Latin America, the authoritarian right in Brazil is a growing force, positioning itself to take power as the center-left adopts a neoliberal agenda throughout the region. Parties dubbed center-left—like the Broad Front in Uruguay, the pro-government Party for Victory in Argentina—are deepening their ties with agro-mineral corporate capitalism.

Uninformed claims by leftist US writers like Noam Chomsky that 'Latin America is the vanguard against neoliberalism' are at best a decade late and now certainly misleading. Such commentators are deceived by populist policy pronouncements and refuse to acknowledge the decay of the center-left regimes; they thus fail to recognize how the neoliberal political actions are fostering mass popular discontent. Regimes that adopt regressive socioeconomic policies do not constitute a vanguard for social emancipation.

Conclusion

What accounts for these abrupt reversals and swiftly broken promises by recently elected supposedly 'left' parties in Europe and Latin America?

One has come to expect this kind of behaviour from the Obama Democrats in North America or the New Democratic Party in Canada. But we were led to believe that in France, with its red republican traditions, a socialist regime backed by anti-capitalist leftists would at least implement progressive social reforms. An army of progressive bloggers told us that Syriza, with its charismatic leader and radical rhetoric, would at least fulfil its basic promises by lifting the yoke of Troika domination and begin to end destitution, including returning electricity to 300,000 candle-lit households. 'Progressives' had repeatedly told us that the Workers' Party lifted thirty million out of poverty. They claimed that a former 'honest auto worker' (Lula Da Silva) would never allow the Workers' Party to revert back to neoliberal budget cuts and embrace its supposed 'class enemies'. US leftist professors refused to give credence to the crass billion-dollar robbery of the Brazilian National Treasury under two Workers' Party presidents.

Several explanations for these political betrayals come to mind. First, despite their popular or 'workerist' claims, these parties were run by middle-class lawyers, professionals and trade union bureaucrats, who were organically disconnected from their mass base. During election campaigns, seeking votes, they briefly embraced workers and the poor, but then spent the rest of their time in pricey restaurants working out 'deals' with bankers, business bribe granters and overseas investors to finance their next election, their children's private schools and their mistresses' luxury apartments.

For a time, when the economy was booming, big corporate profits, payoffs and bribes went hand in hand with wage increases and poverty programs. But when the crisis broke, the 'popular' leaders doffed their Party hats and pronounced 'fiscal austerity was inevitable' while going with their begging cups before their international financial overlords.

In all these countries faced with difficult times, the middle-class leaders of the left feared both the problem (capitalist crisis) and the real solution (radical transformation). Thus, they turned to the 'only' solution: they approached capitalist leaders and sought to convince business associations and, above all, their financial overlords that they were 'serious and responsible', willing to forsake social agendas and embrace fiscal discipline. For domestic consumption they cursed and threatened the elites, providing a little theater to entertain their plebeian followers before they capitulated!

None of the academics-turned-left-leaders have any deep or abiding links to mass struggle. Their 'activism' involves reading papers at social forums and giving papers at conferences on emancipation and equality. Political sell-outs and fiscal austerity will not jeopardize their economic positions. If their parties are ousted by angry constituents and radical social movements, the left leaders pack their bags and return to comfortable tenured jobs or rejoin their law offices. They do not have to worry about mass firings or reduced subsistence pensions. At their leisure they will sit back and write another paper on the how the 'crisis of capitalism' undermined their well-intentioned social agenda or how they experienced the 'crisis of the left'.

Because of their disconnect from the suffering of the impoverished, unemployed voters, the middle-class leftists in office are blind to the need to make a break with the system. In reality, they share the worldview of their supposedly conservative adversaries: they too believe that 'it's capitalism or chaos'. This cliché is passed off as a deep insight into the dilemmas of democratic socialists. The middle-class leftist officials and advisers always use the alibi of 'institutional constraints'. They 'theorize' their political impotence; they never recognize the power of organized class movements.

Their political cowardice is structural and leads to easy moral betrayals: they plead that 'crisis is not a time to tinker with the system'.

For the middle class, 'time' becomes a political excuse. Middle-class leaders of popular movements, lacking audacity or programs of struggle, talk of change … in the future.

Instead of mass struggle, they run to and fro between centers of financial power and their central committees, confusing 'dialogues' that end in submission with consequential resistance.

182 Ideology of Empire

In the end the people will repay them by turning their backs and reject-ing their pleas to re-elect them for 'another chance'.

There will not be another chance. This 'left' will be discredited in the eyes of those whose trust they betrayed.

The tragedy is that the entire left will be tarnished. Who can believe the fine words of 'liberation', 'the will to hope' and the 'return of sovereignty' after experiencing years of the opposite?

Left politics will be lost for an entire generation, at least in Brazil, France and Greece.

The right will ridicule the open zipper of Hollande, the false humility of Rousseff, the hollow gestures of Tsipras and the clowning of Varoufakis.

The people will curse their memory and their betrayal of a noble cause.

Note

1 On the political dynamics of this 'progressive cycle' see J. Petras and H. Velt-meyer (2019). *Latin America in the Vortex of Social Change*. London: Routledge.

Chapter 26

An Empire Built on Fear at Home and Abroad

Political leaders and the mass media deluge the public with a constant stream of frightening incidents caused by the enemy of the week: nerve gas killing dozens of little babies in Syria, Russian-directed poison assassination attempts in England and terror incidents throughout Europe—all requiring an increase in domestic police state surveillance and spying. Extensively monitored bank records, intrusive workplace controls and all personal and, especially, political communications are in the hands of state security officials or corporate security contractors.

Hundreds of prosecuting attorneys look forward to career-enhancing investigations in perpetuity, tracking the complex networks of extended personal and family links, including long-forgotten acquaintances and the contents of casual conversations. Everyone may be subject to interrogations without warrant or explanation. And the media cheers on the process.

Political trials and convictions in court and the media are rampant. Social, workplace and academic self-censorship and blacklisting of dissident voices have become pervasive and accepted. Elections and appointments are rigged by corporate and special interests to favor the most bellicose ideologues who manufacture the pretexts for war.

Political intimidation, trade wars and sanctions run amok.

'Exceptional' people in authority are defined by their power to bludgeon the majority into passive submission. Corporate mass media propaganda repeats brief and lurid messages calling for the death and destruction of the latest 'fill-in-the-blank' enemy.

War fever is everywhere infesting the minds of local opinion leaders, who echo the rants and raves of psychotic leaders without pausing to question them.

Mexican immigrant workers are described as dangerous invaders, drug dealers, rapists and a threat to the everyday life of ordinary citizens. Walls are being constructed and thousands of National Guards are called to the border to confront the invading agricultural workers and their families. Before this, Muslims were broadly described as brainwashed terrorists, programed to plant bombs at their first opportunity anywhere and everywhere—on mass transport, in congested amusement parks, in any public space where the innocent may be harmed. A draconian ban of the entry of Muslims has been instituted, affecting even elderly parents joining their citizen sons or daughters.

After the latest maniacal massacre of students, understaffed public schools (but not private, elite schools) are urged to arm their teachers with baseball bats, rocks and guns. Instead of multiplication drills, terrified teachers hold daily and weekly drills in their over-crowded classrooms—stuffing their pupils into closets and bathrooms. Elementary school lunchtimes have become prison-like exercises in 'total silence' as if to fool a would-be shooter. Images of little Oliver Twist meekly whispering to an armed guard for a bathroom pass come to mind. Haunting some outraged parents is the fear that a mad intruder might set fire to the school, suffocating scores of children locked in closets and bathroom stalls because fire drills have been superseded by 'shooter' drills.

Fear stalks the land! Where will it end?

An Empire Built on Fear

Domination is the driving force of US empire builders. But today's empire is built on fragile economic foundations. An empire that aimed to dominate the world for the long duration now stumbles over a series of military defeats abroad and increasingly relies on aiming propaganda at and instilling fear in its domestic citizenry to regain its dominance. Inculcating fear, especially at home, is the method of choice.

Since the ruling class of the '1 percent' seeks to maintain its world domination, based on increasing exploitation and widening inequalities, voluntary submission of the majority cannot be taken for granted.

The vast majority of citizens no longer trust the ruling elite. The school lessons in democracy and civic responsibility have lost their credibility. How can public school children, who now cower in closets, believe in citizen and constitutional rights?

Unending economic insecurity and increasingly phony patriotic sideshows are beginning to stir up popular discontent. Large-scale, long-term trillion-dollar bank bailouts and exorbitant military budgets are financed by the slash and burn of workers' wages, job security, public services and the social safety net. Soaring medical costs are the primary cause of personal bankruptcy among the working and lower middle classes. A physician-pharmaceutical industry fuels an opioid addiction crisis that narcotizes millions and kills well over a hundred Americans each day. The unemployed are prescribed multiple mood-altering drugs to numb their anxieties about the future. Fear, incompetent medical care, self-destruction, despair and pain all lead to premature death, causing the life expectancy among workers to drop for the first time in US history.

Professionals and opinion leaders, from teachers and physicians to journalists, have abandoned their ethics and enabled the mass deception and oppression of their students, patients and readers.

An empire that fails to reward its supporters, like President Trump's marginalized voters, and repeatedly reneges on its promises can only rely on fear.

The fear we experience is introduced by the ruling class; repeated and embellished by the mass media; and made legitimate by local opinion leaders through face-to-face daily encounters. Teachers and terrified parents instill this fear into the very young without stopping to analyze the origins and motives behind the fear-mongering.

The mass message tells us that we face daily threats from terrorists; that we must increase our vigilance; that we must constantly strengthen police-state powers; that we must accept the use of advanced lethal police weaponry on our streets; that we must inform on our neighbours and co-workers and see them as potential terrorists, militants, activists, critics and immigrants embedded in offices, factories, schools, churches and neighbourhoods. Meanwhile, our oligarch-leaders bless themselves with massive tax cuts and enjoy the greatest concentration of wealth in history.

Fear diverts attention from the imperial state as it engages in dozens of wars and occupies several hundred overseas military bases. The simple comment that this has resulted in countless thousands of deaths and countless millions of destroyed lives, not to speak of the countless billions of dollars funnelled into the bulging pockets of the ruling class, is censored from all public debate.

Fear permeates society; communications are bugged and manipulated. People are afraid to discuss, let alone move to solve, their common socio-economic problems for fear of reprisals. The message to the many is 'keep it to yourself or to your closest kin'.

Fearful people are compelled to publicly demonstrate their loyalty to the state—wear flag pins and repeat illogical propaganda about the 'enemy of the week'.

Peaceful objections to worshipping the symbols of the state are demonized and non-conformists, even those who are talented athletes, are punished by the state and see their careers publicly demolished—collective punishment for any who resist injustice.

Fear and hopelessness feed the opioid epidemic—with millions of workers addicted, a direct result of work place injury and job insecurity, as well as incompetent medical care in the absence of a truly accountable national health care system. Physicians may have been 'pressured' to prescribe highly addictive drugs, but they grew rich in the process.

Fear prevents speaking out and collective struggle. Just turn on the television news: the demagogues for the ruling class direct the masses to look downward instead of upward, to fear the poor or the immigrant rather than the banker or the militarist.

Fear is converted into anger directed at foreigners, Muslims, Afro-Americans, 'deplorable' (meaning poor, marginalized, working-class) whites, war protestors and strikers.

Islamophobes, Russophobes and Sinophobes monopolize the channels of opinion. Any critic of Israel is fired and permanently blacklisted. Critics identifying the 'neo-cons' behind the current march to war are denounced as crypto-anti-Semites. The loudest war criminals are re-appointed to high political office—despite their blood-drenched past.

Fear and self-loathing go hand in hand to secure submission to the ruling class, which channels self-hatred toward political adversaries, external economic competitors and domestic victims (the poor, the marginalized and unemployed)—who cannot die or be locked up fast enough.

Pervasive fear is constantly invented and re-invented to keep the populace on edge, unbalanced and in search of seemingly innocuous distractions to reduce their anxieties.

Russia is described as an advancing murderous juggernaut in order to induce popular compliance with unending arms build-ups and provide cannon fodder for an impending nuclear war.

US-organized and -funded 'regime changes' led by terrorist proxies in the Ukraine, direct invasions in Iraq, Libya and Syria, and the NATO encirclement of Russian borders and economic sanctions rely on fear-mongering. The message? We must bomb them first or they (Russia, China, Syria, Iran ... fill in the blank) will launch a sneak attack on 'us'.

Conclusion

Fear is the last desperate weapon for retaining an unchallenged world empire. Fearful adversaries are compelled to negotiate away their defenses and disarm, like Iraq and Libya, and then allow the empire to commence slaughter at will. Military threats directed against Iran are naked attempts to force them to dismantle their defensive missiles and cut ties with regional allies. The plan is to disarm and isolate Tehran in order to launch an attack with impunity and force eighty million Persians to submit to the combined wills of US, Israeli and Saudi Arabian oligarchs.

China is threatened with trade wars and air and maritime encirclement by the US military. This aims to strike fear in the Chinese leadership and force them to surrender economic sovereignty, financial markets and industrial competitiveness in order to reverse China's growth and advances.

Step-by-step concessions by targeted nations will lead to great takeovers. The ultimate goal, since the time of President Harry Truman, is the reconquest of the Asian giant, reducing the Chinese to beg with a rusty iron rice bowl.

Russia will be accused of poison gas attacks and war crimes everywhere, from Ukraine to the quiet lanes of England to the US–Saudi-funded war against its ally Syria. These serve as a pretext for greater economic sanctions, eliminating all possibility for debate and diplomatic resolution, leading to economic blockades and global war.

The American ruling-class's dream is to rule over a radiated world from the luxury of billion-dollar bunkers! Even as they strike fear and hysteria in the citizenry, they expose their methods: the only real fear is the power of manufactured fear itself.

The ruling class has planted fear-mongers throughout both political parties. They only seem to compete over which is more successful in sowing confusion and fear among voters: numerous immigrants are rounded up from work and home; missile strikes and wars expand into three continents; media and mass communications are largely controlled by the military-industrial complex; secret police investigations are routine; prosecutors seek to investigate even our grandfathers, long cold in their graves.

Fearful Americans are just spectators, 'quiet Americans' waiting for the next massacre, the next bomb to fall. They are told to cower in their bedrooms, while their children are shoved into closets. They are now fearful that the Russians (or this week's fill-in-the-blank intruder) will poison our pizzas or bomb us to the Stone Age.

Wall Street fears that they will lose China, the biggest financial market in the world, as trade wars turn 'hot'.

The Pentagon fears that its ships will collide in the Potomac River and some 'temp' contractor will push the wrong button.

Senators fear losing their perks as they drag their young interns into basement bunkers … for their own safety.

The president, his cabinet, UN representatives and senior advisers are afraid that the population might wake up to find that missiles and nukes can move in both directions.

By the time the masses finally discover that the greatest menace stalking the country is the fear-mongering propaganda, they will be reading an epitaph for their untimely nuclear death.

Chapter 27

Imperial Road to Conquest
Peace and Disarmament Agreements

In recent years US imperial strategy has sought to lessen the cost of defeating and overthrowing independent countries. The means and method are fairly straightforward. Worldwide propaganda campaigns which demonize the adversary; the enlistment and collaboration of European and regional allies (the UK, France, Saudi Arabia and Israel); the recruitment, contracting, training and arming of local and overseas mercenaries dubbed 'rebels' or 'democrats'; economic sanctions to provoke domestic social tensions and political instability of the government; proposals to negotiate a settlement; negotiations which demand non-reciprocal concessions and which include changes in strategic weapons in exchange for promises to end sanctions, diplomatic recognition and peaceful co-existence.

The strategic goal is disarmament in order to facilitate military and political intervention leading up to and beyond defeat, occupation, regime change; 'client regime' impositions to facilitate the pillage of economic resources and the securing of military bases, international alignment with the US empire and a military springboard for further conquests against neighbours and independent adversaries.

We will apply this model to recent and current examples of US tactical and strategic empire building in diverse regions, especially focusing on North Africa (Libya), the Middle East (Iraq, Palestine, Syria and Iran), Asia (North Korea), and Latin America (FARC in Colombia).

Case 1: Libya

After several decades of failed efforts to overthrow the popular Libyan government of Muammar Gaddafi via local tribal and monarchist armed terrorists, and international economic sanctions, the US proposed a policy of negotiations and accommodation.

The US opened negotiations to end sanctions, offered diplomatic recognition and acceptance in the 'international community', in exchange for Gaddafi's demobilization and abandonment of Libya's strategic arms including its long-range ballistic missiles and other effective deterrents. The US did not reduce its military bases, ready and alert, targeting Tripoli.

In 2003 Gaddafi signed off on the agreement with the George W. Bush regime. Major US Libyan oil agreements and diplomatic accords were signed. US security adviser Condoleezza Rice visited President Gaddafi as a symbol of peace and friendship, even as US military aid was channeled to armed US clients.

In February 2011 the US, led by President Obama and Secretary of State Hillary Clinton, joined with its EU allies (France, UK ...) and bombed Libya—its infrastructure, ports, transport centers, oil facilities, hospitals and schools ... . US and EU-backed terrorists seized control of the major cities and captured, tortured and murdered President Gaddafi. Over two million immigrant workers were forced to flee to Europe and the Middle East or return to Central Africa.

Case 2: Iraq

Iraq under Saddam Hussein received arms and support from Washington to attack and invade Iran. This de facto agreement encouraged the Iraqi leader to assume that collaboration between nationalist Iraq and imperial Washington reflected a common agenda. Subsequently, Baghdad believed that they had tacit US support in a territorial dispute with Kuwait. When Saddam invaded, the US bombed, devastated, invaded, occupied and partitioned Iraq.

The US backed the Kurds' territorial seizure in the north and imposed a no-fly zone. Subsequently, President William Clinton engaged in several bombing attacks that failed to dislodge Saddam Hussein.

Under President G. W. Bush, the US launched a full-scale war, invasion and occupation, killing several hundred thousand Iraqis and alienating an entire nation. The US systematically dismantled the modern secular state and its vital institutions while fomenting the most brutal religious and ethnic wars between Shia and Sunni Iraqis.

The attempt by Iraq in the 1980s to collaborate with Washington against its nationalist neighbor Iran led to the invasion, the destruction of the country, the killing of thousands of secular leaders, including Saddam Hussein, as well as the entire secular and scientific intelligentsia, and the transformation of Iraq into a toothless vassal state.

Case Three: Syria

Syria's president Bashar al-Assad, unlike Gaddafi and Hussein, retained a degree of independence in the face of Washington's overtures, even as he sought to accommodate US incursions in Lebanon and its support for the largely minority Christian and pro-Western opposition.

In 2011, the US broke its tacit accommodation and provided arms and finance to its local Islamist clients for an uprising that seized control of most of the countryside and major cities, including half of Damascus. In response, Assad sought the support of Russia, Iran and the Lebanese Hezbollah fighters. Over the next seven years, the US and EU-backed terrorists were defeated and forced to retreat, despite massive military, financial and logistic support from the US, EU, Israel, Saudi Arabia and Turkey.

Unlike Libya and Iraq, Syria has managed to reconquer most of its territory because it was able to secure an armed alliance with strategic allies who succeeded in neutralizing domestic insurgents.

Case 4: FARC

The FARC was formed in the early 1960s as a largely peasant army which had grown, by 2000, to nearly 30,000 fighters and millions of supporters, mostly in the countryside. In effect a dual system of power predominated outside the major cities.

The FARC made several attempts to negotiate a peace settlement with the Colombian oligarchical regime. In the late 1970s a temporary agreement led sections of the FARC to shed arms, form an electoral party, the Patriotic Union, and participate in elections. After several electoral gains, the oligarchy abruptly broke the agreement, unleashed a campaign of terror, and assassinated 5,000 party activists and several presidential and congressional candidates and elected officials. The FARC returned to armed struggle.

During subsequent negotiations, between 1980 and 1981, the oligarchical regime broke off talks and raided the meeting site in an attempt to assassinate the FARC representatives, who successfully evaded capture. Despite the repeated failures, in 2016 the FARC agreed to enter into 'peace negotiations' with the Colombian regime of President Juan Manuel Santos, a former defense minister who was a leading force during the 2001–2010 extermination campaign in the countryside and urban slums. However, major political changes took place within the FARC. During the previous decade the historic leaders of the FARC had either been killed or died and were replaced by a new cohort that lacked the experience and commitment to secure agreements that advanced peace with justice while retaining their arms in case the untrustworthy oligarchical regime, which had repeatedly sabotaged negotiations, reneged on the so-called peace agreement.

In blind pursuit of peace, the FARC agreed to demobilize and disarm its revolutionary army; it failed to secure socio-economic reforms, including land reform; it turned security over to the regime's military forces linked to landlords, the seven US military bases and narco-death squads.

The 'peace agreement' destroyed the FARC. Once disarmed, the regime reneged on the agreement: dozens of FARC combatants were assassinated or forced to flee; the oligarchs retained total control over land from dispossessed peasants, natural resources, public funding and elections; FARC leaders and activists were jailed and subject to death threats and a constant barrage of hostile public and private media propaganda.

The FARC's disastrous peace agreement led to internal splits, divisions and isolation. By the end of 2017, the FARC disintegrated: each fraction went its own way. Some rejoined reduced guerrilla groupings; others abandoned the struggle and sought employment; others pursued opportunities to collaboration with the regime or became coca farmers.

The oligarchy and the US secured the surrender and defeat of the FARC—which it had failed to accomplish in four decades of military warfare—through negotiations.

Case 5: Iran—The Nuclear Accord

In 2016 Iran signed a peace accord with seven signatories: the US, the UK, France, Germany, China, Russia, and the European Union. The agreement stipulated that Iran would limit its manufacture of enriched uranium which had dual use—civilian and military—and ship it out of the country. Iran permitted Western inspection of nuclear facilities—which found Teheran in full compliance.

In exchange the US and its collaborators agreed to end economic sanctions, unfreeze Iranian assets and end restrictions on trade, banking and investment.

The Iranians fully complied. Enriched uranium laboratories ceased producing and shipped-out remaining stock. Inspections were granted full access of Iranian facilities.

In contrast, the Obama regime did not fully comply. Partial sanctions were lifted but others were reinforced, deeply restricting Iran's access to financial markets—in clear violation of the agreement. Nevertheless, Iran continued to maintain its part of the agreement.

With the elections of Donald Trump, the US rejected the agreement ('it's the worst deal ever') and in compliance with the Israeli prime minister B. Netanyahu's military agenda, demanded the total restoration of sanctions, the dismantling of Iran's entire military defenses and its submission to the US, Israeli and Saudi Arabian dictates in the Middle East.

In other words, President Trump discarded the agreement in opposition to all the major countries in Europe and Asia, in favor of Israel's demands to isolate, disarm and attack Iran and impose a puppet regime in Teheran.

French prime minister Emmanuel Macron sought to 'modify' (sic) the agreement to include some of Trump's demands to secure new military concessions from Iran, including that it (1) abandon its allies in the region (Syria, Iraq, Yemen, Palestine, Lebanon-Hezbollah, and Islamic mass movements), (2) dismantle and end its advanced inter-continental ballistic missile defense system, (3) accept US (Israeli) supervision and inspection of all its military bases and scientific centers.

President Macron's posture was to 'save' the form of the 'agreement' by ... destroying the substances. He shared Trump's objective but sought a step by step approach based on 'modifying' the existing agreement. Trump chose the Israeli approach; a frontal repudiation of the entire agreement, accompanied by overt threats of a military attack, if Iran rejected concessions and refused to capitulate to Washington.

Case 6: Palestine

The US pretended to broker a peace agreement between Israel and Palestine in which Israel would recognize Palestine, end colonization and pursue a peace settlement based on mutually agreed to a two-state solution based on pre-1967 territorial and historical rights. The United States under President Clinton hailed the settlement ... and then proceeded to back each and every one of Israel's present and future violations. Over 600,000 of Israel's colonists seized land and expelled tens of thousands of Palestinians. Israel regularly invades the West Bank and has assassinated and jailed tens of thousands of Palestinians. Israel seized total control of Jerusalem. The US endorsed, armed and financed, Israel's step-by-step ethnic cleansing and the Judaification of Palestine.

Case 7: North Korea

The US has recently stated that it favors a negotiated agreement initiated by North Korean President Kim Jong-Un. Pyongyang has offered to end its nuclear programs and testing, and to negotiate a permanent peace treaty including the denuclearization of the peninsula and the retention of US military forces in South Korea.

President Trump has pursued a strategy of 'support' of the negotiation ... while tightening economic sanctions and continuing military exercises in South Korea. In the run-up to negotiations the US has made no reciprocal concessions. Trump overtly threatens to scuttle the negotiations if North Korea does not submit to Washington's insistence that North Korea disarm and demobilize their defenses. In other words, President Trump wants North Korea to follow the policies that led to the US's successful invasion and military conquest and destruction of Iraq, Libya and the FARC.

Washington's negotiations for a Korean peace agreement will follow the same path as its recent broken 'nuclear agreement' with Iran, the one-sided disarmament of Teheran and the subsequent reneging of the agreement.

For empire builders like the US, negotiations are tactical diversions to disarm independent countries in order to weaken and attack them, as all of our case studies demonstrate.

Conclusion

In our studies we have highlighted how Washington uses 'negotiations' and 'peace processes' as tactical weapons to enhance empire building. By disarming and demobilizing adversaries it facilitates strategic goals like regime change.

Knowing that empire builders are perfidious enemies does not mean countries should reject peace processes and negotiations—because that would give Washington a propaganda weapon. Instead, imperial adversaries could follow the following guidelines.

Negotiations should lead to reciprocal concessions—not one-sided, especially non-reciprocal reductions of arms programs. Negotiations should never demilitarize and demobilize its defense forces—this increases vulnerability and permits sudden attacks. Negotiators should retain their ability to impose a high cost for imperial violations and, especially, sudden reversals of military and economic agreements. Imperial violators hesitate to invade when the human and national costs are high and politically unpopular.

Imperial opponents should not remain isolated. They must secure military allies. The case of Syria is clear. Assad built a coalition of Russia, Iran and Hezbollah that effectively countered the US-EU-Israeli-Turkish and Saudi-backed terrorist 'rebels'.

Iran did agree to dismantle its nuclear capacity but it retained its ICBM program, which can retaliate to surprise military attacks by Israel or the US. Almost surely Israel will insist that the US suffer the cost of Middle East wars, to Tel Aviv's advantage.

North Korea has already made unilateral, non-reciprocal concessions to the US and to a lesser degree to South Korea. If it is unable to secure allies (like China and Russia), and if it ends its nuclear deterrent, it invites pressure for more concessions.

Lifting economic sanctions can be reciprocated but not by compromising strategic military defenses. The basic principles are reciprocity, strategic defense and tactical economic flexibility. The guiding idea is that there are no permanent allies, only permanent interests. Misguided trust in lofty Western imperial 'values' and not realistic recognition of imperial interests can be fatal to independent leaders and destructive to a people, as was clearly the case for Iraq, Libya and Palestine and near fatal for Syria. The most recent example is the case of Iran: the US signed a peace agreement in 2016 and repudiated it in 2017. It behooves North Korea to learn from the Iranian experience.

The imperial time frame for repudiating agreement may vary; Libya signed a disarmament agreement with the US in 2003 and Washington bombed them in 2011. In all cases the principle remains the same. There is no historical example of an imperial power renouncing its interests in compliance with a paper agreement. It only abides with agreements when it has no other options.

Chapter 28

Mapping Trump's Empire
Assets and Liabilities

The US empire spans the globe; it expands and contracts according to its ability to secure strategic assets, willing and able to further military and economic power to counter emerging adversaries.

The map of empire is a shorthand measure of the vectors, reach and durability of global power and wealth. The map of empire is changing—adding and subtracting assets and liabilities according to the successes and retreats of domestic and overseas power centers. While the US empire has been engaged in intense conflicts in the Middle East, elsewhere the imperial map has been enlarged at lower cost and greater success.

Expanding the Empire

The US empire has substantially increased its scope and presence in several regions, especially in Latin America. The additions and enlargements include Argentina, Brazil, Colombia, Mexico, Central America, Peru and the Caribbean. The most important asset redrawing the empire in Latin America is Argentina. The US has gained military, economic and political advantages. In the case of Argentina, political and economic advances preceded military expansion.

The US provided ideological and political support to secure the election of its client Mauricio Macri. The new Argentinian president immediately transferred over $5 billion dollars to the notorious Wall Street 'Vulture' speculator, Paul Singer, and proceeded to open the floodgates for a lucrative multi-billion-dollar flow of financial capital. President Macri then followed up by inviting the Pentagon and US intelligence services to establish military bases, spy stations and training operations along its borders. Equally important, Argentina embraced the US directives designed to overthrow the government of Venezuela, undermine Bolivia's nationalist government under Evo Morales and pursue a policy of US-centered regional integration. However, while Argentina is a useful political and military addition to the US empire, it lacks access to the US market—it still depends on China—and has failed to secure a strategic trade agreement with the European Union. Washington has enlarged its military presence with a one-legged client.

Colombia and Mexico, long-time US client states, have provided springboards for enlarging US influence in Central America, the Andean region and the Caribbean. In the case of Colombia, the US has financed its war of extermination against anti-imperialist insurgents and their peasant and working-class supporters and secured seven military bases as launch pads for Washington's destabilization campaign against Venezuela.

Mexico has served a multitude of military and economic functions—from billion-dollar manufacturing platforms to multi-billion-dollar laundering of narco-profits to US banks.

Brazil is the new addition to the empire, with the ousting and arrest of the leaders of the Workers' Party. The shift in political and economic power has enhanced US influence through its leverage over the wealthiest country in the continent. In short, the US has enlarged imperial influence and control via its acquisition of Latin America. There is one caveat: at least in the cases of Brazil and Argentina, the US advance is tentative and subject to reversal as it lacks firm economic and political foundations.

If Latin America reflects an enlargement and upsurge of US imperial influence, the rest of the global map is mostly negative or at best contradictory. The empire-building mission has failed to gain ground in Northeast Asia, the Middle East and North Africa. In Europe, the US retains influence but appears to face obstacles to enlarging its presence.

The key to the enlargement or decline of empire revolves around the performance of the US domestic economy.

Imperial Decline: The China Factor

The determination of the US in remapping its global empire is most evident in Asia. The most notable shift in US political and economic relations in the region has taken place with China's displacement of the US as the dominant investment, trading, infrastructure-building and lending country in the region. Moreover, China has increased its role as the leading exporter to the US, accumulating trade surpluses of hundreds of billions of dollars each year. In 2017, China's trade surplus reached $375 billion dollars.

Washington has compensated for the relative economic decline of the US by widening the scope of its maritime-military presence in the South China Sea and increasing its air and ground forces in South Korea, Japan, Australia, the Philippines and Guam. But how this bolstering of its military presence affects the US's 're-mapping' of its imperial presence depends on the dynamics of the US domestic economy and its ability to retains its existing principal military clients—South Korea, Japan, Australia and the Philippines. Recent evidence suggests that South Korea shows signs of slipping outside of the US economic and military orbit. Seoul has trade issues with the US 'protectionist agenda' and opportunities to expand its trading links with China. Equally important, South Korea has moved toward reconciliation with North Korea and downgraded the US military escalation. As goes South Korea, so goes the US military power base in northern Asia.

The US military strategy is premised on sustaining and expanding its client network. However, its protectionist policies led to the rejection of a multi-lateral trade agreement that erodes its economic ties with existing or potential military partners. In contrast to Latin America, the US remaking of the imperial map has led to economic shrinkage and military isolation in Asia. US military escalation has poured even more deadly strategic US arms into the region but failed to intimidate or isolate China or North Korea.

Chapter 29

Latin America in the Time of Trump

I think the Monroe Doctrine is as relevant today as it was the day it was
written [two centuries ago].

Rex Tillerson, Secretary of State, 1 February 2018

President Trump cancelled his attendance at the 2018 Summit of the
Americas meeting of all 35 presidents of the region designed to debate and
formulate a common policy. Trump delegated Vice President Michael
Pence to take his place. The choice of VP Pence, a known nonentity with
zero experience and even less knowledge of Latin America–US relations,
was indicative of the Trump regime's disdain and low opinion of the eighth
meeting of the tri-annual Summit.

President Trump did not feel obligated to attend because the agenda,
decisions and outcome had already been decided in accordance with the
best interests of the empire. Former Secretary of State Rex Tillerson made
clear that Latin America is Washington's backyard, that the Monroe Doctrine is alive and well.

The revival of the Monroe Doctrine is a work in progress—a collective
effort that preceded the Trump regime and is now on full display. To
understand the ascendancy of the two-century-old Monroe Doctrine
requires that we examine the process—the means and methods that installed
Trump's satraps.

Many Roads, Common Outcomes

The 21st century began with a series of upheavals that challenged incumbent neoliberal client states and installed a series of center-left regimes that
increased social spending and declared their independence from the US.
The progressive politicians wrote premature death certificates for the
Monroe Doctrine as they were co-signed by local bankers, generals and
business oligarchs. In other words, Latin America experienced a series of
temporary reforms based on oligarchical foundations.

A decade and a half later, the Trump regime proclaimed the resurrection of Monroeism: puppets, pillage and plunder became the new order of the day throughout Latin America. Client legislators successfully plotted a series of coups, ousting elected presidents in Brazil, Paraguay and Honduras, replacing them with bona fide US-approved satraps.

The Secretary General of the Organization of American States (OAS), Luis Almagro, a former foreign minister of a center-left regime in Uruguay, blessed Washington's mouthpieces. Rigged elections in Mexico and Guatemala ensured Washington a pair of reliable flunkies. Death squads and a narco-President Santos in Colombia provided the Pentagon with seven military bases and US investors with several oil fields. Swindlers and fraudsters with intimate ties to Wall Street took office in Argentina and Peru. An ex-leftist in Ecuador Lenin Moreno appealed to the people to win an election and once taking office worked for the oligarchs. In other words, through diverse routes that combined rigged elections and political violence, presidents Bush and Obama set the stage for President Trump to inherit a servile entourage of self-styled democratic ... satraps.

President Trump did not need to join the Summit meeting since Donald's scribes had already written the program and the policies to be followed.

In the run-up to the Summit, the Latin American presidents spent their time in office demonstrating their fealty to the Trump version of the Monroe Doctrine.

On taking office, Argentina president Mauricio Macri paid $6 billion to a Wall Street speculator; contracted a $100-billion debt to US and UK bankers; lowered and/or eliminated corporate taxes for agro-exporters; quadrupled charges on gas, electric and water utilities for households and small and medium businesses; privatized mines and oil fields; fired several thousand public sector medical and educational professionals, impoverishing health and educational facilities; extended US military bases across the country; and welcomed chemical companies that contaminate the countryside. In exchange, Trump overlooked Macri's swindles and overseas bank accounts and praised his police-state measures.

Brazil's president Michel Temer was installed in office via a congressional coup, promising to privatize the public transport, infrastructure, mining, oil and electrical sectors as well as the financial and banking system. Temer and his congressional and judicial allies ensured that military and diplomatic alliances served Washington's drive to overthrow the Venezuelan, Cuban and Bolivian governments. Temer and his judicial allies jailed the leading opposition presidential candidate, Lula Da Silva.

Trump's satraps in the Brazilian military joined the US in policing the continent. In exchange, President Temer, with 95 percent popular disapproval and facing jail, secured President Trump's permission to seek asylum in Miami and membership in his golf club once out of office.

Mexican president Peña Neto privatized the national patrimony—the oil fields, mines and banks. Neto collaborated with police, military and paramilitary groups murdering dozens of opposition students, critical journalists and human rights workers. Neto allowed drug trafficking, bankers and business leaders to launder billions of dollars in overseas accounts to evade taxes. President Peña Neto was an active supporter of Washington's international policies—in particular its efforts to isolate and overthrow the Venezuelan government. Because of Peña Neto's subservience to Washington, President Trump demanded further concessions, including US control of the Mexican border, immigration and internal policing.

Colombia under presidents Uribe and Santos provided the US with seven military bases. President Santos signed a peace agreement with the FARC and proceeded to disarm and murder over fifty former FARC guerrillas and order the jailing and extradition of one of its leaders, Jesús Santrich. President Santos signed off on lucrative oil concessions with US and other multinationals.

Newly elected Ecuadorian president Lenin Moreno followed Brazilian, Mexican, Peruvian, Argentine and Chilean presidents in handing over strategic natural resources to US multinationals. All of these political clients supported US efforts to exclude Venezuelan president Maduro from the Summit of the Americas for opposing coups, Trump and the Monroe Doctrine.

The oligarchs backed Washington's efforts to delegitimize the Venezuelan elections in May 2018 and to paralyze its economy in order to overthrow the elected president.

The Triumph of Neo-Monroeism

President Trump presides over the Americas—with the exception of Cuba, Venezuela and Bolivia. Washington has successfully orchestrated the conversion of Latin America to a major political, military and diplomatic launch pad for US global domination.

None of the regimes have any legitimacy. They all came to power through illicit means—their elections fuelled by corruption, force, violence and US complicity.

The Americas receive 42 percent of US manufacturing exports (most going to Mexico and Canada) and are a major market for US arms and toxic agro-chemicals. Nevertheless, Washington is losing its economic competition with China in the region—and as a result Trump is attempting to pressure its clients to reduce their ties, accusing China of being 'imperialist'. However, Latin America's rulers want to serve both powers: the US politically and China economically.

Conclusion

President Trump has embraced the Monroe Doctrine in his pursuit of dominance in Latin America. Washington takes for granted the oligarchs' submission and makes no pretence of consultation: it simply dictates policies via US emissaries.

Under President Trump's tutelage, Latin American subjects negotiate the terms of their surrender of sovereignty in order to secure a share of the economic pillage for their oligarchs and US military protection.

Trump is particularly proud that US dominance is virtually free of cost and effort. The Latin oligarchs do not demand any economic or military aid: the clients pay for policing the empire and contract neoliberal economists to hand over their public patrimony.

Latin American clients mouth speeches that echo Trump's interventionist policies. Latin American oligarchs ignore President Trump's domestic crises and political instability as well as his nuclear war threat to Syria and sanctions against Russia.

Only in one area does the Latin American oligarchy not follow Washington's orders: it refuses to boycott China. Argentina, Chile, Peru and Brazil's major exports of agro-mineral commodities depend on Beijing—which has also become a principle source of loans and foreign investments.

Washington has secured political dominance (or 'hegemony', as polite pundits call it) but it wants more!

President Trump demands a joint military force to overthrow the Venezuelan government and install a client regime. Trump can count on OAS boss Luis Almagro to provide the rhetoric, but his clients need the military to prop up their own rule.

Trump tells his Latin American clients to isolate and lessen ties to China. However, they fear fuelling domestic elite opposition. At most, Washington can count on clients in Honduras, Paraguay and Argentina to follow Trump's lead.

Trump secured Peña Neto's agreement to revise NAFTA in order to increase US trade advantages, allow the US greater control over the border and increase the flow of laundered money through US banks. Mexico assumes the costs of collaborating with the Trump regime.

So far the Trump regime has had a free ride running the Latin American imperial provinces on the cheap! So much so that it has ignored these clients and relegated them to Washington's backyard. Trump, Wall Street and Pentagon supporters are reasonably content with the running of the Americas: they are reaping high-interest loans and pay backs; grabbing thousands of public enterprises at bargain basement prices; benefiting from cost-free military bases including ports and airbases; and they have control over pliable client generals at their beck and call.

What and who can spoil Trump's imperial party in Latin America?

Venezuela holds elections. President Maduro wins, defeats coup plots and proceeds to diversify the economy and markets, lower inflation and begin an economic recovery.

Cuba renews its revolutionary program and leadership; democratizes its economy and socializes its political system. Brazilian trade unions and social movements organize general strikes, paralyze the economy, free Lula. He is re-elected to advance the struggle far beyond the crooked court and corrupt electoral system.

Argentina explodes; trade unions, the unemployed and the dispossessed unleash general strikes and face-off against the police; they take over the presidential palace and President Macri flees overseas; stopping off in Panama and the Bahamas to cash in his illicit holdings.

Mexico has a free and democratic election and AMLO wins, takes office and ends corruption. Trump pays for the wall.

Paraguay, Honduras and Colombia persist—death squads flourish, forcing pacified guerrillas to return to the struggle and peasants to occupy plantations.

The US mass media claim that it's all a Russian plot. Putin is accused of being behind the low beef prices in Buenos Aires and the flight of capital from Sao Paulo.

The US ambassador to the UN, Nikki Haley, claims Bashar Assad is organizing Arab border conflicts between Bolivia and Chile and narco-traffickers in Paraguay and plotting corruption in Brazil.

Trump tweets: populist resistance is all 'fake news' and fake plots. He denounces Latin oligarchs opposing his trade war as supporters of Chinese imperialism. He praises US oligarchs since they are only crooks signing business deals!

Trump organizes a barbecue for his backyard oligarchs. Only money launderers are invited.

Chapter 30

Trump's Protectionism
A Great Leap Backward

US presidents, European leaders and their academic spokespeople have attributed China's growing market share, trade surpluses and technological power to its 'theft' of Western technology, 'unfair' or non-reciprocal trade and restrictive investment practices. President Trump has launched a trade war—raising stiff tariffs, especially targeting Chinese exports—designed to pursue a protectionist economic regime.

The China-bashers of the Western world ignore the developmental experiences of the past 250 years, starting with the post-revolutionary United States policy of protecting 'infant' industries.

In this essay we will proceed to criticize the model underlying the current Western attack on China. We will then turn to outlining the experience of countries that overcame backwardness in the course of successfully industrializing their economies.

Development in Historical Perspective

Western ideologists claimed that 'backward economies' should follow a development path originally established by successful countries, namely the UK. They argued that 'stages of development' begin by embracing liberal free market policies, specializing in their 'comparative advantages', namely exporting raw materials. Economic 'modernization' would lead, stage by stage, to a mature high-consumption society.

The advocates of the liberal stage theory dominated the economic departments of major US universities and served as the planning strategy advocated by US policymakers.

Early on, dissenting economic historians pointed out serious anomalies. For example, 'early developers' like the UK secured trade advantages as a result of worldwide empires that forced colonies to exporting raw materials under unfavorable terms of trade, an advantage which 'later' countries lacked. Second, the post-revolutionary US led by Treasury Secretary Alexander Hamilton successfully promoted protectionist industrial policies to protect US 'infant' industries from the established UK empire. The US civil war was fought precisely to prevent US plantation owners from linking their exports to British liberal free traders and manufacturers.

In the mid-19th and early 20th centuries, developing countries like Germany, Japan and Soviet Russia rejected the ideology of free trade and open markets in favor of state-centered protected industrialization. They succeeded in overcoming backwardness, competing and overtaking early developers like the UK.

In the post-World War II period, after unsuccessful attempts to follow the Western free market model, South Korea, Taiwan and Malaysia successfully pursued statist, protectionist, export models of development.

Regions and countries that followed Western free-market policies specializing in primary goods exports like Latin America, Africa, the Middle East and the Philippines failed to overcome stagnation and backwardness.

A leading economic historian, Alexander Gerschenkron, argued that economic backwardness provided emerging countries with certain strategic advantages; these involved the systematic substitution of imports by domestic industries, leading to dynamic growth and subsequently competitive export strategies (*Economic Backwardness in Historical Perspective: A Book of Essays*).

The successful late developing countries borrowed and acquired the latest productive techniques while the early industrializers remained with their existing outmoded methods of production. In other words, the developing countries, guided by the state, 'jumped' stages of growth and surpassed their competitors.

China is a superb example of Gerschenkron's model. Through state intervention it overcame the constraints imposed by the monopoly controls of existing imperial countries and rapidly advanced through borrowing the most advanced technology and innovations and then moved on to become the most active filer of advanced patents in the world. In 2017 China surpassed the US, filing 225 patents in 2017 while the US lagged behind with ninety-one (*Financial Times*, 3/16/18, p. 13).

An excellent example of China's advances in technological innovation is the Huawei Group, which spent $13.8 billion on research and development in 2017 and plans to increase its annual R&D budget to $20 billion a year. Chinese companies will lead standard setting in next-generation technologies, including networking (*Financial Times*, 3/31/18, p. 12). Washington's resort to excluding China from US markets has nothing to do with China 'stealing' US patents and secrets and everything to do with Huawei's R&D spending directed at obtaining talent, technology, equipment and international partnerships. The White House's protectionist Sinophobia is driven by fear of Chinese advances in fifth-generation high-speed data networks, which are undermining the US ability to compete in cutting-edge technology.

China's competitive excellence was the result of the state's systematic substitution of advanced technology, which allowed the economy to gradually liberalize and out-compete the US in global and domestic markets.

China has followed and exceeded the example of earlier late-developing countries (Germany and Japan). It combined advanced industrial export growth as the leading sector with a relatively backward agricultural sector providing cheap, low-cost foodstuffs.

China is now moving up the development ladder, deepening its domestic market, advancing its high technology sector and gradually reducing the importance of the low-value consumer and rust belt industries.

Cry-Baby Economies Revert to Protectionism

The US failure to compete with China and its resulting trade deficits are a result of its inability to incorporate new technologies and apply them to domestic civilian production, increasing income and upgrading and incorporating the force into competitive sectors that could defend the domestic market.

The state has surrendered its leading role to the financial and military elites that have eroded US industrial competitiveness. Moreover, unlike China the state has failed to provide leadership in identifying priority targets compatible with intensified competition from China.

While China exports economic products, the US exports arms and wars. The US has a surplus of arms exports and a growing commercial deficit.

China has multi-billion-dollar infrastructure investments in over fifty countries that enhance its trade surplus. The US has multi-billion-dollar expenditures in over 800 overseas military bases.

Conclusion

US charges that China has emerged as a world economic power by unfair trade and theft of US technology ignore the entire history of all late developing countries, beginning with the US rise and eclipse of the UK during the 19th century.

The US's attempt to turn back the clock to an earlier stage of protectionism will not raise US competitiveness or increase its share of the domestic market.

US protectionism will simply result in higher prices, unskilled labor, war debts and financial monopolies. A US trade war will simply allow the Chinese state to divert trade from the US to other markets and re-direct its investments toward deepening its domestic economy, and increasing ties with Russia, Asia, Africa, Latin America and Oceana.

The US 'blame game' with China is misplaced. Instead, it should re-examine its reliance on a laissez faire economy with neither plan nor reason.

Its resort to tariffs will increase costs without raising income and improving innovation.

Current US protectionism was stillborn from the start. The White House has already downgraded its tariff that targeted competitors. Moreover, its $60 billion tariff on China affects less than 3 percent of its exports.

Instead of seeking to blame outside competitors like China it would be wiser to learn from its experience and absorb its technological advances while making strategic investments in infrastructure and domestic consumption. Until the US reduces its military spending by two-thirds, and subordinates its finance sector to industry and domestic households, it will continue to fall behind China.

Instead of returning to the strategy of backward countries reliant on the protection of infantilized industries, the US should accept that it must now compete through state-directed development linked to upgrading its workforce, raising skill levels and expanding social welfare.

Chapter 31

Trump Marches Onward and Downward

Journalists, academics, pundits and experts have ignored the complexity of President Trump's impact on the state of the US empire. To properly assess the geopolitical configuration of power, we consider the military, economic, political and diplomatic advances and setbacks of the Trump regime in Latin America, the European Union and Asia (including the Middle East). Second, we examine the time frame—the shifting direction of the present configuration of forces. We will conclude by discussing how the influence and results of foreign policy shape domestic political power.

The Background to President Trump's Empire Building

First and foremost we must take account of the fact that many of Trump's policies build on and reflect the policies of his predecessors, namely presidents Bush and Obama. The US wars in Afghanistan, Iraq, Libya and Syria were started by presidents Clinton, Bush and Obama. The US bombings of Libya and the destruction and uprooting of millions of Africans was inaugurated by Obama. The expulsion of millions of Central American and Mexican immigrants from the US was common practice prior to Trump. In short, President Trump continued, and in some cases exacerbated, the socio-economic and military policies of his predecessors. In a few areas Trump reversed policies, as was the case with Obama's nuclear agreement with Iran.

The successes and failures of Trump's empire-building policies cannot be attributed solely to his regime. Nevertheless, President Trump must be held responsible for the current state of the empire and its direction.

Trump Marches Forward in Latin America

President Trump has built upon and extended US imperial victories throughout most of Latin America. A satellite regime is in place in Brazil thanks largely to the judicial-legislative coup that overthrew president elect Dilma Rousseff. The puppet regime of Michel Temer privatized the economy, embraced Trump's dominance and aligned with efforts to over-throw Venezuela's government.

Similarly, Trump inherited from Obama the present client regimes in Argentina (President Mauricio Macri), Peru (President Martin Vizcarra), Honduras (President Hernandez) Paraguay (President Cartes), Chile (President Piñera), Ecuador (President Moreno), and most of the ruling elites in Central America and the Caribbean. Trump has added to the list current efforts to overthrow the Daniel Ortega regime in Nicaragua.

Under President Trump, Washington succeeded in reversing relations with Cuba and the so-called peace accord in Colombia between the guerrillas and the Juan Manuel Santos regime. In July 2018, Trump succeeded in backing the accession to power of Ivan Duque, a protégé of the far-right party of Alvaro Uribe in Colombia. President Obama's reversal of center-left regimes via coups have been consolidated and expanded by Trump, with the important exception of Mexico. Trump partially reversed Obama's opening of relations with Cuba and threatens to militarily invade Venezuela.

Trump's imperial empire in Latin America is, for the most part, inherited and largely sustained ... for now. But there are several crucial caveats. First, Mexico's new president Andrés Manuel López Obrador (AMLO) is likely to pursue independent and progressive foreign and domestic policies, rene-gotiating NAFTA, oil contracts and border disputes. Second, Brazil and Argentina's neoliberal economic policies are in deep crisis and the incum-bent puppet regimes are economically unstable, face mass social opposition and will likely suffer electoral defeats. Third, Venezuela and Cuba have successfully resisted economic and diplomatic sanctions.

Militarily, President Trump retains US military bases in Colombia and has incorporated Bogota into NATO; he has also secured military operations in Argentina and Ecuador. The biggest challenge to Trump's empire building in Latin America is in the all-important economic realm.

Trump has failed to gain ground in trade, investment and raw materials in the face of competition from China. Despite the political and military sub-ordination of Latin American regimes to Washington, the bulk of their trade ties are with China. Moreover, Brazil and Argentina will increase their agro-exports to China in line with Beijing's trade tariffs on US exports. In the so-called trade war not a single Latin American client state has sided with the US. On the contrary, all are taking advantage of Washington's loss of the China market to enhance their exports.

Clearly the US does not exercise 'hegemony' over Latin America's trad-ing relations. Worse still (from an imperialist perspective), Trump's dumping of the Trans-Pacific Partnership and threats to withdraw from NAFTA have reduced Washington's leverage over Latin America and Asia.

Trump's boasts and claims of dominance over Latin America is largely a product of his predecessors' imperial policies. At most, Trump's policies have hardened the far right, which, however, is weakening politically and economically and has provoked the rise of the left to power in Mexico and increased opposition in Colombia, Brazil and Argentina. In short, the Trump regime's empire-building project retains a decided influence in Latin America, but it faces major challenges and reversals.

Trump in Asia: One Step Forward, Two Steps Back

Washington has gained prestige for its diplomatic overtures to North Korea but is losing the trade war with the world's second greatest power: China.

Faced with Trump's economic war, China has diversified its trading partners, thus undermining key US agribusiness enterprises. China has implemented tariffs on canola, soybeans, corn, cotton, pork and beef. Moreover, China has replaced the US as the main trading partner throughout Asia. While Japan, South Korea and Australia provide military bases for the US, they are eager to replace Washington's export to China. Moreover, China's multi-billion-dollar Belt and Road Initiative has secured sixty-eight nations as partners, with the prominent absence of the self-excluded United States.

US economic sanctions against Iran have failed to undermine the government's oil exports, while banking transactions and imports of manufacturing and service products are replaced by China, Russia, India and most of Asia. All of which will increase their trade with Teheran.

In the Middle East and South Asia, the US can no longer count on clients or allies other than Israel and Saudi Arabia. Moreover, the Saudis rejected Trump's demand to increase oil production to lower oil prices for US consumers.

Israel is a 'loyal ally' to Washington when it is to their economic advantage and suits their hegemonic aspirations. For example, Israel has continued to substantiate ties with Russia even in violation of US sanctions. Pakistan, Myanmar and Cambodia have moved closer to China as a result of increasing financial and infrastructure aid.

On balance, the US continues to exercise military dominance in Asia via its bases in South Korea, Japan and Australia. However, it is losing economic influence and presence in the rest of Asia. If history is any precedent, imperial empires without economic foundations sooner or later crumble, especially when rising regional powers are capable of replacing them.

The EU and Trump's Empire: Partner, Client or Rival?

The European Union (EU) is the largest market in the world and yet remains a political and military dependency of Washington. The EU has suffered from its lack of an independent foreign policy, its reliance on NATO, a US subsidiary, is one of the main reasons.

President Trump has exploited the EU's weakness to defy its policies on several strategic issues, ranging from the Paris Agreement on climate change to the nuclear agreement with Iran to Trump's recognition of Jerusalem as the Israeli capital. Trump's tariff on EU exports is the latest and most provocative effort to defy and dominate the region.

Moreover, the EU is increasingly divided over immigration and the UK departure (Brexit), as well as the economic and political split between Germany, Italy and Poland. This means that the Trump regime can no longer count on a powerful unified alliance at its behest in its quest for a global empire. Instead, the US under Trump seeks to secure economic supremacy and supreme political-military dominance.

President Trump demands that EU countries double their military budgets in order to increase the Pentagon's arms spending. As a result of the divisions and hostilities between the US and EU, President Trump's imperial policies reflect a contradictory strategy that couples enhancing economic protectionism with overtures to 'enemy' Russia. By adopting the nationalist slogan 'Make America Strong' by 'Making the EU Weak' it appears that Trump is using nationalist slogans to promote imperial goals.

Domestic growth and imperial decline

To date, mid-2018, Trump is riding a wave of domestic growth of the economy, trade and employment. Critics claim that this is a short-lived conjuncture that faces powerful counter-currents. They argue that the trade war and decline of the overseas markets of China, the EU, Mexico, Canada and elsewhere will provoke a decline of the US.

Trump's strategic gamble is that the US trade war will succeed in opening China's market while reducing China's exports. Trump hopes that US multinationals will relocate to the US and increase jobs and exports. A pipe dream.

Moreover, the corporate tax windfall has not been accompanied by a decrease in inequalities and increases in wages. The result is that Trump faces the real prospect of a decline in both exports and popular electoral support, especially from those adversely affected by declining markets and deep cuts in spending on health, education and the environment.

Political consequences of 'America First' in a corporate world

Trump's nationalist economic policies are highly unlikely to enhance empire building. To the contrary, the trade war will force the major corporate tax beneficiaries with overseas trade links with the EU, North America and China to turn against Trump.

Empire building trumps America First. Without an economic empire the US will lack the means to secure the markets necessary to stimulate local exports and production.

Conclusion

President Trump has to some extent succeeded and benefited from temporarily achieving dominance in Latin America by expanding the domestic economy and imposing demands on China, the EU and North America.

Nevertheless, his policies have undermined allies, antagonized competitors and provoked retaliation. All of which increases the economic cost of running an empire.

Trump has failed to provide viable substitutes for the EU and China markets. Nor has he secured the markets of his remaining clients in Latin America. The notion that Trump can build 'national capitalism in one country' is a chimera. At most it would require intensive exploitation of US labor and high rates of investment, sacrificing profits and salaries. The electoral oligarchy and the mass media will force him to retreat from trade wars and surrender to the globalizing elites.

Chapter 32

Trump Against the World Order

A Teapot in a Tempest?

Political leaders, media moguls and journalists in recent years have saturated the public airwaves and media outlets across the world with claims and accusations that President Trump is destroying the post-war 'world order' that has underpinned over seventy years of relative peace and development for a majority of countries in the world system, undermining historic alliances, Western values and the world trade organizations and violating national and international constitutions and institutions.

In the United States, legislators, judges and leaders from both parties have accused President Trump of being a traitor for fraternizing with and serving as a tool of Russian president Putin. This essay will analyze and discuss these claims and accusations. We will begin by looking at the actions and reactions of President Trump's predecessors to determine whether there has been a break with the past. This requires an examination of his 'inheritance'—what actions preceded his presidency. Second, we will evaluate what President Trump has said and what he has done and their significance. We will conclude by examining whether the conflicts are of world historical significance or a tempest in a teapot and whether President Trump has acted against the current 'world order' and the apparent decline in the power and status of the US in search of a new world order dominated by the United States.

President Trump's Inheritance: What 'World', What 'Order'?

The word 'world' is an abstraction—our life is built around many micro, local, regional and macro worlds that are connected and disconnected. The world of President Trump is the imperial world, centered on US supremacy; the regional world is centered on its allies and satellites. In so far as Trump has forced divisions within the European Union and threatened China he has called into question the existing world order. However, he has so far failed to construct a new world order.

Trump inherited a world *dis*order, a world riven by prolonged regional wars in Africa, the Middle East and South Asia. Under the previous four presidents, imperial values replaced democratic ideals, as witnessed by the millions slaughtered in Iraq, Syria, Libya, Yemen, Somalia and Palestine over the past two decades.

Trump is attempting to reconfigure the world order—or 'remake' a US-centered world order—through economic pressure, military threats and political bluster. Part of the process involves generating chaos in order to strengthen his hand in future negotiations and settlements. Trump's so-called 'craziness' is a tactic to secure a better deal, an approach with short-term gains and unforeseen medium-term consequences.

In fact, Trump has done little to unmake the existing order. The US militarily surrounded China under ex-president Obama, a policy Trump follows to the letter. Washington remains in NATO and trades with the EU. The Pentagon continues wars in the Middle East. The Treasury finances Israeli ethnic cleansing. In other words, Trump has been either unwilling or unable to extricate the US from the political mess of his predecessors. He has increased the military budget but not been able to project power. Trump has threatened trade wars across the globe, but in fact trade has increased and deficits remain in place.

Despite Trump's claims of great transformation and his enemies' charge of systematic destruction, the question remains—what has really changed?

Rhetoric is Reality Under Trump and Anti-Trump

Few signpost changes have taken place despite the bluster and the rhetoric in the political 'playpen'.

Despite changes in personalities, the underlying political structures remain in place and promise to continue, despite elections and unending investigations and revelations. The so-called 'trade war' has failed to reduce world trade; employment is unchanged; inequalities persist and deepen. Policies threatening war alternate with peace overtures. Increases in military budgets are spent by and for armchair generals.

Democrats and Republicans denounce each other, then share cocktails and dinner, believing they have done an 'honest day's work'. Immigrants are seized, interned and expelled to nations run by death squads funded by elected US politicians from both parties.

Trump threatens a catastrophic war against Iran while sanctions fail to deter Teheran from developing ties with Europe and Asia. Domestic agendas promising 'transformations' come and go, while trillion-dollar infrastructure promises disappear down the memory hole. Rousing denunciations echo in the legislative chambers but are suspended to secure bipartisan approval so that multi-billions of dollars can be added to the military budget.

Tax giveaways to the very rich provoke inconsequential debates. Armchair assassins pretend to be journalists and direct the Pentagon to disobey the 'traitor' president and launch a war, prompting a response by the president—threatening new wars. None of these players will risk their own skin!

Employers claim there is a shortage of skilled workers, forgetting to fund vocational education or raise wages and salaries.

Candidates for office spend millions, but the more they spend, the fewer the voters. Abstention is the majoritarian response to phony trade wars, fake Russian meddling, bipartisan charades, porn politics and tweets as hand-shaped turds.

Conclusion

The overwhelming reality is that 'chaos' is like foam on a stale beer: very few if any changes have taken place. The world order remains in place, unmoved by inconsequential trade tiffs between Europe and North America.

Washington's angry voices are hollow farts compared to China's multi-billion-dollar infrastructure expansion of the Belt and Road across West Africa.

In the ongoing world order, Washington increases its Israeli handouts to thirty-eight billion for the next decade and budgets four percent of its GNP to robotize the military-industrial complex.

The president alternates tweet commands on war and peace to his trusted and disloyal cabinet members and honest and dishonest intelligence operatives. Under the same tent, investigators investigate each other. None of which is a bad thing because nothing changes for the worst—at least up to now: no treason or impeachment trials; no peace or new wars in the Middle East, no trade or nuclear wars!

But there is no reason to believe that threats will not become a reality. Netanyahu could lead Trump by the nose to a catastrophic war against Iran. Trump could provoke a trade war with China. Climate change can lead to seven plagues of Biblical proportions. Economic bubbles can burst and central banks may be unable to bail out the banks too big to fail. Every disaster that has been promised and not happened could become reality.

In the meantime, prophets of doom and gloom cash their weekly checks and tick off the list of inequities of their chosen adversaries. The 10 percent who defend or oppose the world order still determine who rules the rest—the 90 percent. No wonder there is bipartisan support to increase police powers!

Chapter 33

A Decalogue of American Empire Building

Few Americans, if any, believe what they hear and read from leaders and media publicists. Most choose to ignore the cacophony of voices claiming vices and virtues. This essay provides a set of theses that purports to lay out a basis for dialogue between and among those who choose to abstain from elections with the aim of engaging them in political struggle.

Thesis 1

US empire builders of all colors and persuasions practice donkey tactics: waving the carrot and wielding the whip to move the target government along the chosen path. For Washington, this means offering dubious concessions and threatening reprisals.

Washington applied the tactic successfully in several recent encounters. In 2003 the US offered the Libyan government of Muammar Gaddafi a peaceful accommodation in exchange for disarmament and the abandonment of nationalist allies in the Middle East, Africa and Asia. In 2011, the US with its European allies applied the whip—bombing Libya, financing and arming retrograde tribal and terrorist forces, destroying the infrastructure, murdering Gaddafi and uprooting millions of Africans and Libyans who fled to Europe. Washington recruited mercenaries for its subsequent war against Syria in order to destroy the nationalist Bashar Assad regime.

Washington succeeded in destroying an adversary but did not establish a puppet regime in the midst of perpetual conflict. The empire's carrot weakened its adversary, but the stick failed to recolonize Libya. Moreover, its European allies are obligated to pay the multi-billion-euro price of absorbing millions of uprooted immigrants and the ensuing domestic political turmoil.

Thesis 2

The empire builders' policy of reconfiguring the economy in order to regain imperial supremacy makes domestic and overseas enemies. President

Trump launched a global trade war, replaced political accommodation with economic sanctions against Russia and a protectionist agenda at home, and sharply reduced corporate taxes. He provoked a two-front conflict. Overseas, he provoked opposition from European allies and China while facing perpetual harassment from domestic free-market globalists and Russophobic political elites and ideologues.

Two-front conflicts are rarely successful. Most successful imperialists conquer adversaries in turn—first one and then the other.

Thesis 3

Leftists frequently reverse course: they are radicals out of office and reactionaries in government, eventually falling between the two chairs. We witness the phenomenal collapse of the German Social Democratic Party, the Greek Socialist Party (PASOK), (and its new version Syriza) and the Workers' Party in Brazil. Each attracted mass support, won elections, formed alliances with bankers and the business elite—and in the face of their first crisis were abandoned by both the populace and elite.

Shrewd but discredited elites frequently recognize the opportunism of the left and in time of distress have no problem in temporarily putting up with left rhetoric and reforms as long as their economic interests are not jeopardized. The elite knows that the left signals left and turns right.

Thesis 4

Elections, even those won by progressives or leftists, frequently become springboards for imperially backed coups. Over the past decade, newly elected presidents who are not aligned with Washington face congressional and/or judicial impeachment on spurious charges. The elections provide a veneer of legitimacy that a straight-out military coup lacks.

In Brazil, Paraguay and Venezuela, legislatures under US tutelage attempted to oust a popular president. They succeeded in the former and failed in the latter.

When electoral machinery fails, the judicial system intervenes to impose restraints on progressives, based on tortuous and convoluted interpretation of the law. Opposition leftists in Argentina, Brazil and Ecuador have been hounded by ruling party elites.

Thesis 5

Even crazy leaders—and President Trump is known for his midnight outbursts and nuclear threats against any and all, ranging from philanthropic

world-class sports figures (LeBron James) to NATO-respecting EU allies—
sometimes speak truth to power.

President Trump has denounced and exposed the repeated deceits and
ongoing fabrications of the mass media. Never before has a president so
forcefully identified the lies of the leading print and TV outlets. The *New
York Times, Washington Post, Financial Times*, NBC, CNN, ABC and CBS
have been thoroughly discredited in the eyes of the wider public. They
have lost legitimacy and trust. Where progressives have failed, a war-
monger billionaire has accomplished, speaking a truth to serve many
injustices.

Thesis 6

When a bark turns into a bite, Trump proves the homely truth that fear
invites aggression. Trump has implemented or threatened severe sanctions
against the EU, China, Iran, Russia, Venezuela, North Korea and any
country that fails to submit to his dictates. At first, it was bombast and
bluster that secured concessions.

Concessions were interpreted as weakness and invited greater threats.
The disunity of opponents encouraged imperial tacticians to divide and
conquer. But by attacking all adversaries simultaneously that tactic is
undermined. Threats everywhere limit choices to dangerous options at
home and abroad.

Thesis 7

Anglo-American empire builders are master meddlers in the politics of
sovereign states. But what is most revealing is the current ploy of accusing
the victims of the crimes that are committed against them.

Following the overthrow of the Soviet regime, the US and its European
acolytes 'meddled' on a world-historic scale, pillaging over two trillion
dollars of Soviet wealth and reducing Russian living standards by two-thirds
and life expectancy to under sixty years—below the average life expectancy
of a Bangladeshi.

With Russia's revival under President Putin, Washington financed a large
army of self-styled non-governmental organizations to organize electoral
campaigns, recruited moguls in the mass media and directed ethnic uprisings. The Russians are retail meddlers compared to the wholesale multi-
billion-dollar US operators.

Moreover, the Israelis have perfected meddling on a grand scale—they
intervene in Congress, the White House and the Pentagon. They set the
Middle East agenda, budget and priorities and secure the biggest military
handouts on a per capita basis in US history!

Apparently, some meddlers meddle by invitation and are paid to do it.

Thesis 8

Corruption is endemic in the US, where it effectively has legal status and where tens of millions of dollars change hands and buy Congress people, presidents and judges.

In the US the buyers and brokers are called 'lobbyists'—everywhere else they are called fraudsters. Corruption (lobbying) greases the wheels of billion-dollar military spending, technological subsidies, tax-evading corporations and every facet of government—out in the open, all the time.

Corruption as lobbying never arouses the least criticism from the mass media. On the other hand, when corruption takes place under the table in Iran, China and Russia, the media denounce the political elite—even where in China over two million officials, high and the low, are arrested and jailed.

When corruption is punished in China, the US media calls it a 'political purge' even if it directly reduces conspicuous consumption by the elite. In other words, imperial corruption defends democratic value; anti-corruption is a hallmark of authoritarian dictatorships.

Thesis 9

Bread and circuses are integral parts of empire building—exemplified by prompting urban street mobs to overthrow independent, elected governments.

Imperially financed mobs provided the cover for CIA-backed coups in Iran (1954), Ukraine (2014), Brazil (1964), Venezuela (2003, 2014 and 2017), Argentina (1956), Nicaragua (2018), Syria (2011) and Libya (2011)—just some places and times.

Masses in this context involve paid and voluntary street fighters who speak for democracy and serve the elite. 'Mass cover' is especially effective in recruiting leftists who look to the street for opinion and ignore the suits that call the shots.

Thesis 10

The empire is like a three-legged stool: its invasions kill millions, capture and kill rulers and then rule by homicide—police assassinating dissenting citizens. The cases of Iraq and Libya come to mind. The US and its allies invaded, bombed and killed over a million Iraqis, captured and assassinated its leaders and installed a police state.

A similar pattern occurred in Libya: the US and EU bombed, killed and uprooted several million people, assassinated Gaddafi and fomented a lawless terrorist war of clans, tribes and Western puppets.

'Western values' reveal the inhumanity of empires built to murder à la carte—stripping the victim nations of their defenders, leaders and citizens.

Conclusion

The ten theses define the nature of 21st-century imperialism—its con-
tinuities and novelties. The mass media systematically write and speak lies to
power: their message is to disarm their adversaries and arouse their patrons
to continue to plunder the world.

Bibliography

Petras on US Imperialism

Petras, J. and R. Rhodes (1976). 'The Reconsolidation of US Hegemony', *New Left Review*, 97, May/June: 35–53.

Petras, James and Henry Veltmeyer (2001). *Globalization Unmasked: Imperialism in the 21st Century*. Halifax: Fernwood Publications.

Petras, James and Henry Veltmeyer (2007). *Multinationals on Trial: Foreign Investment Matters*. London: Ashgate.

Petras, James and Henry Veltmeyer (2000). 'Globalization or Imperialism?', *Cambridge Review of International Affairs*, 14(1): 41–82.

Petras, James and Henry Veltmeyer (2000). *Hegemonia dos Estados Unidos no Nova Milênio*. Petrópolis: Editorial Vozes.

Petras, James and Henry Veltmeyer (2005). *Empire with Imperialism: Dynamics of Globalizing Capitalism*. Halifax: Fernwood Publications.

Petras, James and Morris Morley (1975). *The United States and Chile: Imperialism and the Overthrow of the Allende Government*. New York: Monthly Review Press.

Petras, James (1978). *Critical Perspectives on Imperialism and Social Class*. New York: Monthly Review Press.

Petras, James (1995). *Empire or Republic, Global Power, Domestic Decay: The US in the 1990s*. Abingdon: Routledge.

Petras, James (2003). *The New Development Politics: The Age of Empire Building and New Social Movements*. Aldershot: Ashgate Publishing.

Petras, James (2007). *Rulers and Ruled in the US Empire: Bankers, Zionists and Militants*. Clarity Press.

US Imperialism – Studies and Debate

Ahmad, A., ed. (2001). *On the National and Colonial Questions: Selected Writings of Marx and Engels*. New Delhi: Leftwords Books.

Amin, S. (2001). 'Imperialism and Globalization', *Monthly Review*, 53(2): 19–27.

Arrighi, G. (1994). *The Long Twentieth Century*. London: Verso.

Arrighi, Giovanni (2002). 'Lineage of Empire', *Historical Materialism*, 10(3): 3–16.

Arrighi, Giovanni (2005). 'Hegemony Unravelling – I', *New Left Review*, 32 (March/April): 23–80.

Ashman, S. and A. Callinicos (2006). "Capital Accumulation and the State System: Assessing David Harvey's The New Imperialism', *Historical Materialism*, 14(4): 107–131.

Bacevieh, Andrew (2002). *American Empire. The Realities and Consequences of US Diplomacy*. Cambridge, MA: Harvard University Press.

Barnet, Richard and John Cavenagh (1994). *Global Dreams: Imperial Corporations and the New World Order*. New York: Simon & Schuster.

Barone, C. (1985). *Marxist Thought on Imperialism*. Armonk: M. E. Sharpe.

Berberoglu, Berch (1987). *The Internationalization of Capital: Imperialism and Capitalist Development on a World Scale*. New York: Praeger.

Berberoglu, Berch (1992). *The Legacy of Empire: Economic Decline and Class Polarization in the United States*. New York: Praeger.

Berberoglu, Berch (2002). *Labour and Capital in the Age of Globalization*. Lanham: Rowman & Littlefield.

Berberoglu, Berch (2003). *Globalization of Capital and the Nation-State: Imperialism, Class Struggle, and the State in the Age of Global Capitalism*. Lanham: Rowman & Littlefield.

Berberoglu, Berch (2005). *Globalization and Change: The Transformation of Global Capitalism*. Lanham: Lexington Books.

Boot, Max (2002). *The Savage Wars of Peace: Small Wars and the Rise of American Power*. New York: Basic Books.

Borón, A. (2005). *Empire and Imperialism*. London: Zed Press.

Brenner, R. (1998). 'The Economics of Global Turbulence', *New Left Review*, 229 (May/June): 1–264.

Brenner, R. (2006). 'What Is, and What is Not, Imperialism?', *Historical Materialism*, 14(4): 79–105.

Brewer, A. (1980). *Marxist Theories of Imperialism*. London: Routledge.

Brewer, Anthony (1990). *Marxist Theories of Imperialism: A Critical Survey*, 2nd edn. London: Routledge.

Bukharin, Nikolai (1972 [1930]). *Imperialism and World Economy*. London: Merlin Press.

Callinicos, A. (2002). 'Marxism and Global Governance', in D. Held and A. McGrew, eds, *Governing Globalization*. Oxford: Polity.

Callinicos, A. (2007). 'Does Capitalism Need the State System?', *Cambridge Review of International Affairs*, 20(4): 533–549.

Callinicos, A. (2009). *Imperialism and Global Political Economy*. Cambridge: Polity.

Eland, I. (2002). 'The Empire Strikes Out: The "New Imperialism" and its Fatal Flaws', *Policy Analysis*, 459, 26 November: 1–27.

Ferguson, Niall (2004). *Colossus: The Price of America's Empire*. London: Penguin.

Fine, B. (2006). 'Debating the "New" Imperialism', *Historical Materialism*, 14(4): 133–156.

Foster, J. B. (2006). *Naked Imperialism: The US Pursuit of Domination*. New York: Monthly Review Press.

Frieden, J. (2006). *Global Capitalism: Its Fall and Rise in the 20th Century*. New York: W. W. Norton.

Gerschenkron, A. (1962). *Economic Backwardness in Historical Perspective: A Book of Essays*. Cambridge, MA: Belknap Press of Harvard University Press.

Gindin, S. (2013). *The Making of Global Capitalism: The Political Economy of Global Empire*. London: Verso.

Goldman, M. (2005). *Imperial Nature: The World Bank and Struggles for Social Justice in the Age of Globalization*. New Haven and London: Yale University Press.

Gordon, D. (1988). 'The Global Economy: New Edifice or Crumbling Foundation', *New Left Review*, 168: 24–64.

Gowan, Peter (1999). *The Global Gamble: Washington's Faustian Bid for World Domination*. London: Verso.

Grandin, G. (2006). *Empire's Workshop: Latin America, the United States and the Rise of the New Imperialism*. New York: Henry Holt & Co.

Hardt, M., and A. Negri (2000). *Empire*. Cambridge: Harvard University Press.

Harvey, D. (2003). *The New Imperialism*. New York: Oxford University.

Hilferding (2006 [1910]). *Finance Capital*. London: Routledge.

Hilferding, R. (1981). *Finance Capital*. London: Routledge.

Hobsbawm, E. (1989). *The Age of Empire 1875–1914*. New York: Vintage Books, Random House.

Hobson, J. A. (1948). *Imperialism: A Study*. London: Allen & Unwin.

Hobson, J. A. (1972). *Imperialism: A Study*. Ann Arbor: University of Michigan Press.

Hudson, M. (2003). *Super Imperialism. The Origins and Fundamentals of US: World Dominance*, 2nd edn. London: Pluto.

Kautsky, K. (1970). 'Ultra-Imperialism', *New Left Review*, 59 (January/February): 41–46.

Kemp, T. (1967). *Theories of Imperialism*. London: Dennis Dobson.

Kinzer, S. (2007). *Overthrow: American Century of Regime Change from Hawaii to Iraq*. New York: Henry Holt & Co.

Lenin, V. I. (1965). *Imperialism: The Highest Stage of Capitalism*. Peking: Foreign Language Press.

Lenin, V. I. (1968). 'Notebooks on Imperialism', in *Collected Works*, vol. 39. Moscow: Progress Publishers.

Luxemburg, R. (1951). *Accumulation of Capital*. London: Routledge & Kegan Paul.

Magdoff, H. (1978). *Imperialism: From the Colonial Age to the Present*. New York: Monthly Review Press.

Magdoff, H. (2003). *Imperialism Without Colonies*. New York: Monthly Review. Press.

Mandel, E. (1970). *Europe Versus America: Contradictions of Imperialism*. New York: Monthly Review Press.

Mann, M. (2003). *Incoherent Empire*. London: Verso.

McLean, David (1995). *War, Diplomacy and Informal Empire*. London: Tauris.

Morley, Morris (1994). *Washington, Somoza and the Sandinistas: State and Regime in US Policy Toward Nicaragua, 1969–1981*. New York: Cambridge University Press.

Panitch, L. (2000). 'The New Imperial State', *New Left Review*, 2(2): 5–20.

Panitch, L. and C. Leys (2004). *The New Imperial Challenge*. New York: Monthly Review Press.

Parenti, Michael (1995). *Against Empire*. San Francisco: City Lights Books.

Peet, R. (2003). *Unholy Trinity: The IMF, World Bank and TWO*. London: Zed Books.

Radice, H. ed. (1975). *International Firms and Modern Imperialism*. New York: Penguin.

Razack, S. (2004). *Dark Threats and White Knights: The Somalia Affair, Peacekeeping and the New Imperialism*. Toronto: University of Toronto Press.

Robinson, W. (2007). 'Beyond the Theory of Imperialism: Global Capitalism and the Transnational State', *Societies Without Borders*, 2: 5–26.

Rowthorn, R. (1971). 'Imperialism in the 1970s: Unity or Rivalry?', *New Left Review*, 69: 31–54.

Said, E. (1993). *Culture and Imperialism*. New York: Knopf.

Saxe-Fernández, J. and O. Núñez (2001). *Globalización, Imperialismo y Clase Social*, edited by J. Saxe-Fernández et al. Buenos Aires: Editorial Lúmen.

Sutcliffe, B. (2006). 'Imperialism Old and New: A Comment on David Harvey's *The New Imperialism* and Ellen Meiksins Wood's *Empire of Capital*', *Historical Materialism*, 14(4): 59–78.

Tarbuck, J. K. (1972). *Imperialism and the Accumulation of Capital*. London: Penguin.

Veltmeyer, H., ed. (2010). *Imperialism, Crisis and Class Struggle*. Leiden: Brill.

Veltmeyer, H. (2012). 'The Natural Resource Dynamics of Post-Neoliberalism in Latin America: New Developmentalism or Extractivist Imperialism?', *Studies in Political Economy*, 90 (Autumn)): 57–86.

Veltmeyer, H., ed. (2008). *New Perspectives on Globalization and Antiglobalization: Prospects for a New World Order*. Farnham: Ashgate Publishing.

Veltmeyer, H., ed. (2010). *Imperialism, Crisis and Class Struggle: The Verities of Capitalism*. Leiden: Brill Publishers.

Veltmeyer, H. (2005). 'Development and Globalization as Imperialism', *Canadian Journal of Development Studies*, 26(1): 89–106.

Veltmeyer, H. (2005). ''Foreign Aid, Neoliberalism and Imperialism', in Alfredo Saad-Filho and Deborah Johnston (eds), *Neoliberalism: A Critical Reader*. London: Pluto Press.

Veltmeyer, H. (2012). 'The Latin American Left in the Face of the New Imperialism', in J. Webber and B. Carr (eds), *The New Latin American Left: Cracks in the Empire*. Lanham: Rowman & Littlefield.

Wallerstein, I. (2003). *The Decline of American Power: The US in a Chaotic World*. New York: New Press.

Warren, B. (1980). *Imperialism, Pioneer of Capitalism*. London: Verso.

Weaver, F. (2000). *Latin America in the World Economy: Mercantile Colonialism to Global Capitalism*. Boulder: Westview.

Webber, J. and B. Carr, eds (2012). *The New Latin American Left: Cracks in the Empire*. Lanham: Rowman & Littlefield.

Wood, E. M. (2003). *Empire of Capital*. London and New York: Verso.

Index

Note: Page numbers followed by 'n' refer to notes

Abrams, E. 46
Abreu, Katia 179
Academi (formerly Blackwater) 143–145
accumulation 13
Affordable Care Act (2010) 61
Afghanistan 5, 21–26, 45–49, 53, 86, 155, 159, 169–171, 206; economic beneficiaries 16; and immigration 105–107; proxy wars 16, 26–27, 32–39, 56–57, 93; and US-NATO-EU re-mapping 137–139
Africa 3, 6, 51, 54, 57, 72, 203; public health systems collapse 78–79
Against Empire (Parenti) viii
Agency for International Development (USAID) 123
agro-business 4, 7, 118–120, 178; mineral 6–8, 12, 110, 118, 125, 178, 180, 200; mining 20; reform policies 54
Al Qaeda 5, 47
Albania 152
Algeria 55
Alliance for Progress 4, 19, 122–126
alliances 43–44, 48; client and puppet regimes 50, 54–58
Almagro, Luis 198–200
American Century Will Survive the Rise of China (Nye) 167
American Federation of Labor and Congress of Industrial Organizations (AFL-CIO) 90
American Israel Public Affairs Committee (AIPAC) 170
Angola 5, 15, 55

anti-authoritarian rhetoric 50
Arellano, López 144
Argentina 8–12, 16–20, 23, 67, 72, 123, 127, 149, 156–158, 198–201, 207–208, 215–217; bonds and financial blackmail 162; Party for Victory 180
arms trade 46, 107, 204
Arria, Diego 145
Aruba 127
Ashcroft, John 145
Asian Infrastructure Investment Bank (AIIB) 133–134, 141, 172–174
Assad, Bashar 27, 33, 44, 70, 189–190, 193
austerity 9, 125, 128, 177, 181
Australia 6, 24, 57, 71, 153–154, 195, 208
authoritarianism 52
Aznar, José María 144

Bachelet, Michelle 125
Bahrain 46
Balkan states 21, 24–26, 33, 52, 138, 152
ballistic missiles 189–192
Baltic states 21, 24–26, 33, 52, 138, 152, 160, 163
Bank of America 176
banks xi, 4, 29, 176, 208; deregulation 19, 179; elite 12, 117–120; and illicit financial flows 119–120; trillion-dollar transfers (bailouts) 93, 102–104
battalions, neo-fascist 72
battle of ideas 124
beheading atrocities 78

Bernanke, B. 46
Big Pharma 94
big stick approach 124
Birceño, Gustavo Tarre 145
Blackwill, R., and Tellis, A. 130–135
blowback 21, 35
Bolivarian Alliance for the Americas
    (ALBA) 23, 124
Bolivarian Revolution (1999–) 51,
    140–141
Bolivia 4, 7, 10, 16–19, 23, 57, 66,
    72–73, 123, 127, 147–149,
    156–157, 194, 198
bombings 22, 25, 29, 37, 70–72, 145,
    206; EU–US in Libya 24, 27, 176,
    206, 212, 217; suicide 38
Boone, Laurence 176
Bound to Lead (Nye) 167
boycotts 7, 131, 134, 147
Brazil 4–12, 18–20, 23, 57, 72, 123,
    127–129, 149, 156–158, 198–201,
    206–208; austerity program 125; cuts,
    corruption and mass revolts 175,
    178–182, 217; Workers Party 67,
    118, 175, 178–180, 195, 215
BRICS (Brazil/Russia/India/China/
    South Africa) 65, 134, 158, 172–174
British East India Company 30
Burelli, Pedro M. 145
Bush, George W. 31, 81, 91, 94, 124,
    145, 189, 198, 206
Bush, H. W. 16, 22, 25, 65, 91

Calderon, Felipe 144
Cambodia 154, 208
Canada 6, 152, 180
capital, dispossession of 115
Capital Financial Integrity Group 118
capital flight 91
capitalism ix–xi, 3, 14; China's turn
    21–22; crisis of 115, 181; productive
    116, 120; and the welfare
    state 88–95
Capriles, Henrique 147
Caracazo massacre (1989) 140
Cardoso, Fernando 67
Caribbean 20, 127, 158, 207
CARICOM (Caribbean
    Community) 143
Carter, James (Jimmy) 15, 90–91, 147
Caucasus 6, 28, 33, 35, 72
Cedeño, Eligio 145

Central America 15–17, 72; and
    Washington's Two-Track policy
    122–128
Central Intelligence Agency (CIA)
    16–17, 20, 44, 60
Central Unica dos Trabalhadores
    (CUT) 179
Chamorro, Violeta 17
Chaney, Dick 82
chaos 159–163, 213
Chávez, Hugo Rafael 10, 14, 50–51,
    66, 124, 127; and anti-imperialist
    struggle 140–142, 145; misones (social
    programs) 140
Chavez, Rebecca 145
Chevron 81
Chile 4, 11, 16–19, 54, 71, 125–127,
    144, 149, 156–157, 199–201, 207
China 4–10, 13, 18, 24–27, 34–36,
    54–58, 62, 65, 71–73, 83, 147,
    153–154, 162, 172–173, 217; aid
    package to Brazil 129; alternative
    grand strategy 135–136; Belt and
    Road Initiative 208, 213; capitalism,
    growth and economy leader 14,
    20–23, 56, 103, 109, 124, 168–169,
    186–187; Civil War and Communist
    Party 131; and the commercial deficit
    102–104; denounced by Washington
    110–111; elite illicit financial flows
    118–120; and human rights 50–51;
    power political capabilities 133–134;
    threat recommendations (contra-
    dictions/incoherence) 133–135; and
    Trump 102–104, 194–196, 200,
    207–216; US policies and mistaken
    assumptions 130–133; US pro-
    tectionism and blame game 202–205
Chomsky, Noam 180
Christian Democrats 125
CIA 16–17, 20, 44, 60
class inequalities x, 26, 96–99, 116–117;
    poor pay and vulnerability 91–95;
    struggles 89, 128; working and wel-
    fare 88–95, 195
climate change 209
Clinton, Hilary 106, 124, 189
Clinton, William (Bill) 22, 25, 65, 106,
    122, 138, 189, 206; and welfare state
    88, 92–95
Cohen, E. A. 46
collaborator rulers 51–53, 170

collectivism 55
Colombia 9–12, 18–19, 51, 71–73,
    106–107, 126–127, 144, 149, 157,
    195; military aid 72–73; Patriotic
    Union 190; and US military threat
    10, 190–192, 198–201, 207–208
colonialism, internal 100–104
color revolutions 35
commodity production 7–8, 17, 20,
    23, 125
communism 25, 55
Community of Latin American and
    Caribbean States (CELAC) 23,
    141, 147
concentration camps 23
conditionality 18
Congress 45–49, 68, 92
Conoco Phillips 81
contested terrain 9
copper 54
corporate elite (US) 4
Correa, Rafael 10, 66
corruption 9, 12, 36–37, 46, 57, 78,
    116, 119, 155, 178–180, 198, 217
Council on Foreign Relations (CFR)
    134–135
coups 7–10, 14, 17, 27, 29, 33, 48, 147,
    170, 207, 215; and collaborators 52;
    makers 60–62; Pentagon-backed 16,
    23, 54, 66–68, 72, 106, 124, 129,
    156, 217; as restoration formula 19;
    Ukraine 37; Venezuela 10, 140–150
Crimea 37, 68, 73
Cristie, Chris 80
Croatia 152
Cuba 19, 149, 198, 199–201, 207;
    blockade 23, 122; health services
    77; revolution 19, 106, 122–123,
    156–157; secret CIA invasion and
    missile crisis 123; and Washington's
    Two Track policy 122–127
Cuomo, Andrew 80
Curacao 127
Czech Republic 21, 152

Da Silva, Lula 118
De la Rua, Fernando 67
death squads 12, 15, 57, 107, 157, 198
debt 18
Defense Department 130
degradation 23
deindustrialization 91

demagogues 93–95, 177
democracy 65–74; free elections and
    client rejection 65–66; subversion
    and globalizing threats 66–71;
    Washington and Latin America
    66–68; and world power 65–74
Democrats 90–94, 138, 180
Deng Xiaoping 131
Denmark 152
depression 91
deregulation 8, 19, 79, 91–92, 119, 179
destabilization campaigns 4, 8, 19, 73;
    single track 123–125; Washington's
    Two-Track policy 122–129
destitution 53
diplomacy, gun boat 6
dis-accumulation 3–4, 115–121
disinvestment 7, 12
displacement 29–32, 45, 93, 171, 195
dispossession 7, 85; and illicit financial
    flows 115–121
Dominican Republic 54, 123, 156
Drug Enforcement Administration
    (DEA) 10, 66, 123
drugs 17, 107; trafficking 12, 199
Duque, Ivan 207

Eastern Europe 24
Ebola virus 75–80; and Nurse Kaci
    79–80
economics 3–13, 8, 29–31, 53–58, 94,
    128–129, 162, 178–181; backward
    and protectionism 202–205; Chinese
    109–111, 131–136; crisis and decline
    14, 17–18, 46, 78, 125, 155, 184;
    expansion and market domination
    18, 124; and global warfare results
    31–35; globalization doctrine 25;
    integration 7; and internal colonial-
    ism 100–104; progressive projects 17;
    reconfiguration 214–215; stagnation
    142; versus military at national level 5
Ecuador 9–10, 18–20, 23, 66, 72–73,
    123, 127, 141, 147–149, 157,
    198–199, 207, 215
education 79, 95–99, 170
Egypt 26, 44–48, 54, 57–58,
    69, 155
El Salvador 5, 16–17, 106
elections 12, 17, 18, 45, 88, 157, 212,
    215; and democratic transitions 123;
    rigged (stage-managed) 17, 35,

65–66, 72–73, 147, 170,
  179–181, 198
elite, corporate 4
elite factions 98–99, 108, 215; financial
  115–121; political 9, 30, 49,
  53, 81, 170
Emanuel, R. 46
embargoes 46
empire, decline and fall 22–28
empirical tiers *see* tiers
Environmental Protection Agency
  (EPA) 90
epidemics 75–80
Erdogan, Recep Tayyip 47–48
Estonia 152
Ethiopia 119
European Central Bank (ECB) 176
European Commission (EC) 176
European Union (EU) 14, 21–28, 33–35,
  51–52, 57, 62, 68, 78, 101, 147, 160,
  172, 178, 194; and Trump's empire
  208–212, 216; and US-NATO
  empirical tiers 152–156, 171
expansion, priority areas 3–4
exploitation 3, 7, 38, 52, 93; by business
  and bankers 91; cheap labor 22, 120;
  EU 21; and immigration 105–108;
  oil 27, 81; and pillage of wealth
  115–117; resources 14;
  and war 52–54
exports 5, 22, 27, 46, 57, 208
extractivism 3, 6–12, 79, 129, 141–142
extremists 15–16, 69–70
Exxon 81–83

false flag demolitions 25
family allowances 9
fear 183–187
fearmongering 79–80
Federal Bureau of Investigation (FBI) 60
Federal Reserve 92
Feith, D. 46, 82
Fernandez, Cristina 20, 67
financial backing 15, 36, 115–121
financial deregulation 91–92, 119
financial investigation agencies 117–119
Financial Times 78, 116, 130, 178, 216
financialization 101–102
FIRE (finance/insurance/real estate)
  135, 160
Fischer, S. 46
Ford, Gerald 15

Fox, Vicente 144
fracking 83
France 78, 152, 160–161; French
  Socialism 175–176, 180–182
Franco, Frederico 68
free markets x, 5, 19, 43, 129, 215
Freedom House 144
Froman, M. 46
Fujimori, Alberto 12
funding 21, 53; Medicare 61; oil and
  refineries 82–83; terrorists 36,
  46–47, 56, 161, 217

Gadhafi, Muammar 32, 69, 82, 107,
  137, 188–189, 214, 217
Gandhi, Mahatma 173
gas 27, 62, 81
Gates Foundation 79
Geary, Thomas W. 145
genocide 49–50, 73, 160, 171
Georgia 33, 58
Germany 21–22, 26, 55, 78, 83, 101,
  138, 143–144, 152, 158, 176–178,
  203; Social Democratic Party 215
Gerschenkron, Alexander 203
GI Bill 89
globalization 3–5, 91, 110, 152
golpistas (coup-makers) 149
Gorbachev, Mikhail 131
governments *see* left-wing governments
Great Depression 94, 110
Great Financial Crash
  (2008–2011) 93
Great Society 92–94
Greece 78, 152; Socialist Party
  (PASOK) 178, 215; and Syriza
  176–182; and Troika (IMF/EC/
  ECB) 176–180
Greenspan, A. 46
Grenada 16, 157
Guantanamo 126
guarimbas (street gangs) 142
Guatemala 16–17, 54, 106, 198
guerrilla warfare 5, 32, 207
gun boat diplomacy 6
'guns without butter' 90
Guyana 149, 156

Haiti 77, 147
Haley, Nikki 201
Hamilton, Alexander 202
Hariri, Saad 70

Harvard University John F. Kennedy
   School 135, 173
health, public *see* national health services
hedge funds 10
Hezbollah 27, 44, 70, 155–156, 190
Holland 78
Hollande, François 160, 175–176, 182
home ownership access 97
Homeland Security 56, 60
homelessness 93, 97
Honduras 7–9, 16–19, 23, 66–67,
   72–73, 106–107, 147, 157, 198–201,
   207; and Washington's
   Two-Track policy
   123–124, 127
Hong Kong 54, 71, 154
Huawei Group 203
Humala, Ollanta 10–12
human rights rhetoric 50–52, 150, 160
Hussein, Saddam 25, 69, 189

ideologies 14, 110; anti-terrorism and
   Islamic 50; power configurations 14
illicit debts 18
illicit transactions 9
immigrants 106–107, 111, 185–187,
   206, 212, 214
immigration 52, 199; exploitation and
   anti- policies 105–108
imports 5, 8, 208; substitution
   policies 55
India 6, 10, 58, 71, 153, 208; illicit
   financial flows 119–120
Indonesia 54, 119–120, 153
inflation 8–9, 142
Inman, Bobby R. 145
insurgency 19, 37, 49, 83, 121–122,
   170, 190, 195
integration, US-centered 7, 18, 23,
   123–124
intelligence agencies 15–16, 36, 43, 46,
   56, 62, 83; and global spy
   networks 170
internal colonialism 100–104
International Center for Non-Profit
   Law (ICNL) 144
International Monetary Fund (IMF)
   6–7, 18, 28, 79, 120, 125,
   129, 134, 172
International Republican Institute
   (IRI) 144
investments x, 5, 14

Iran 4, 26–28, 45–47, 54–57, 62,
   69–70, 137, 142, 155, 159, 162, 174,
   206–208, 216–217; nuclear
   negotiations 47; peace and
   disarmament negotiations 191–193,
   212–213; and punitive sanctions 34
Iraq 4–5, 11, 21–27, 33–34, 45–49,
   53–57, 69–73, 76–78, 85–87, 155,
   159–161, 169–171; and immigration
   105–107; and oil exploitation 81–82;
   peace and disarmament negotiations
   189, 192–193; pillage and state
   dismantlement 25, 31, 36–39, 93,
   178, 206, 212, 217; as shared imperial
   outpost 137; and US-NATO-EU
   re-mapping 137–139
Is the American Century Over? (Nye) 167
Islamic Development Bank (IDB) 18
Islamic nations 20, 154–156, 171;
   destruction 20, 25; forces and extremists 15–16, 69–70; and nationalism
   16, 27; supported wars against 72–73
Islamic State of Iraq and Syria (ISIS) 27,
   32–33, 76, 82, 155
Islamophobia 21, 50, 56, 176
Israel 15–17, 21–27, 34, 54, 57, 62,
   85–87, 99, 137, 155, 170–171, 176,
   208–209, 216; annexation and war
   against Palestine 65, 69–70, 159–163,
   212; and Chavista personalities
   murder 144; citizenship 33; drive for
   supremacy 56; oligarchs 21, 55; peace
   and disarmament negotiations
   190–193; US military subsidies 56,
   213; as US power axis 44–49
Italy 78, 152
Ivy League 99

Jacobson, Roberta 126
jail without trial 170
Japan 5, 24, 54, 57–58, 62, 71, 83,
   153–154, 195, 203, 208
jihadi movements 46–47, 72, 161
job creation 88–89
job security 91
Johnson, Lyndon B. 90, 94
Jordan 26, 44, 54, 57–58, 155
Justice Department 117

Karzai, Harmad 32
Kennedy, John F. 19, 90, 122–123, 126
kidnapping 170

Kim Jong-Un 192
Kirchner, Néstor 10, 20, 67
kleptocrats 37, 118–120, 137
Korea 172
Korean War (1950–1953) 131
Kosovo 152
Kurdish people 5, 27, 37, 44, 47–48,
    156, 159, 189

land grabs 9, 33, 52, 85; and reform 106
Landless Rural Workers' Movement
    (MST) 179
Laos 154
Latin America 3–12, 26, 50–51, 57–58,
    170–171, 195, 203, 206–210;
    domestic rebellions 23; extractive
    versus military 6–13; and immigra-
    tion 105–108; and integration 7;
    regimes 6, 9–10; shifting priorities
    and global constraints 17–20; strate-
    gies and contingencies 17–20; theo-
    retical reflections 20–21; tiers of
    empire 156–158; and Trump
    197–201; and Washington 66–68,
    72–73, 122–129
Latvia 152
Lebanon 23–27, 44–47, 69–70, 106,
    169, 174, 189–190
Ledezma, Antonio 143, 146
left-wing governments 175–182, 215;
    Brazil's cuts, corruptions and mass
    revolts 175, 178–182; French
    Socialism 175–176, 180–182; Greece
    and Syriza's Instant transformation
    175–182
Levy, D. 46
Levy, Joaquin 179
Lew, J. L. 46
Libby, S. 46
Libya 4, 11, 23, 26, 36–39, 45–46, 49,
    69–73, 137, 150, 155, 161, 169–171;
    and Big Oil 81–82; EU–US bomb-
    ings 24, 27, 176, 206, 212, 217; from
    trading partner to failed state 32; and
    immigration 105–107; peace and
    disarmament agreements 188–189,
    192–193, 214
Lithuania 152
living standards 52, 79, 89, 91–92,
    96–99, 123
lobbyists 62, 81–86
Lockheed Martin (LMT) 85–86

Lopez, Leopoldo 148
Lugo, Fernando 67–68
Lula da Silva, Luiz Inácio 10, 198, 201

McCarthyism 61, 89, 173
Macedonia 152
Machado, Maria Corina 143, 145
Macri, Mauricio 20, 194, 198
Macron, Emmanuel 138, 176, 191–192
Madoff, Bernard (Bernie) 93
Maduro, Nicolás 127–128, 140–150,
    199–201; assassination plan 148
Malaysia 54, 153, 203
Mali 176
mapping 195; US–NATO–EU 137–139
Marshall Plan 53
Mearsheimer, J., and Walt, S. 170
media 45, 48, 60–62, 73, 78, 143;
    propaganda and meddling 215–218
Medicaid 90, 94
Medicare 61, 90, 94
mega-cycles 125
Menem, Carlos 67
mercenaries 14, 17, 23, 26–27, 47, 137,
    156, 159
MERCOSUR (South American
    Common Market) 68, 149
Merkel, Angela 178
Mexican Petroleum (PEMEX) 11
Mexico 9–12, 18, 57–58, 71–72, 107,
    118, 144, 149, 195, 198–201,
    206–209; as militarized detention
    center 161; triple alliance 11
Meysan, T. 143–146, 150n1
Miami Herald 126
Middle East 3, 6–9, 12–13, 17, 20, 23,
    50, 54–55, 171, 203, 208; and
    immigration 105–107; multi-tiered
    empire 154–156; re-mapping
    (US–NATO–EU) 137–139, 212; as
    US power axis 44–49, 72
militarist faction 19, 43, 54, 90
military 3–13; academy graduates 99;
    bases 14, 21, 51, 54, 127, 152, 194,
    198, 207–208; budgets (spending)
    and bureaucracy 14–15, 133, 212;
    and China policies 131–135; deficits
    101; dependencies 153–154;
    encirclement 69–73, 133–135, 155;
    and global warfare results 31–35; high
    capacity/declining economic perfor-
    mance 169–171; interventions and

proxy wars 15–28, 33, 53–54, 73, 76–77, 122–129, 137–139; metaphysics as crackpot realism 172–173; and Middle East as power axis 44–49, 56; pacts and puppet regimes 54–58; platforms reliance 122, 172; strategic priorities 14–28; US subsidies 55–58; versus economy at national level 5; versus extractive in Latin America 6–13; veterans and IMC lobby budget fight 87

military aid, Colombia 72–73

military threat, US to Colombia 10, 190–192, 198–201, 207–208

militias, Peshmerga 33, 44

Milken, Michael 93

minerals, agro- 6–8, 12, 110, 118, 125, 178, 180, 200

mining 4, 7, 20, 23

mispricing 118

missiles: ballistic 189–192; sites 21, 159

Mobil 81–83

money laundering xi, 5, 107, 117, 120, 195, 199–201

Monroe Doctrine 197–200

Morales, Evo 66, 194

Moreno, Lenin 198–199

Morsi, Mohamed 46, 69

mortality rates 11, 26, 29, 32, 36–38, 94–97; Bolivia 140; Iraq 137; Mexicans 72; Syria 71

Mossad 20, 44, 145–146

Mozambique 15, 55

Mubarak, Hosni 69

Mujahedeen al Khalq 44–46

multinational corporations (MNCs) 3–12, 14–17, 26, 51, 54, 82–84, 101–103; EU 22, 27; extractive 6–8; and US global strategies 3–5, 17–20, 23–28; wealth hoarding 118–120

Muslim Brotherhood 46–48, 69

Myanmar 154, 208

El Nacional 145

Namibia 55

National Democratic Institute (NDI) 144

National Endowment for Democracy (NED) 37, 127, 144–145

National Guard 77–78

national health services 75–80; as big business (for profit model) 76–79; care deterioration and inadequacy 76–80; guidelines 75; and political priorities 76–79; procedures and protocols 76

national interest viii–ix

National Security Agency (NSA) 67, 73, 161; rhetoric 21, 61–62, 76, 110

National Security Council (NSC) 45, 144

nationalism 16, 27, 109–111

negotiations 10, 19, 188–193; FARC 190–192; Iran 191–193; Iraq 189, 192–193; and Israel 190–193; Libya 188–189, 192–193; North Korea 192–193; Palestine 192–193; Syria and Lebanon 189–190, 193

neocolonialism 140

neoliberalism 4, 16–19, 110; Latin American regimes 6–13

Netanyahu, B. 191, 213

Neto, Peña 199–200

networks 50–58; client and puppet regimes 54–58; collaborator central roles 50–53; expansion 133; and exploitation 52–54

New Deal 88–91, 94

New York Times 146, 216

New Zealand 57, 153

Newark Liberty International Airport 80

Nicaragua 5, 16–18, 36–37, 55, 106, 123, 127, 149, 157, 207, 217; Sandinista revolution (1961–1990) 16

Nisman, Alberto 20

Nixon, Richard 5, 90, 131

no strike production 91

non-governmental organizations (NGOs) 8–10, 68–69, 72, 144, 174

North American Free Trade Agreement (NAFTA) 57, 92, 118, 200, 207

North Atlantic Treaty Organization (NATO) 21, 26, 33, 48, 53, 69–72, 82, 101, 171–172, 178, 212; air assaults 24, 105; coalition 32, 47, 52, 57; dominance 152; and EU empirical tiers 152–156, 208; missile sites 33–35; shock troops 68

North Korea 153, 192–193, 196, 208, 216

Northrop Grumman (NOG) 85–86

Norway 152

nuclear arms 138, 160, 215–216

Nye, Joseph 167–174; high military capacity/declining economic performance consequences 169–171; and historical fallacies 172; military metaphysics as crackpot realism 172–173; soft and hard power segmentation 167–174

Obama, Barack 24, 46, 51, 56, 61, 76–77, 81–83, 86, 106, 162–163, 189–191, 198, 206–207; China policy 133–134; and Cuba 124–125; electoral donor-owners and tax evasion 93–94; and the Iron Dome 163; Marines sent to Central America 126; Venezuela war threat and national emergency declaration 143–150; welfare and war 93–96, 159, 212
Obrador, Andrés Manuel López 207
Occupational Health and Safety Administration (OSHA) 90
Oceana 51, 57
oil 16, 27, 46, 56, 62, 189, 199; Big and the Pentagon 81–84; corporations 4, 31, 54; deals 5; exploitation 27, 81; fields appropriation 11; gateways 21; price manipulation 142; producing regions 20; profits 81–84; trade losses 45
oligarchs 33, 60, 68, 96, 106, 120, 139, 160, 190–191, 197–201; Israel 21, 55; Russia 21, 33, 55
open markets doctrine 109
Operation Jericó 143–146
Organization of American States (OAS) 124, 141, 145–147, 198–200
Ortega, Daniel 207
Orthodox Christians 72
overseas funds channeling 115–121

Pakistan 15, 23, 26, 36, 46, 49, 54–58, 105, 155, 159, 208
Palestine 25, 36, 44–45, 57, 65, 70–72, 85, 137, 155, 212; ethnic slaughter 45, 49, 159–160; Hamas government 70; peace and disarmament negotiations 192–193; people's rights 48; and protests in France 160
Palestinian slaughter, Congress endorsement 49
Pan Pacific agreements 71

Panama 16–18, 145
Papandreou, George 178
Paraguay 7–9, 18–20, 23, 67–68, 123, 127, 157, 198–201, 207, 215
Parenti, Michael viii–x
Paris Match 177
Patriot Act (2001) 93
patronage system 9
Pax Americana viii
Pax Britannica 156
Pence, Michael 197
pensions 8–9, 97; plunder of 117–121
Pentagon 15–16, 36, 44–45, 60–61, 77, 81–87, 93, 126–128, 135, 145–149, 167–173, 187, 194, 198–200, 209, 212–216; and Big Oil 81–84
Pérez, Carlos Andrés 140
Peru 4, 10–12, 16–20, 71, 127, 149, 156–157, 198–200, 207
Peshmerga militias 33, 44
Petras, J. ix–xi, 170
Petro-Caribe 124, 147
Petrobas 67
Philippines 24, 54, 58, 153, 195, 203
pillage viii–ix, 18, 38, 55, 65, 140, 198–200; Golden Age 138; US Treasury 15–16, 23, 26, 45–46, 49; and wealth concentration 115–121
Piñera, Sebastián 144
Pinochet, Augusto 124
pivot from war 5; to Asia 24; to realism 138
Plan Colombia 106–107
plutocrats 111
Poland 21, 37, 152, 160
populism 10–12, 125
Poroshenko, Petro 68
Portugal 78
poverty 79, 88–89, 93, 159; reduction programs 6, 90
power centers 59–62; countervailing forces 59; and executive officials as rulers 59–61; President counter-attacks 61; September 2018 showdown 61–62; soft and hard segmentation 167–174
Powers, Samantha 73
pressure groups 56
privatization 4, 9, 15, 177, 206–207
profits 3–7, 16, 26, 30, 39, 53, 81–88, 93–109, 115–120, 161, 178, 181,

195, 210; oil 81–84; and social costs 85–87
propaganda 12, 51, 60, 66–67, 94, 169–171, 215–218; adversary demonization and negotiations 188, 193; and fear 183–187; Horror Shows 78–79; against Venezuela 143–144
prostitution 107
protectionism 89, 110, 195, 202–205, 215; and cry-baby economies 204
protests 12
proxy wars 26–27, 33, 53–54, 73, 86, 193; Afghanistan 16, 26–27, 32–39, 56–57, 93; Central America 15–17, 72; Tiananmen Square 131
public health 75–80
puppet regimes see regimes
Putin, Vladimir 22, 33, 68, 138, 160, 201, 211, 216

quarantine 75

racism 89–90
Rasmussen, Anders Fogh 161
Raytheon (RTN) 85–86
Reagan, Ronald 16, 90–91, 94
reason of force 74
recession 31, 78
refugees 79, 93, 153, 159–161
regimes 10, 14, 20, 24–25, 123; Afghan 15; Ba'thist 27, 47; Broad Front 125; center-left 23; client 50, 54–58, 122–128, 137–139, 197, 200, 207; collapsing 19; death squad 15–16; destabilizing strategy 19; Islamic 16; Kiev failure 33–35; Maliki 33, 47; progressive cycle of change 175, 182n1; puppet 5, 32–34, 46, 54–58, 170–172, 191, 197, 206–207, 217; secular nationalist populist 46–47, 54; US/Israeli-backed 16–17
rent control 89
repression 56
Republicans 90, 94
resources 14, 26, 54, 55; pillage 18, 52–53, 78–79
retrenchment 137
Revising US Grand Strategy Toward China (Blackwill and Tellis): mistaken assumptions 130–133; policy

recommendations contradictions and incoherence 133–135
Revolutionary Armed Forces of Colombia (FARC) 10, 19, 126–127, 199; peace and disarmament negotiations 190–192
Rice, Condoleezza 189
rights 88; to work laws 89
robber barons 138
Romer, Henrique Salas 145
Roosevelt, Franklin D. 94
Rosneft 83
Rothschild Bank 176
Rousseff, Dilma 10, 67, 118, 125, 179–182
royalty reductions 8
Rubio, Marco 144
rulers, collaborator 51–53, 170
Rumsfeld, Donald 82
Russia 10, 24–28, 34–37, 48, 62–73, 83, 93, 129, 138–139, 142, 153–155, 158–163, 172, 178, 190, 203, 208, 217; impoverishment and pillage 22, 100–101, 216; military encirclement 155, 176; oligarchs 21, 33, 55; plots 201; sanctions and concessions 215–216
Russiagate investigation 138

Samper, Ernesto 126
sanctions 4–5, 24, 27–29, 34, 45–46, 68–69, 83–85, 105, 131, 153, 159–163, 178, 208; and hard/soft power 172–174; peace and disarmament negotiations 188, 191–193, 212, 215–216; against Venezuela 144
Sandinista 16–17; revolution (1961–1990) 16
Santos, Juan Manuel 10, 19, 126, 190, 198, 207
Santrich, Jesús 199
satraps 49, 52, 70, 197–198
Saudi Arabia 15, 26–27, 54, 57–58, 62, 69–70, 137, 142, 155, 190–191, 208; absolutist monarchy and US power axis 44–49; Taliban and Al Qaeda financing 47
scorched earth policy 12
secret agencies 56
Security Exchange Commission 117
Sendic, Raul 149

separatists 137
Serbia 36
sharing of revenues 30
Shear, D. 130
shell companies 116–120
Singapore 54
Singer, Paul 194
Sisi, Abdel Fattah 46–48, 69
Slovakia 152
Slovenia 152
Smoot-Hawley tariff 110
social costs 85–87
social crisis 52
social expenditure cuts 8
social security 61, 88–89, 94
Somalia 23–26, 36–38, 53–57,
    73, 93, 137, 162,
    169–171, 212
Somoza, Anastasio 16
South Africa, proxy wars 15–17
South Asia 4–6, 54–56, 72
South Korea 5, 54, 57–58, 120,
    153–154, 192, 203, 208; and North
    reconciliation 195–196
South Sudan 137
SOUTHCOM (United States
    Southern Command) 145
Spain 6, 78, 152
Special Forces (US) 21–24, 37–38, 83,
    127; Green Berets and counter-
    insurgency 122, 126
specialization doctrine 109
spoiler tactics 124
squalidos (domestic fifth column) 150
State Department 124–126
stigmatization 23
sting operations 161
street riots 8
strikes 12, 88, 91, 94
suicide 85; bombers 38
Summit of the Americas: (2010)
    124–126; (2018) 197
Surinam 149
Sweden 152
swindles 117–120
Syria 4, 21–28, 36–39, 44–49,
    69–73, 76–78, 86–87, 150,
    159–161, 169–171, 174; and
    immigration 106–107; peace and
    disarmament negotiations 189–190,
    193; and US-NATO-EU
    re-mapping 137–139, 206,

212, 217; wars on behalf of terrorists
    32–33, 155–156, 176–178
Syriza (Coalition of Greek Radical Left)
    175–182

Taft Hartley Act (1947) 89
Taiwan 5, 57–58, 153, 203
Taliban 5, 16, 27, 32, 38, 47, 155
tariffs 205–207
tax evasion 91; and offshore shell
    companies 116–120; overseas havens
    92–94, 97–98
tax reductions 8, 198
tax system 97–98, 102; corporate 209,
    215; and cuts 110; gains 110–111,
    158; giveaways 213; middle class
    payers 111; reforms 139
technology 92–94
telecommunications 54
Tellis, A., and Blackwill, R. 130–135
Temer, Michel 198, 206–207
territory losses 58
terror doctrine 23
terrorism 5–6, 10, 70–71, 155; and 9/11
    93, 217; reciprocal 21, 24
terrorists: funding 36, 46–47, 56, 161,
    217; wars on behalf of (Syria) 32–33,
    155–156, 176–178
Thailand 153
theses 214–218; corruption and
    lobbyists 217; coups 215; economic
    reconfiguration 214–215; leftist
    governments 215; Libya 214;
    meddling 216; media propaganda
    215–218; sanctions 215–216; state
    financed mobs 217; Western values
    and terrorist wars 217
thinktanks 68
Tibet 154
tiers, empirical 151–158; Eastern
    153–154; and the global myth 158;
    Latin American 156–158; Middle
    East 154–156; overview 151–152;
    Western allies 152–153
Tillerson, Rex 197
torture 23, 170
trade ix–xi, 4–9, 14, 26–28, 203,
    209–212; agreements 4–5, 51, 56–58,
    127, 158, 194; arms 46, 107, 204;
    barrier elimination 9; deficit 58,
    102–104; diversified 18; embargoes
    7; oil 45; and past empire building

29–30; war 101–104, 110, 139, 183, 186–187, 201–215, 215
trafficking, drugs 12, 199
Trans Pacific Partnership (TPP) 133, 207
Trans-Pacific Alliance 11
Treasury 15–16, 23, 26, 45–46, 49, 117, 212
Tricare 87
Truman, Harry S. 186
Trump, Donald 59–61, 94–96, 110, 138–139, 185, 191–192, 214–216; America First political consequences 209–210; in Asia 208; assets and liabilities 194–196; and the China factor 102–104, 194–196, 200, 207–215; empire expansion and decline 194–195, 206, 209; and the EU 208–212; fake news and plots 201; and Latin America 197–201, 206–210; and Presidential counter-attacks 61; protectionist-militarism and the commercial deficit 101–104, 202–205; trickle-down 94, 102; against the world order 211–213
Tsipras, Alexis 176–178, 182
Tunisia 155
Turkey 27, 56–57, 106, 155, 190; as US power axis 44, 47–49
Two-Track policy 122–129

Uighur separatists 71
Ukraine 24–28, 36–38, 58, 68–69, 72–73, 86–87, 153, 169–172, 217; coup 37; economy decimation 27; Kiev junta 24, 68, 160, 176–178; power grab and sanctions 33–35
unemployment 18, 52–53, 177, 181
Union of South American Nations (UNASUR) 23, 126, 141, 147–149
unions 10–11, 18, 88, 91, 94, 106–107, 201; activists 89–90; membership 88–90; sabotage of militants abroad (hand in glove) 91–92; and shop stewards 89; and war policy collaboration 89–90
unipolar world 5, 22, 52, 55, 65, 101, 111, 138
United Fruit Company 54
United Kingdom (UK) 102, 116, 143–144, 152, 172, 188–191, 198, 202–204, 209

United Nations (UN) 73, 77, 147
uprisings (resistance movements) 10, 23–24, 37–38, 52, 55, 58, 73, 106; anti-war and urban 89, 92–93; Islamic 155; and peace movement demise 107; Tibetan and Uyghur 131; Venezuelan 144–145
Uribe Vélez, Alvaro 107, 144, 207
Uruguay 4, 16–19, 23, 123, 127, 149, 157, 198; Broad Front regime 125, 180
USAID 66, 72
USSR, collapse of 5, 21–22, 33, 58, 100, 131

Valls, Manuel 176
Varoufakis, Yanis 176–178, 182
Vázquez, Tabaré 125
Veltmeyer, Henry viii–xi
Venezuela 8–14, 18–20, 23, 36–37, 51, 57, 66–67, 72–73, 157–158, 178, 194, 207, 215–217; bombings 145; Constitution 145; coups 10, 140–150; failed coup anatomy (2015) 143–146; national Emergency declaration purpose 148–149; as national security threat 126; and Obama 143–150; offensive against 140–150; United Socialist Party (PSUV) 66; US imperialism and strategy 142–143, 198–201; war threat and political failure response 147–148; and Washington's Two Track policy 123–124, 127
Veteran Health Administration (VHA) 87
veterans 87–90
Vietnam 25, 54, 92, 154; African American veterans 90
Volker Plan 90

wages 8–12, 52, 91–99, 107, 120, 178, 213; inequality 97–99
Wall Street 25, 49, 55, 61–62, 67, 73, 79, 86, 91–94, 110, 132, 135, 162, 187, 194, 198–200
Wall Street Journal 118
Walt, S., and Mearsheimer, J. 170
warfare, guerrilla 5, 32, 207
warlords 137
wars 5, 8, 11, 14–28, 99, 159, 183–187, 212; contingencies, priorities and

constraints 17–20; costs 27–28, 36,
46–49, 56–58, 72, 85–87, 94, 137,
168–169; on drugs 9; and epidemics
75–80; and exploitation 52–54;
global results 29–39; Gulf 31; and
healthcare consequences 75–80; and
immigration 105–108; and industry
53; and Latin America 20–21; lost
(failed) 36–39; of nerves 149; profits
and budget fighting 85–87; on terror
5–6, 10, 23–25, 28n1, 71, 78,
101–102; without end 27, 55–56;
zones 26, *see also* proxy wars
Warsaw Pact 21, 171
Washington 122–129; Consensus 100;
single track policy 123–125; Two-
Track Policy origins and re-intro-
duction 122–129
Washington Post 146, 216
wealth 115–121; and dis-accumulation
role 118–119; exploitation and pillage 115–117; inverted pyramid 117;
overseas funds channeling 115–121;
private accumulation 115–121
weapons transfers 85
welfare programs 26, 53, 121; age of
Demagogues 93–95; debacle and
Obamacare 90–95; hospital closures
161, 184; last wave and reforms
89–91; and the New Abolitionists
92–93; New Deals and Big Wars
88–89; spending transfers 98–99; state
and capitalist opposition 88–95

welfare state 88, 92–95
Whitaker, Kevin 145
White House 45, 68, 73, 123–125,
145–147
Wolfowitz, P. 46, 82
workers 12, 213; disappearing 96–99;
and falling living standards 96–98;
protests 52–53, 88, 91; wages and
welfare 88–95
Workfare 88, 93–94
World Bank (WB) xi, 6, 18, 120
world leadership rhetoric 14
World Trade Organization (WTO) 131
World War II (1939–1945)
89–91, 156

Xi Jinping 119

Yellen, J. 46
Yeltsin, Boris 21, 33, 131
Yemen 23, 46, 53, 57, 73, 155, 159,
169–170, 212
Yugoslavia 5, 22, 25, 55, 93, 150

Zelaya, Manuel 7, 66–67,
106–107, 124
Ziff, Benjamin 145
Zionist-Militarist State 54–57,
160, 170; power configuration
15–21, 25–28, 45–49, 70, 156;
war profits and social
costs 85–87
Zuniga, Ricardo 144